CANON EOS 40D GUIDE TO DIGITAL PHOTOGRAPHY

David D. Busch

Course Technology PTR
A part of Cengage Learning

COURSE TECHNOLOGY
CENGAGE Learning™

Australia, Brazil, Japan, Korea, Mexico, Singapore, Spain, United Kingdom, United States

COURSE TECHNOLOGY
CENGAGE Learning

Canon EOS 40D Guide to Digital Photography
David D. Busch

Publisher and General Manager, Course Technology PTR: Stacy L. Hiquet

Associate Director of Marketing: Sarah O'Donnell

Manager of Editorial Services: Heather Talbot

Marketing Manager: Jordan Casey

Executive Editor: Kevin Harreld

Project Editor: Jenny Davidson

Technical Reviewer: Michael D. Sullivan

PTR Editorial Services Coordinator: Erin Johnson

Interior Layout Tech: Bill Hartman

Cover Designer: Mike Tanamachi

Indexer: Katherine Stimson

Proofreader: Sara Gullion

For product information and technology assistance, contact us at
Cengage Learning Customer & Sales Support Center, 1-800-354-9706

For permission to use material from this text or product, submit all requests online at **cengage.com/permissions**
Further permissions questions can be emailed to
permissionrequest@cengage.com

Library of Congress Catalog Card Number: 2007938244

ISBN-13: 978-1-59863-510-2

ISBN-10: 1-59863-510-7

Course Technology
25 Thomson Place
Boston, MA 02210
USA

Cengage Learning is a leading provider of customized learning solutions with office locations around the globe, including Singapore, the United Kingdom, Australia, Mexico, Brazil, and Japan. Locate your local office at: **international.cengage.com/region**

Cengage Learning products are represented in Canada by Nelson Education, Ltd.

For your lifelong learning solutions, visit **courseptr.com**

Visit our corporate website at **cengage.com**

Printed in the United States of America
4 5 6 7 11 10 09 08

For Cathy

Acknowledgments

Once again, thanks to the folks at Course Technology PTR, who have pioneered publishing digital imaging books in full color at a price anyone can afford. Special thanks to executive editor Kevin Harreld, who always gives me the freedom to let my imagination run free with a topic, as well as my veteran production team including project editor Jenny Davidson and technical editor Mike Sullivan. Also thanks to Bill Hartman, layout; Katherine Stimson, indexing; Sara Gullion, proof-reading; Mike Tanamachi, cover design; and my agent, Carole McClendon, who has the amazing ability to keep both publishers and authors happy.

About the Author

David D. Busch has written nine bestselling guidebooks for specific digital SLR models, and five other popular books devoted to dSLRs, including *Mastering Digital SLR Photography* and *Digital SLR Pro Secrets*. As a roving photojournalist for more than 20 years, he illustrated his books, magazine articles, and newspaper reports with award-winning images. He's operated his own commercial studio, suffocated in formal dress while shooting weddings-for-hire, and shot sports for a daily newspaper and upstate New York college. His photos have been published in magazines as diverse as *Scientific American* and *Petersen's PhotoGraphic*, and his articles have appeared in *Popular Photography & Imaging*, *The Rangefinder*, *The Professional Photographer*, and hundreds of other publications. He's currently reviewing digital cameras for CNet and *Computer Shopper*.

When About.com recently named its top five books on Beginning Digital Photography, occupying the #1 and #2 slots were Busch's *Digital Photography All-In-One Desk Reference for Dummies* and *Mastering Digital Photography*. During the past year, he's had as many as five of his books listed in the Top 20 of Amazon.com's Digital Photography Bestseller list—simultaneously! Busch's 90-plus other books published since 1983 include bestsellers like *QuickSnap Guide to Digital SLR Photography*.

Busch earned top category honors in the Computer Press Awards the first two years they were given (for *Sorry About The Explosion* and *Secrets of MacWrite, MacPaint and MacDraw*), and he later served as Master of Ceremonies for the awards.

Contents

Chapter 3
Setting Up Your Canon EOS 40D   43

Chapter 4
Getting the Right Exposure   107

Chapter 5
Advanced Shooting with Your Canon EOS 40D   133

Chapter 6
Working with Lenses   175

Chapter 7
Working with Light   207

Chapter 8
Downloading and Editing Your Images   233

Chapter 9
Canon EOS 40D: Troubleshooting
and Prevention   257

Appendix A
Upgrading to the Canon EOS 40D   283

Glossary   293

Index   305

Preface

You've unpacked your Canon EOS 40D digital SLR. The slim little book included in the box is complete, but it's difficult to wade through. You know everything you need to know is in there, somewhere, but you don't know where to start. In addition, the camera manual doesn't offer much information on photography or digital photography. Nor are you interested in spending hours or days studying a comprehensive book on digital SLR photography that doesn't necessarily apply directly to your 40D.

All you want at this moment is a guide that explains the purpose and function of the 40D's basic controls, how you should use them, and why. Ideally, there should be information about file formats, resolution, aperture/priority exposure, and special autofocus modes available, but you'd prefer to read about those topics only after you've had the chance to go out and take a few hundred great pictures with your new camera. Why isn't there a book that summarizes the most important information in its first two or three chapters, with lots of illustrations showing what your results will look like when you use this setting or that?

Now there is such a book. If you want a quick introduction to the 40D's focus controls, flash synchronization options, how to choose lenses, or which exposure modes are best, this book is for you. If you can't decide on what basic settings to use with your camera because you can't figure out how changing ISO or white balance or focus defaults will affect your pictures, you need this guide.

Introduction

I sincerely believe that this book is your best bet for learning how to use your new camera, and for learning how to use it well.

If you're a Canon EOS 40D owner who's looking to learn more about how to use this great camera, you've probably already explored your options. There are DVDs and online tutorials—but who can learn how to use a camera by sitting in front of a television or computer screen? Do you want to watch a movie or click on HTML links, or do you want to go out and take photos with your camera? Videos are fun, but not the best answer.

Of course, there's always the manual furnished with the camera. It's compact and filled with information, but there's really very little about *why* you should use particular settings or features, and its organization may make it difficult to find what you need. Multiple cross-references may send you flipping back and forth between two or three sections of the book to find what you need. The basic manual is also hobbled by black-and-white line drawings and tiny monochrome pictures that aren't very good examples of what you can do.

Also available are third-party guides to the 40D, like this one. I haven't been happy with some of these guidebooks, which is why I wrote this one. The existing books range from skimpy and illustrated by black-and-white photos to lushly illustrated in full color but too generic to do much good. Photography instruction is useful, but it needs to be related directly to the Canon EOS 40D as much as possible.

I've tried to make *Canon EOS 40D Guide to Digital Photography* different from your other 40D learn-up options. The roadmap sections use larger, color pictures to show you where all the buttons and dials are, and the explanations of what they do are longer and more comprehensive. I've tried to avoid overly general advice, including the two-page checklists on how to take a "sports picture" or a "portrait picture" or a "travel picture." Instead, you'll find tips and techniques for using all the features of your Canon EOS 40D to take *any kind of picture* you want. If you want to know where you should stand to take a picture of a quarterback dropping back to unleash a pass, there are plenty of books that will tell you that. This one concentrates on teaching you how to select the best autofocus mode, shutter speed, f/stop, or flash capability to take, say, a great sports picture under any conditions.

This book is not a lame rewriting of the manual that came with the camera. Some folks spend five minutes with a book like this one, spot some information that also appears in the original manual, and decide "Rehash!" without really understanding the differences. Yes, you'll find information here that is also in the owner's manual, such as the parameters you can enter when changing your 40D's operation in the various menus. Basic descriptions—before I dig in and start providing in-depth tips and information—may also be vaguely similar. There are only so many ways you can say, for example, "Hold the shutter release down halfway to lock in exposure and focus." But not *everything* in the manual is included in this book. If you want a large table showing which settings are available in each of the various Basic Zone and Creative Zone modes, you'd better have the Canon Function Availability Table available in the original manual. But if you need advice on when and how to use the most important functions, you'll find the information here.

Canon EOS 40D Guide to Digital Photography is aimed at both Canon and dSLR veterans as well as newcomers to digital photography and digital SLRs. Both groups can be overwhelmed by the options the 40D offers, while underwhelmed by the explanations they receive in their user's manual. The manuals are great if you already know what you don't know, and you can find an answer somewhere in a booklet arranged by menu listings and written by a camera vendor employee who last threw together instructions on how to operate a camcorder.

Once you've read this book and are ready to learn more, I hope you pick up one of my other guides to digital SLR photography. Three of them are offered by Course Technology PTR, each approaching the topic from a different perspective. They include:

Quick Snap Guide to Digital SLR Photography

Consider this a prequel to the book you're holding in your hands. It might make a good gift for a spouse or friend who may be using your 40D, but who lacks even basic knowledge about digital photography, digital SLR photography, and Canon EOS photography. It serves as an introduction that summarizes the basic features of digital SLR cameras in general (not just the 40D), and what settings to use and when, such as continuous autofocus/single autofocus, aperture/shutter priority, EV settings, and so forth. The guide also includes recipes for shooting the most common kinds of pictures, with step-by-step instructions for capturing effective sports photos, portraits, landscapes, and other types of images.

Mastering Digital SLR Photography, Second Edition

This book is an introduction to digital SLR photography, with nuts-and-bolts explanations of the technology, more in-depth coverage of settings, and whole chapters on the most common types of photography. While not specific to the EOS 40D, this book can show you how to get more from its capabilities.

Digital SLR Pro Secrets

This is my more advanced guide to dSLR photography with greater depth and detail about the topics you're most interested in. If you've already mastered the basics in *Mastering Digital SLR Photography*, this book will take you to the next level.

Why the Canon EOS 40D Needs Special Coverage

There are many general digital photography books on the market. Why do I concentrate on books about specific digital SLRs like the EOS 40D? One reason is that I feel dSLRs are the wave of the future for serious photographers, and those who join the ranks of digital photographers with single lens reflex cameras deserve books tailored to their equipment.

When I started writing digital photography books in 1995, digital SLRs cost $30,000 and few people other than certain professionals could justify purchasing them. Most of my readers a dozen years ago were stuck using the point-and-shoot low-resolution digital cameras of the time—even if they were advanced photographers. I myself took tons of digital pictures with an Epson digital camera with 1024×768 (less than 1 megapixel!) resolution, and which cost $500.

As recently as 2003 (before the original Digital Rebel was introduced), the lowest-cost dSLRs were priced at $3,000 or more. Today, anyone with around $600 can afford one of these basic cameras, and around $1,400 buys you a sophisticated model like the Canon EOS 40D (with lens). The digital SLR is no longer the exclusive bailiwick of the professional, the wealthy, or the serious photography addict willing to scrimp and save to acquire a dream camera. Digital SLRs have become the favored camera for anyone who wants to go beyond point-and-shoot capabilities. And Canon cameras have enjoyed a dominating position among digital SLRs because of Canon's innovation in introducing affordable cameras with interesting features and outstanding performance (particularly in the area of high ISO image quality). It doesn't hurt that Canon also provides both full-frame and smaller format digital cameras and a clear migration path between them (if you stick to the Canon EF lenses that are compatible with both).

You've selected your camera of choice, and you belong in the Canon camp if you fall into one of the following categories:

- Individuals who want to get better pictures, or perhaps transform their growing interest in photography into a full-fledged hobby or artistic outlet with a Canon 40D and advanced techniques.

- Those who want to produce more professional-looking images for their personal or business website, and feel that the EOS 40D will give them more control and capabilities.

- Small business owners with more advanced graphics capabilities who want to use the EOS 40D to document or promote their business.

- Corporate workers who may or may not have photographic skills in their job descriptions, but who work regularly with graphics and need to learn how to use digital images taken with a Canon EOS 40D for reports, presentations, or other applications.

- Professional webmasters with strong skills in programming (including Java, JavaScript, HTML, Perl, etc.) but little background in photography, but who realize that the 40D can be used for sophisticated photography.

- Graphic artists and others who already may be adept in image editing with Photoshop or another program, and who may already be using a film SLR (Canon or otherwise), but who need to learn more about digital photography and the special capabilities of the 40D dSLR.

Who Am I?

You may have seen my photography articles in *Popular Photography & Imaging* magazine. I've also written about 2,000 articles for (late, lamented) *Petersen's PhotoGraphic*, plus *The Rangefinder, Professional Photographer,* and dozens of other photographic publications. First, and foremost, I'm a photojournalist and made my living in the field until I began devoting most of my time to writing books. Although I love writing, I'm happiest when I'm out taking pictures, which is why I took 14 days off right smack in the middle of writing this book for a solo visit to Spain—not as a tourist, because I've been to Spain no less than a dozen times in the past—but solely to take photographs of the people, landscapes, and monuments that I've grown to love.

Like all my digital photography books, this one was written by someone with an incurable photography bug. My first Canon SLR was a Pellix back in the 1960s, and I've used a variety of newer models since then. I've worked as a sports photographer for an Ohio newspaper and for an upstate New York college. I've operated my own commercial studio and photo lab, cranking out product shots on demand and then printing a few hundred glossy 8 × 10s on a tight deadline for a press kit. I've served as a photo-posing instructor for a modeling agency. People have actually paid me to shoot their weddings and immortalize them with portraits. I even prepared press kits and articles on photography as a PR consultant for a large Rochester, N.Y., company, which shall remain nameless. My trials and travails with imaging and computer technology have made their way into print in book form an alarming number of times, including a few dozen on scanners and photography.

Like you, I love photography for its own merits, and I view technology as just another tool to help me get the images I see in my mind's eye. But, also like you, I had to master this technology before I could apply it to my work. This book is the result of what I've learned, and I hope it will help you master your EOS 40D digital SLR, too.

Chapter Outline

Chapter 1: Shooting Your First Canon EOS 40D Picture
Just what you need to know to take your camera out of the box, make basic settings, and begin shooting good pictures within minutes.

Chapter 2: Canon EOS 40D Roadmap
This chapter is a guided tour of the external buttons, dials, and controls of the EOS 40D.

Chapter 3: Setting Up Your Canon EOS 40D
Here you'll learn how to make all the key menu settings needed to customize and tailor the operation of your EOS 40D.

Chapter 4: Getting the Right Exposure
Learn how to use the EOS 40D's metering modes, select the best ISO setting, and use exposure compensation and histograms to fine-tune your exposure.

Chapter 5: Advanced Shooting with Your Canon EOS 40D
This chapter explains autofocus modes, white balance, continuous shooting, and custom image parameters including Picture Styles.

Chapter 6: Working with Lenses
Everything you need to know about Canon lenses, compatibility, choosing and using prime lenses and zooms, and much more.

Chapter 7: Working with Light
This chapter includes Canon EOS 40D flash basics, as well as tips for working with other types of illumination, including studio flash.

Chapter 8: Downloading and Editing Your Images

There are plenty of good Photoshop books available, but this isn't one of them. Instead, you'll find the information you need for choosing the right editing software, noise reduction utilities, RAW converters, and other aids.

Chapter 9: Canon EOS 40D: Troubleshooting and Prevention

This chapter provides some tips for bringing a dead camera back to life, troubleshooting common problems, and ways to maintain the health of your 40D and its accessories.

Appendix A: Upgrading to the Canon EOS 40D

This is a succinct guide to what's new about the EOS 40D, for those who are contemplating an upgrade and need to know what they're getting (and getting into). This resource is perfect for 30D owners, those who currently have Digital Rebel/Rebel XT/Rebel XTi models, and those coming to Canon from other brands.

Glossary

Want a quick definition of an unfamiliar word? You'll find it here.

1

Shooting Your First Canon EOS 40D Picture

If I were a betting person, I'd be willing to wager that you've already taken—at least—a few hundred shots with your new Canon EOS 40D. As valuable as a book like this one is, nobody can suppress their excitement long enough to read the instructions before initiating play with a new toy. My first photo with this camera was a snapshot of the owner of the photo store where I bought my 40D. As a long-time Canon owner, I purchased just the 40D body (sans lens), but I remembered to take a favorite lens and a Compact Flash card with me when I picked up the camera. Because the 40D had just been introduced, there was enough of a maintenance charge in the fresh-off-the-boat battery to allow capturing a few images on the spot, even before the ink on my check was dry.

That's how easy the EOS 40D is to set up and use: it's not a point-and-shoot camera, but if you have some experience with film or digital SLRs (especially if you have worked with the EOS 30D or 20D), you can assemble all the pieces, flip the power switch, remove the lens cap, and then point—and shoot. And, even if you were not already familiar with this camera, you were able to figure out what that big switch on the back labeled OFF and ON does, and, probably, aligned the big 'ole dial on the top surface with one of the icons representing things like a person (portrait), flower (close-up), mountain scene (landscape), or runner (sports activity). (These are the Basic or "scene" modes.) So, this first chapter is not likely to be your first exposure to using the Canon EOS 40D.

Still, this is my opportunity to review the setup procedures for the camera for those among you who are already veteran users, and to help ease the more timid (and those who have never worked with a digital SLR before) into the basic pre-flight checklist that needs to be completed before you really spread your wings and take off. For the uninitiated, the EOS 40D *does* have lots of dials and buttons and settings that might not make sense at first, but will surely become second nature after you've had a chance to use the camera for awhile.

But don't fret about wading through a manual to find out what you must know to take those first few tentative snaps. I'm going to help you hit the ground running with this chapter, which will help you set up your camera and begin shooting in minutes. You won't find a lot of detail in this chapter. Indeed, I'm going to tell you just what you absolutely must understand, accompanied by some interesting tidbits that will help you become acclimated. I'll go into more depth and even repeat some of what I explain here in later chapters, so you don't have to memorize everything you see. Just relax, follow a few easy steps, and then go out and begin taking your best shots—ever.

First Things First

The Canon EOS 40D comes in an impressive gray-and-red box filled with stuff, including connecting cords, booklets, CDs, and lots of paperwork. The most important components are the camera and lens (if you purchased your 40D with a lens), battery, battery charger, and, if you're the nervous type, the neck strap. You'll also need a Compact Flash memory card, as one is not included. If you purchased your EOS 40D from a camera shop, as I did, the store personnel probably attached the neck strap for you, ran through some basic operational advice that you've already forgotten, tried to sell you another Compact Flash card, and then, after they'd given you all the help you could absorb, sent you on your way with a handshake.

Perhaps you purchased your 40D from one of those mass merchandisers that also sell washing machines and vacuum cleaners. In that case, you might have been sent on your way with only the handshake, or, maybe, not even that if you resisted the hard-sell efforts to sell you an extended warranty. You save a few bucks, but don't get the personal service a professional photo retailer provides. It's your choice. There's a third alternative, of course. You might have purchased your camera from a mail order or Internet source, and your 40D arrived in a big brown (or purple/red or yellow/red) truck. Your only interaction when you took possession of your camera was to scrawl your signature on an electronic clipboard.

In all three cases, the first thing to do is to carefully unpack the camera and dou-ble-check the contents with the checklist on one end of the box, helpfully desig-nated with a CONTENTS heading. At a minimum, the box should include a Digital Camera EOS 40D, Wide Strap EW-100DGR, Battery Charger CG-580, Battery Pack BP-511A, Interface Cable IFC-200U, Video Cable VC-100, and a software CD-ROM. It's possible that the camera was accompanied by a lens, as well, and that the contents I've listed above will vary slightly depending on when and where you bought the camera.

While this level of setup detail may seem as superfluous as the instructions on a bottle of shampoo, checking the contents *first* is always a good idea. No matter who sells a camera, it's common to open boxes, use a particular camera for a demonstration, and then repack the box without replacing all the pieces and parts afterwards. Someone might actually have helpfully checked out your camera on your behalf—and then mispacked the box. It's better to know *now* that something is missing so you can seek redress immediately, rather than discover two months from now that the video cable you thought you'd never use (but now *must* have) was never in the box.

Initial Setup

The initial setup of your Canon EOS 40D is fast and easy. Basically, you just need to charge the battery, attach a lens, and insert a Compact Flash card. I'll address each of these steps separately, but if you already feel you can manage these setup tasks without further instructions, feel free to skip this section entirely. You should at least skim its contents, however, because I'm going to list a few options that you might not be aware of.

Battery Included

Your Canon EOS 40D is a sophisticated hunk of machinery and electronics, but it needs a charged battery to function, so rejuvenating the BP-511A lithium-ion battery pack furnished with the camera should be your first step. A fully charged power source should be good for approximately 1,100 shots, based on standard tests defined by the Camera & Imaging Products Association (CIPA) document DC-002. If half your pictures use the built-in flash, you can expect about 800 shots before it's time for a recharge.

All rechargeable batteries undergo some degree of self-discharge just sitting idle in the camera or in the original packaging. Lithium-ion power packs of this type typ-ically lose a few percent of their charge every day, even when the camera isn't turned on. The small amount of juice used to provide the "skeleton" outline on

A BATTERY AND A SPARE

My experience is that the CIPA figures are often a little optimistic, so it's probably a good idea to have a spare battery on hand. In addition to the BP-511A, the 40D will also work with Canon BP-511, BP-512, and BP-514 battery packs if you have one handy. The chief difference among them is that the BP-511 and BP-512 provide 1,100 mAh of juice, while the BP-511A and BP-514 furnish 1,390 mAh—more than 25 percent more power.

I always recommend purchasing Canon brand batteries (for about $50) over less-expensive third-party packs, even though the $30 substitute batteries may offer more capacity (some top 1,500 mAh) at a lower price. My reasoning is that it doesn't make sense to save $20 on a component for a $1,000-plus camera, especially since batteries (from Canon as well as other sources) have been known to fail in potentially harmful ways. Canon, at least, will stand behind its products, issue a recall if necessary, and supply a replacement if a Canon-brand battery is truly defective. A third-party battery supplier that sells under a half-dozen or more different product labels and brands may not even have an easy way to get the word out that a recall has been issued.

If your pictures are important to you, always have at least one spare battery available, and make sure it is an authentic Canon product.

the top panel monochrome LCD when the 40D is turned off isn't the culprit; Li-ion cells lose their power through a chemical reaction that continues when the camera is switched off. So, it's very likely that the battery purchased with your camera is at least partially pooped out, so you'll want to revive it before going out for some serious shooting.

Power Options

Several battery chargers are available for the Canon EOS 40D. The compact CG-580, shown in Figure 1.1, is furnished with the camera, and so is the charger that most 40D owners end up using. Purchasing one of the optional charging devices offers more than some additional features: You gain a spare that can keep your camera running until you can replace your primary power rejuvenator. Here's a list of your power options:

- **CG-580:** The standard charger for the 40D (and also compatible with earlier cameras that use the same batteries), this one is the most convenient, because of its compact size and built-in wall plug prongs that connect directly into your power strip or wall socket and requires no cord.

- **CB-5L:** This is similar to the CG-580, and also charges a single battery, but requires a cord. That can be advantageous in certain situations. For example, if your power outlet is behind a desk or in some other semi-inaccessible location, the cord can be plugged in and routed so the charger itself sits on your desk or another more convenient spot. The cord itself is a standard one that works with many different chargers and devices (including the power supply for my laptop), so I purchased several of them and leave them plugged into the wall in various locations. I can connect my 40D's charger, my laptop computer's charger, and several other electronic components to one of these cords without needing to crawl around behind the furniture. The cord itself draws no power when it's not plugged into a charger.

- **Compact Power Adapter CA-PS400:** This handy device can charge a pair of batteries at once. You'll want this charger if you are using the 40D's BG-E2N battery-vertical grip (which holds two power packs) or if you do a lot of shooting at any given time and run through your batteries quickly.

- **Dual Battery Charger CG-570:** This is another charger that can juice up two 500-series batteries at once when connected to either the Car Battery Cable CB-570 (plug into your vehicle's lighter or accessory socket) or the Compact Power Adapter CA-570 (connect to an AC power source). The vehicle battery option allows you to keep shooting when in remote locations that lack AC power.

- **Battery Grip BG-E2N:** This accessory holds two batteries (or six AA cells with the BGM-E2 battery holder). You can potentially increase your shooting capacity to 1,900–2,200 shots (1,400–1,600 with flash), while adding an additional shutter release, main dial, AE lock/FE lock, and AF point selection controls for vertically oriented shooting.

- **AC Adapter Kit ACK-E2:** This device allows you to operate your EOS 40D directly from AC power, with no battery required. Studio photographers need this capability because they often snap off hundreds of pictures for hours on end and want constant, reliable power. The camera is probably plugged into a flash sync cord (or radio device), and the studio flash are plugged into power packs or AC power, so the extra tether to this adapter is no big deal in that environment. You also might want to use the AC adapter when viewing images on a TV connected to your 40D, or when shooting remote or time-lapse photos.

Charging the Battery

When the battery is inserted into the CG-580 charger properly (it's impossible to insert it incorrectly), a Charge light begins flashing. It flashes on and off until the battery reaches a 50 percent charge, then blinks in two-flash cycles between 50-75 percent charged, and in a three-flash sequence until the battery is 90 percent charged, usually within about 90 minutes. You should allow the charger to continue for about 60 minutes more, until the status lamp glows steadily, to ensure a full charge. When the battery is charged, flip the lever on the bottom of the camera and slide the battery in. (See Figure 1.2.)

Figure 1.1 The flashing status light indicates that the battery is being charged.

Figure 1.2 Insert the battery in the camera; it only fits one way.

Final Steps

Your Canon EOS 40D is almost ready to fire up and shoot. You'll need to select and mount a lens, adjust the viewfinder for your vision, and insert a Compact Flash card. Each of these steps is easy, and if you've used an EOS 30D or 20D (or one of the Digital Rebels), you already know exactly what to do. I'm going to provide a little extra detail for those of you who are new to the Canon or digital SLR worlds.

Mounting the Lens

As you'll see, my recommended lens mounting procedure emphasizes protecting your equipment from accidental damage, and minimizing the intrusion of dust. If your 40D has no lens attached, select the lens you want to use and loosen (but do not remove) the rear lens cap. I generally place the lens I am planning to mount vertically in a slot in my camera bag, where it's protected from mishaps, but ready to pick up quickly. By loosening the rear lens cap, you'll be able to lift it off the back of the lens at the last instant, so the rear element of the lens is covered until then.

After that, remove the body cap by pressing the release button next to the lens mount, and rotating the cap towards the shutter release button. You should always mount the body cap when there is no lens on the camera, because it helps keep dust out of the interior of the camera, where it can settle on the mirror, focusing screen, the interior mirror box, and potentially find its way past the shutter onto the sensor. (While the 40D's sensor cleaning mechanism works fine, the less dust it has to contend with, the better.) The body cap also protects the vulnerable mirror from damage caused by intruding objects (including your fingers, if you're not cautious).

Once the body cap has been removed, remove the rear lens cap from the lens, set it aside, and then mount the lens on the camera by matching the alignment indicator on the lens barrel (red for EF lenses and white for EF-S lenses) with the red or white dot on the camera's lens mount. (See Figure 1.3.) Rotate the lens toward the shutter release until it seats securely. (You can find out more about the difference between EF and EF-S lenses in Chapter 6.) Set the focus mode switch on the

Figure 1.3
Match the white dot on EF-S lenses with the white dot on the camera mount to properly align the lens with the bayonet mount. For EF lenses, use the red dots.

lens to AF (autofocus). If the lens hood is bayoneted on the lens in the reversed position (which makes the lens/hood combination more compact for transport), twist it off and remount with the "petals" facing outward. (See Figure 1.4.) A lens hood protects the front of the lens from accidental bumps, and reduces flare caused by extraneous light arriving at the front element of the lens from outside the picture area.

Figure 1.4
A lens hood protects the lens from extraneous light and accidental bumps.

Adjusting Diopter Correction

Those of us with less than perfect eyesight can often benefit from a little optical correction in the viewfinder. Your contact lenses or glasses may provide all the correction you need, but if you are a glasses wearer and want to use the EOS 40D without your glasses, you can take advantage of the camera's built in diopter adjustment, which can be varied from −3 to +1 correction. Press the shutter release halfway to illuminate the indicators in the viewfinder, then rotate the diopter adjustment wheel next to the viewfinder (see Figure 1.5) while looking through the viewfinder until the indicators appear sharp.

Figure 1.5
Viewfinder diopter correction from −3 to +1 can be dialed in.

Diopter adjustment knob

If the available correction is insufficient, Canon offers 10 different Dioptric Adjustment Lens Series E correction lenses for the viewfinder window. If more than one person uses your 40D, and each requires a different diopter setting, you can save a little time by noting the number of clicks and direction (clockwise to increase the diopter power; counterclockwise to decrease the diopter value) required to change from one user to the other. There are 18 detents in all.

Inserting a Compact Flash Card

You can't take photos without a Compact Flash card inserted in your EOS 40D (although there is a **Shoot w/o Card** entry in Shooting Menu 1 that enables/disables shutter release functions when a memory card is absent—learn about that in Chapter 3). So, your final step will be to insert a Compact Flash card. Slide the door on the right side of the body toward the back of the camera to release the cover, and then open it. (You should only remove the memory card when the camera is switched off, but the 40D will remind you if the door is opened while the camera is still writing photos to the Compact Flash card.)

Insert the memory card with the label facing the back of the camera, as shown in Figure 1.6, oriented so the edge with the double row of tiny holes goes into the slot first. Close the door, and your preflight checklist is done! (I'm going to assume you remember to remove the lens cap when you're ready to take a picture!) When you want to remove the memory card later, press the gray button (shown at the bottom of Figure 1.7) to make the Compact Flash card pop out.

Figure 1.6 The Compact Flash card is inserted with the label facing the back of the camera.

Figure 1.7 To remove a Compact Flash card, press the gray button at the bottom of the slot to pop the card out of the camera.

HOW MANY SHOTS? GUESS!

You know you have a great camera when the counter that keeps track of the number of shots remaining is its most annoying defect. What's the deal? The counter tops out at a measly 999 shots, which is a ridiculously low number given the capacity of modern Compact Flash cards. If you use a 4GB or 8GB card, it's almost inevitable that the counter will indicate no more than 999 shots remaining if you're shooting JPEG Fine or JPEG Standard—even though you may actually have much more capacity than that remaining.

For example, an 8GB card can hold about 1,450 JPEG Fine shots in full resolution (Large) format, but the counter shows just 999 pictures remaining (as it also will for full resolution JPEG Standard). If you're using a "medium"-sized 4GB card, the counter overflows at 999 exposures when you shoot at JPEG Standard (the actual capacity is about 1,468 exposures). Even puny 2GB cards can cause the counter to falter if you elect to use Medium or Small resolution settings. Ironically, you might have been using JPEG rather than RAW or RAW+JPEG in order to squeeze more images onto your memory card—but the 40D won't tell you just how many more pictures remain, until the count dips below 999. Some other camera brands insert a K (for kilo, or thousands) in the counter (as in 1.4K) to show large numbers of exposures remaining.

There's not much excuse for this, because 8GB and 4GB cards have become so prevalent. The silver lining is that if you shoot RAW or RAW+JPEG, rather than JPEG alone, the counter does its job with any common card capacity (a 4GB card displays 252 shots remaining; an 8GB card bumps the counter up to only 502). While I expect that 16GB Compact Flash cards will become relatively cheap during the life of this book, it's hard to visualize a situation in which an EOS 40D owner will actually *need* to fit 3,000 JPEG Fine pictures onto a single card.

Selecting a Shooting Mode

You can choose a shooting method from the Mode Dial located on the top left edge of the Canon EOS 40D. There are seven Basic Zone shooting modes, in which the camera makes virtually all the decisions for you (except when to press the shutter), and five Creative Zone modes, which allow you to provide input over the exposure and settings the camera uses. There are also three Camera User Settings that can be used to store specific groups of camera settings, which you can then recall quickly by spinning the Mode Dial to C1, C2, or C3. You'll find a complete description of both Basic Zone and Creative Zone modes as well as Camera User Settings in Chapter 4.

Turn your camera on by flipping the power switch to ON, or to the mark above the ON indicator, which is also "on" but which activates the Quick Control Dial above and to the right of the power switch, as shown in Figure 1.8. (You'll want the Quick Control Dial active in virtually all situations.) Next, you need to select which shooting mode to use. If you're very new to digital photography, you might want to set the camera to Auto (the green frame on the Mode Dial) or P (Program mode) and start snapping away. Either mode will make all the appropriate settings for you for many shooting situations. If you have a specific type of picture you want to shoot, you can try out one of the other Basic Zone modes indicated on the Mode Dial with appropriate icons and shown in Figure 1.9:

- **Auto.** In this mode, the 40D makes all the exposure decisions for you, and will pop up the flash if necessary under low light conditions.

- **Portrait.** Use this mode when you're taking a portrait of a subject standing relatively close to the camera and want to de-emphasize the background, maximize sharpness, and produce flattering skin tones.

- **Landscape.** Select this mode when you want extra sharpness and rich colors of distant scenes.

Figure 1.8
Rotate the power switch all the way counterclockwise to activate the Quick Control Dial.

Quick Control Dial

Activate Quick Control Dial

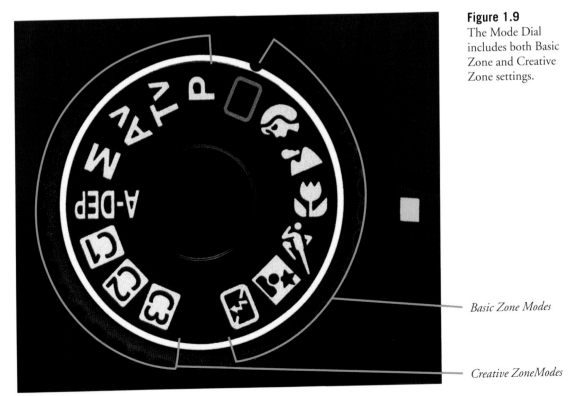

Figure 1.9
The Mode Dial includes both Basic Zone and Creative Zone settings.

Basic Zone Modes

Creative ZoneModes

- **Close Up.** This mode is helpful when you are shooting close-up pictures of a subject from about one foot away or less.

- **Sports.** Use this mode to freeze fast-moving subjects.

- **Night Portrait.** Choose this mode when you want to illuminate a subject in the foreground with flash, but still allow the background to be exposed properly by the available light. Be prepared to use a tripod or an image stabilized (IS) lens to reduce the effects of camera shake. (You'll find more about IS and camera shake in Chapter 6.)

- **Flash Off.** This is the mode to use in museums and other locations where flash is forbidden or inappropriate. It otherwise operates exactly like the Auto setting but disables the pop-up internal flash unit.

If you have more photographic experience, you might want to opt for one of the Creative Zone modes, also shown in Figure 1.9. These, too, are described in more detail in Chapter 4. These modes all let you apply a little more creativity to your camera's settings. These modes are indicated on the Mode Dial by letters A-DEP, M, Av, Tv, and P:

- **A-DEP (Automatic depth-of-field).** Choose this mode if you want to allow the 40D to select an f/stop that will maximize depth-of-field for the subjects in the frame as it adjusts focus and selects an appropriate shutter speed.

- **M (Manual).** Select when you want full control over the shutter speed and lens opening, either for creative effects or because you are using a studio flash or other flash unit not compatible with the 40D's automatic flash metering.

- **Av (Aperture Priority).** Choose when you want to use a particular lens opening, especially to control sharpness or how much of your image is in focus. The 40D will select the appropriate shutter speed for you. Av stands for *aperture value.*

- **Tv (Shutter Priority).** This mode (Tv stands for *time value*) is useful when you want to use a particular shutter speed to stop action or produce creative blur effects. The 40D will select the appropriate f/stop for you.

- **P (Program).** This mode allows the 40D to select the basic exposure settings, but you can still override the camera's choices to fine-tune your image.

Choosing a Metering Mode

You might want to select a particular metering mode for your first shots, although the default Evaluative Metering (which is set automatically when you choose a Basic Zone mode) is probably the best choice as you get to know your camera. To change metering modes, press the Metering Mode/WB button and spin the Main Dial to cycle among the choices shown in Figure 1.10:

- **Evaluative metering.** The standard metering mode; the 40D attempts to intelligently classify your image and choose the best exposure based on readings from 35 different zones in the frame, with emphasis on the autofocus points.

- **Partial metering.** Exposure is based on a central spot, roughly nine percent of the image area.

- **Spot metering.** Exposure is calculated from a smaller central spot, about 3.8 percent of the image area.

- **Center-Weighted Averaging metering.** The 40D meters the entire scene, but gives the most emphasis to the central area of the frame.

You'll find a detailed description of each of these modes in Chapter 4.

Figure 1.10
Metering modes (left to right Evaluative, Partial, Spot, Center-Weighted).

BUTTON, BUTTON

The top panel buttons each have two functions. To set the left function of each pair (that is AF with the AF-Drive button), hold the button and rotate the Main Dial. To set the right function of each pair, rotate the Quick Control Dial.

Choosing a Focus Mode

You can easily switch between automatic and manual focus by moving the AF/MF switch on the lens mounted on your camera. However, if you're using a Creative Zone shooting mode, you'll still need to choose an appropriate focus mode. (You can read more on selecting focus parameters in Chapter 5.) If you're using a Basic Zone mode, the focus method is set for you automatically.

To set the focus mode, press the AF-DRIVE button on the top panel of the camera (see Figure 1.11), and spin the Main Dial until the mode you want appears in the status LCD. The three choices are

- **One Shot.** This mode, sometimes called *Single Autofocus*, locks in a focus point when the shutter button is pressed down halfway, and the focus confirmation light glows in the viewfinder. The focus will remain locked until you release the button or take the picture. If the camera is unable to achieve sharp focus, the focus confirmation light will blink. This mode is best when your subject is relatively motionless. Portrait, Night Portrait, and Landscape Basic Zone modes use this focus method exclusively.

- **AI Servo.** This mode, sometimes called *Continuous Autofocus*, sets focus when you partially depress the shutter button, but continues to monitor the frame and refocuses if the camera or subject is moved. This is a useful mode for photographing sports and moving subjects. The Sports Basic Zone mode uses this focus method exclusively.

- **AI Focus.** In this mode, the 40D switches between One Shot and AI Servo as appropriate. That is, it locks in a focus point when you partially depress the shutter button (One Shot mode), but switches automatically to AI Servo if the subject begins to move. This mode is handy when photographing a subject, such as a child at quiet play, which might move unexpectedly. The Flash Off Basic Zone mode uses this focus method.

Figure 1.11
Set Autofocus mode.

Main Dial

Autofocus Mode button

Selecting a Focus Point

The Canon EOS 40D uses nine different focus points to calculate correct focus. In A-DEP, or any of the Basic Zone shooting modes, the focus point is selected automatically by the camera. In the other Creative Zone modes, you can allow the camera to select the focus point automatically, or you can specify which focus point should be used.

There are several methods to set the focus point manually. You can press the AF Point Selection button on the back of the camera, look through the viewfinder, and use the multi-controller button (to the right and below the viewfinder window) to move the focus point to the zone you want to use. For example, press the multi-controller straight up or down, and the top or bottom focus points are selected. To the left or right, and the side points are selected. Movements to the two o'clock, four o'clock, seven o'clock, or ten o'clock positions choose the in-between focus sensors. Press the multi-controller in, and the center focus point becomes active.

You can also choose a focus point by pressing the AF Point Selection button and then rotating the Main Dial. The focus point will cycle among the edge points counterclockwise (if you turn the Main Dial to the left) or clockwise (if you spin the Main Dial to the right), ending/starting with the center focus point/all nine focus points, as shown in Figure 1.12. The Quick Control Dial can also be used.

Figure 1.12
Select a focus point.

Other Settings

There are a few other settings you can make if you're feeling ambitious, but don't feel ashamed if you postpone using these features until you've racked up a little more experience with your EOS 40D.

Adjusting White Balance and ISO

If you like, you can custom tailor your white balance (color balance) and ISO sensitivity settings. To start out, it's best to set white balance (WB) to Auto, and ISO to ISO 100 or ISO 200 for daylight photos, and ISO 400 for pictures in dimmer light. You'll find complete recommendations for both these settings in Chapter 4. You can adjust either one now by pressing the Metering Mode-WB button (for white balance) and rotating the Quick Control Dial, or ISO-Flash Exposure Compensation button (for ISO sensitivity) and rotating the Main Dial until the setting you want appears on the status LCD. Both buttons are shown in Figure 1.11.

If you've been playing with your camera's settings, or your 40D has been used by someone else, you can restore the factory defaults by selecting **Clear All Camera Settings** from the Setup Menu 3, and/or **Clear All Custom Func**, from the Custom Functions main menu.

Using the Self-Timer

If you want to set a short delay before your picture is taken, you can use the self-timer. Press the AF-Drive button and rotate the Quick Control Dial until the self-timer icon (for a 10-second delay) or the self-timer icon accompanied by the numeral 2 (for a 2-second delay) appear on the status LCD. Canon supplies a rubber eyepiece cover, which attaches to your camera strap and can be slid over the eyepiece in place of the rubber eyecup. This prevents light from entering through the eyepiece, which can confuse the exposure meter. I've found that extraneous light is seldom a problem unless a bright light source is coming from directly behind the camera, in which case I use my hand to shield the viewfinder.

Press the shutter release to lock focus and start the timer. The self-timer lamp will blink and the beeper will sound (unless you've silenced it in the menus) until the final two seconds, when the lamp remains on and the beeper beeps more rapidly.

Reviewing the Images You've Taken

The Canon EOS 40D has a broad range of playback and image review options, and I'll cover them in more detail in Chapter 3. For now, you'll want to learn just the basics. Here is all you really need to know at this time, as shown in Figure 1.13:

- Press the Playback button (marked with a blue right-pointing triangle) to display the most recent image on the LCD.

- Rotate the Quick Control Dial to review additional images. Turn it counterclockwise to review images from most recent to oldest, or clockwise to start with the first image on the Compact Flash card and cycle forward to the newest.

- Use the Jump button to leap ahead 10 or 100 images.

- Press the Info button repeatedly to cycle among overlays of basic image information, detailed shooting information, or no information at all.

- Press the Magnify button repeatedly to zoom in on the image displayed; the Reduce Image button zooms back out. Press the Playback button to exit magnified display.

- Use the multi-controller to scroll around within a magnified image.

Figure 1.13
Review your images.

Reduce image/Show Thumbnails

Magnify image

Scroll around within magnified image

Advance through images

You'll find information on viewing thumbnail indexes of images, jumping forward and backward 10 or 100 images at a time, automated playback, and other options in Chapter 3.

Transferring Photos to Your Computer

The final step in your picture-taking session will be to transfer the photos you've taken to your computer for printing, further review, or image editing. Your 40D allows you to print directly to PictBridge-compatible printers and to create print orders right in the camera, plus you can select which images to transfer to your computer. I'll outline those options in Chapter 3.

For now, you'll probably want to transfer your images either by using a cable transfer from the camera to the computer, or by removing the Compact Flash card from the 40D and transferring the images with a card reader. The latter option is usually the best, because it's usually much faster and doesn't deplete the battery of your camera. However, you can use a cable transfer when you have the cable and a computer, but no card reader (perhaps you're using the computer of a friend or colleague, or at an Internet café).

To transfer images from the camera to a Mac or PC computer using the USB cable:

1. Turn the camera off.

2. Pry back the rubber cover that protects the EOS 40D's USB port, and plug the USB cable furnished with the camera into the USB port. (See Figure 1.14.)

Figure 1.14
Images can be transferred to your computer using a USB cable.

3. Connect the other end of the USB cable to a USB port on your computer.

4. Turn the camera on. Your installed software usually detects the camera and offers to transfer the pictures, or the camera appears on your desktop as a mass storage device, enabling you to drag and drop the files to your computer.

To transfer images from a Compact Flash card to the computer using a card reader, as shown in Figure 1.15:

1. Turn the camera off.

2. Slide open the Compact Flash card door, and press the gray button, which ejects the card.

3. Insert the Compact Flash card into your memory card reader. Your installed software detects the files on the card and offers to transfer them. The card can also appear as a mass storage device on your desktop, which you can open and then drag and drop the files to your computer.

Figure 1.15
A card reader is the fastest way to transfer photos.

2

Canon EOS 40D Roadmap

The Canon EOS 40D has an amazing number of buttons and dials and knobs—and that's actually a *good* thing. While it might take you some time to learn the position and function of each of these controls, once you've mastered them this camera is remarkably easy to use. That's because dedicated buttons with only one or two functions each are much faster to access than the alternative—a maze of menus that must be navigated every time you want to use a feature.

For example, if you need to change the ISO setting on your 40D, would you rather press the ISO button and spin the Main Dial until the desired value appears on the LCD—or would you prefer tapping a menu button, using cursor keys to locate the ISO setting submenu, pressing a button to select the ISO menu, navigating to the ISO value you want, and then pressing an OK button to confirm your choice? Yet, that's the procedure mandated by countless point-and-shoot digital cameras and more than a few digital SLRs. The Canon dedicated button approach (also used by other digital SLR vendors) is a much better design.

Of course, to learn the function and application of all these controls, what you really need is a street-level roadmap that shows where everything is, and how it's used. But what Canon gives you is a world globe with an overall view and many cross-references to the pages that will tell you what you really need to know. Check out the Nomenclature pages in the manual, which offer two tiny line drawings of the camera body that show front, back, two sides, and the top and bottom of the 40D. There are more than 50 callouts pointing to various buttons and dials. If you can find the control you want in this cramped layout, you'll still need to flip back and forth among multiple pages (individual buttons can have as many as five different cross references!) to locate the information. Most other third-party books follow this format, featuring black-and-white photos of front, back, and top views, and many labels.

I'm out to atone for those deficiencies. In this chapter, I'm going to provide a street-level roadmap, rather than a satellite view, using many different views and lots of explanation accompanying each zone of the camera, so that by the time you finish this chapter, you'll have a basic understanding of every control and what it does. I'm not going to delve into menu functions here—you'll find a discussion of your setup, shooting, and playback menu options in Chapter 3. Everything here is devoted to the button pusher and dial twirler in you.

Canon EOS 40D: Full Frontal

The front of the 40D (see Figure 2.1) is the face seen by your victims as you snap away. For the photographer, though, the front is the surface your fingers curl around as you hold the camera, and there are really only three buttons to press, all within easy reach of the fingers of your left hand, plus the shutter button and Main Dial, which are on the top/front of the handgrip. There are additional controls on the lens itself. You'll need to look at several different views to see everything.

Figure 2.2 shows a three-quarters view of the left side of the EOS 40D (when viewed from the front). You can see the flash hot shoe on top and the door for the Compact Flash card at the left edge. The other components you need to know about are as follows:

- **Shutter button.** Angled on top of the handgrip is the shutter release button. Press this button down halfway to lock exposure and focus (in One Shot mode and AI Focus with non-moving subjects).

- **Main Dial.** This dial is used to change shooting settings. When settings are available in pairs (such as shutter speed/aperture), this dial will be used to make one type of setting, such as shutter speed, while the Quick Control Dial (on the back of the camera) will be used to make the other, such as aperture setting.

- **Red-Eye reduction/self-timer lamp.** This LED provides a blip of light shortly before a flash exposure to cause the subjects' pupils to close down, reducing the effect of red-eye reflections off their retinas. When using the self-timer, this lamp also flashes to mark the countdown until the photo is taken.

- **DC power cord cover.** (Not visible.) This cover, on the inside edge of the handgrip, opens to allow the DC power cable to connect to the 40D.

Figure 2.1

Figure 2.2

Red Eye Reduction
Lamp/Self-Timer Lamp

Main Dial

Shutter Release

Compact Flash Door

Handgrip

DC power
cord cover

■ **Handgrip.** This provides a comfortable handhold, and also contains the 40D's battery.

■ **Compact Flash card slot.** Slide the door over this slot towards the back of the camera to provide access to the Compact Flash memory card.

You'll find more controls on the other side of the 40D, shown in Figure 2.3. In the illustration, you can see the Mode Dial on top, and the rubber cover on the side that protects the camera's USB, TV, external flash, and remote control ports.

Figure 2.3

Autofocus/Manual focus lens switch

Mode Dial

Flash button

External connector terminal cover

Lens release button

Depth-of-field preview

Image stabilization switch

The main buttons shown include:

■ **Flash button.** This button releases the built-in flash so it can flip up (see Figure 2.4) and starts the charging process. If you decide you do not want to use the flash, you can turn it off by pressing the flash head back down.

■ **Lens Release button.** Press and hold this button to unlock the lens so you can rotate the lens to remove it from the camera.

■ **Depth-of-Field Preview button.** This button, adjacent to the lens mount, stops down the lens to the taking aperture so you can see in the viewfinder how much of the image is in focus. The view grows dimmer as the aperture is reduced.

■ **Lens switches.** Canon autofocus lenses have a switch to allow changing between automatic focus and manual focus, and, in the case of IS lenses, another switch to turn image stabilization on and off.

Figure 2.4
Pressing the Flash button (which has an arrow/lightning bolt symbol) pops up the built-in flash unit and starts the charging process.

The main feature on this side of the EOS 40D is a rubber cover (see Figure 2.5) that protects the four connector ports underneath from dust and moisture.

Figure 2.5

External connector terminal cover

The four connectors, shown in Figure 2.6, are as follows:

- **USB port.** Plug in the USB cable furnished with your EOS 40D and connect the other end to a USB port in your computer to transfer photos.

- **Video port.** You can link this connector with a television to view your photos on a large screen.

- **PC terminal.** This connector is for a non-dedicated electronic flash unit, including studio flash.

- **Remote control terminal.** You can plug various Canon remote release switches, timers, and wireless controllers into this connector.

Figure 2.6

PC connector

Video port

Remote Control terminal

USB port

The Canon EOS 40D's Business End

The back panel of the EOS 40D (see Figure 2.7) bristles with more than a dozen different controls, buttons, and knobs. That might seem like a lot of controls to learn, but you'll find, as I noted earlier, that it's a lot easier to press a dedicated button and spin a dial than to jump to a menu every time you want to change a setting.

Figure 2.7

You can see the controls clustered on the left side of the 40D in Figure 2.8. The key buttons and components and their functions are as follows:

- **Viewfinder eyepiece.** You can frame your composition by peering into the viewfinder. It's surrounded by a soft rubber frame that seals out extraneous light when pressing your eye tightly up to the viewfinder, and it also protects your eyeglass lenses (if worn) from scratching. It can be removed and replaced by the cap attached to your neck strap when you use the camera on a tripod, to ensure that light coming from the back of the camera doesn't venture inside and possibly affect the exposure reading.

- **Print/Share button.** Used to print and share images when the 40D is connected to a computer with the USB cable.

- **Menu button.** Summons/exits the menu displayed on the rear LCD of the 40D. When you're working with submenus, this button also serves to exit a submenu and return to the main menu.

- **Playback button.** Displays the last picture taken. Thereafter, you can move back and forth among the available images by rotating the Quick Control Dial, to advance or reverse one image at a time, or the Main Dial, to jump forward or back using the jump method selected with the Jump button (described below). To quit playback, press this button again. The 40D also

Figure 2.8

Print/Share button

Menu button

Viewfinder eyepiece

1/250 8.0   100-0567 CF

Jump button

Erase button

Info/Trim Orientation button

Playback button

Picture Styles button

exits Playback mode automatically when you press the shutter button (so you'll never be prevented from taking a picture on the spur of the moment because you happened to be viewing an image).

■ **Erase button.** Press to erase the image shown on the LCD. A menu will pop up displaying Cancel and Erase choices. Rotate the Main Dial or the Quick Control Dial to select one of these actions, then press the Set button to activate your choice.

■ **Jump button.** Specifies the leaps that skip a specified number of images during playback of the shots you've already taken. Jumps can be either 1 image, 10 images, 100 images, jump by date, or jump by screen (that is, by screens of thumbnails when using index mode). Once the Jump button is pressed, rotate the Quick Control Dial to select the jumping method, and press the

Set button to confirm your choice. Thereafter, the Main Dial can be used to jump using your chosen method. This button is also used to leap to the first item in a menu and to display various types of image information in the single image display mode.

- **Info. button.** When pressed repeatedly, changes the amount of picture information displayed. In shooting mode, the color LCD changes from no information, to detailed information (see Figure 2.9), to a shooting information display that provides the same data as the top panel monochrome LCD (see Figure 2.10). The latter mode is especially useful when the 40D is mounted on a tripod and the top panel isn't readily visible. In playback mode, pressing the Info. button cycles among basic displays of the image; a detailed display with a thumbnail of the image, shooting parameters, and a brightness histogram; and a display with less detail but with separate histograms for brightness, red, green, and blue channels. When setting Picture Styles, the Info. button is used to select a highlighted Picture Style for modification. In Live View mode, the Info. button adjusts the amount of information overlaid on the live image that appears on the LCD screen. When trimming an image, the Info. button selects the orientation.

- **Picture Styles.** This button pops up the Picture Styles menu on the LCD, so you can select a given style or modify an existing style. You'll find more about Picture Styles in Chapter 3.

Figure 2.9

Figure 2.10

More buttons reside on the right side of the back panel, as shown in Figure 2.11. The key controls and their functions are as follows:

- **Diopter adjustment knob.** Rotate this knob to adjust the diopter correction for your eyesight.

- **Multi-controller knob.** This joystick-like button can be shifted up, down, side to side, and diagonally for a total of eight directions, or pressed. It can be used for several functions, including AF point selection, scrolling around a magnified image, trimming a photo, or setting white balance correction.

- **AF-ON.** Press this button to activate the autofocus system without needing to partially depress the shutter release. This control, used with other buttons, allows you to lock exposure and focus separately: Lock exposure by pressing the shutter release halfway, or by pressing the AE Lock button; autofocus by pressing the shutter release halfway, or by pressing the AF-ON button.

- **AE/FE (auto exposure/flash exposure) lock/Thumbnail/Zoom Out button.** This button has several functions, which differ depending on the AF point and metering mode. You can find more about these variations in Chapter 4.

In Shooting mode, it locks the exposure or flash exposure that the camera sets when you partially depress the shutter button. The exposure lock indication

(*) appears in the viewfinder. If you want to recalculate exposure with the shutter button still partially depressed, press the * button again. The exposure will be unlocked when you release the shutter button or take the picture. To retain the exposure lock for subsequent photos, keep the * button pressed while shooting.

When using flash, pressing the * button fires an extra preflash that allows the unit to calculate and lock exposure prior to taking the picture.

In Playback mode, press this button to switch from single-image display to nine-image thumbnail index. Move among the thumbnails with the Quick Control Dial. When an image is zoomed in, press this button to zoom out.

Figure 2.11

- **AF Point Selection/Zoom In button.** In Shooting mode, this button activates autofocus point selection. (See Chapter 4 for information on setting autofocus/exposure point selection.) In Playback mode, this button zooms in on the image that's displayed, or the highlighted thumbnail index image.

- **Access lamp.** When lit or blinking, this lamp indicates that the Compact Flash card is being accessed.

- **Quick Control Dial.** Used to select shooting options, such as f/stop or exposure compensation value, or to navigate through menus. It also serves as an alternate controller for some functions set with other controls, such as AF point.

- **Set button.** Selects a highlighted setting or menu option.

- **ON/OFF switch.** Rotate counterclockwise to the ON position to turn the 40D on with the optional features of the Quick Control Dial deactivated. (Which some users prefer for simplicity; most don't bother with this.)

- **Quick Control Dial switch position.** Rotate the ON/OFF switch all the way counterclockwise to this position to activate the Quick Control Dial.

- **LCD.** View your images and navigate through the menus on this screen.

Going Topside

The top surface of the Canon EOS 40D has its own set of frequently accessed controls. The three of them just forward of the status LCD panel have dual functions and are marked with hyphenated labels. Press the relevant button (you don't need to hold it down) and then rotate the Main Dial to choose the left function of the pair, such as Metering Mode, Autofocus, or ISO, and the Quick Control Dial to select the right function, such as white balance, drive mode, or flash exposure compensation. The settings you make will be indicated in the LCD status panel, which is described in the section that follows this one. The key controls, shown in Figure 2.12, are as follows:

- **Mode Dial.** Rotate this dial to switch among Basic Zone and Creative Zone modes, and to choose one of the Camera User Settings (C1, C2, or C3). You'll find these modes and options described in more detail in Chapter 4.

- **Sensor focal plane.** Precision macro and scientific photography sometimes requires knowing exactly where the focal plane of the sensor is. The symbol on the side of the pentaprism marks that plane.

- **Flash hot shoe.** Slide an electronic flash into this mount when you need a more powerful speedlight. A dedicated flash unit, like those from Canon, can use the multiple contact points shown to communicate exposure, zoom

Figure 2.12

setting, white balance information, and other data between the flash and the camera. There's more on using electronic flash in Chapter 7.

■ **LCD Illuminator button.** Press this button to turn on the amber LCD panel lamp that backlights the LCD status panel for about six seconds, or to turn it off if illuminated. The lamp will remain lit beyond the six-second period if you are using the Mode Dial or other shooting control.

■ **Metering Mode-WB button.** This button has two functions. Rotate the Main Dial after pressing this button to change between Evaluative, Partial, Spot, or Center-Weighted metering. Rotate the Quick Control Dial to cycle among AWB (Automatic White Balance), Daylight, Shade, Cloudy/Twilight/ Sunset, Tungsten, White Fluorescent, Flash, Custom, and Color Temperature. You'll find more information about customizing white balance in Chapter 3.

■ **AF-Drive button.** Press once and then rotate the Main Dial to change between One Shot, AI Focus, and AI Servo autofocus modes (you'll find more about those modes in Chapter 5). Drive mode settings include Single Shot, High Speed Continuous (up to 6.5 fps), Low Speed Continuous (up to3 fps), and 10- or 2-second Self-Timer, selected by holding down the button and rotating the Quick Control Dial.

■ **ISO/Flash Exposure Compensation button.** Press and rotate the Main Dial to choose an ISO setting; use the Quick Control Dial to change electronic flash exposure compensation. You'll find more about ISO options in Chapter 3, and flash EV settings in Chapter 7.

■ **Monochrome LCD status panel.** This LCD readout provides information about the status of your camera and its settings, including exposure mode, number of pictures remaining, battery status, and many other settings. I'll illustrate all these in the next section.

■ **Main Dial.** This dial is used to make many shooting settings. When settings come in pairs (such as shutter speed/aperture in manual shooting mode), the Main Dial is used for one (for example, shutter speed), while the Quick Control Dial is used for the other (aperture).

■ **Shutter release button.** Partially depress this button to lock in exposure and focus. Press all the way to take the picture. Tapping the shutter release when the camera has turned off the auto exposure and autofocus mechanisms reactivates both. When a review image is displayed on the back-panel color LCD, tapping this button removes the image from the display and reactivates the auto exposure and autofocus mechanisms.

WHO'S GOT THE BUTTON?

If you're a veteran of the Canon EOS 30D era, you've probably noticed that only a few controls received new assignments when the 40D was designed. The three top panel buttons are the most notorious culprits. With the 30D, the pairings were as follows: AF Mode/White Balance; Drive Mode/ISO; and Metering Mode/Flash Exposure Compensation. On the theory that the most-used features should be controlled by the Main Dial (and thus reside first in the button pairings), the 40D redesign moved the lesser-used Drive Mode option to the right side of a pair, and the more-frequently accessed ISO control to the left side of a pair.

LCD Panel Readouts

The top panel of the EOS 40D (see Figure 2.13) contains a monochrome LCD readout that displays status information about most of the shooting settings. All of the information segments available are shown in Figure 2.14. I've color-coded

Figure 2.13

Figure 2.14

Shutter Speed/AF Point Selection/CF Card Warnings/Error Codes/Busy/Cleaning Image Sensor/Flash Recycling

Automatic Exposure Bracketing

White Balance Correction

Aperture

Shots Remaining/Shots Remaining-WB Bracketing/Self-Timer Countdown/Bulb Exposure Time

Autofocus Mode

White Balance Presets

Image Size/Quality

Flash Exposure Compensation Indicator

Exposure Level/ Exposure Compensation Amount/ Flash Exposure Compensation Amount/ AEB Range/CF Card Writing Status

Battery Level

Monochrome Mode Indicator

Beeper

ISO Speed

Custom Function

Single Shooting/HS Continuous Shooting/LS Continuous Shooting/Self-Timer the display to make it easier to differentiate them; the information does *not* appear in color on the actual 40D. Many of the information items are mutually exclusive (that is, in the White Balance area at upper left, only one of the possible settings illustrated will appear).

Some of the items on the status LCD also appear in the viewfinder, such as the shutter speed and aperture (pictured at top in blue in the figure), and the exposure level (in yellow at the bottom).

Lens Components

The typical lens, like the one shown in Figures 2.15 and 2.16, has seven or eight common features:

- **Filter thread.** Lenses have a thread on the front for attaching filters and other add-ons. Some also use this thread for attaching a lens hood (you screw on the filter first, and then attach the hood to the screw thread on the front of the filter).

Figure 2.15

Filter thread

Lens hood bayonet mount

Zoom ring

Zoom scale

Focus ring

Focus distance

Autofocus/Manual switch

- **Lens hood bayonet.** This is used to mount the lens hood for lenses that don't use screw-mount hoods (the majority).

- **Zoom ring.** Turn this ring to change the zoom setting.

- **Zoom scale.** These markings on the lens show the current focal length selected.

- **Focus ring.** This is the ring you turn when you manually focus the lens.

- **Distance scale.** This is a readout that rotates in unison with the lens' focus mechanism to show the distance at which the lens has been focused. It's a useful indicator for double-checking autofocus, roughly evaluating depth-of-field, and for setting manual focus guesstimates.

- **Autofocus/Manual switch.** Allows you to change from automatic focus to manual focus.

- **Image stabilization switch (not shown).** Lenses with IS include a separate switch for adjusting the stabilization feature.

Figure 2.16

Electrical Contacts

Lens Mount Bayonet

Looking Inside the Viewfinder

Much of the important shooting status information is shown inside the viewfinder of the EOS 40D. As with the status LCD up on top, not all of this information will be shown at any one time. Figure 2.17 shows what you can expect to see. These readouts include:

- **Spot metering reference circle.** Shows the circle that delineates the metered area when Spot Metering is activated.

- **Autofocus zones.** Shows the nine areas used by the 40D to focus. The camera can select the appropriate focus zone for you, or you can manually select one or all of the zones, as described in Chapter 4.

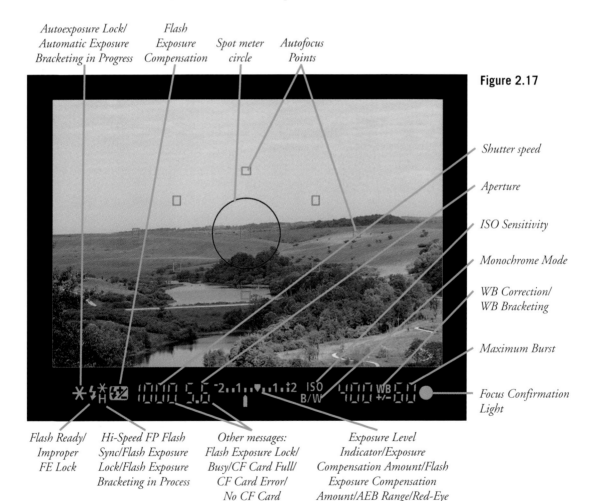

*Autoexposure Lock/
Automatic Exposure
Bracketing in Progress*   *Flash
Exposure
Compensation*   *Spot meter
circle*   *Autofocus
Points*

Figure 2.17

Shutter speed

Aperture

ISO Sensitivity

Monochrome Mode

*WB Correction/
WB Bracketing*

Maximum Burst

*Focus Confirmation
Light*

*Flash Ready/
Improper
FE Lock*   *Hi-Speed FP Flash
Sync/Flash Exposure
Lock/Flash Exposure
Bracketing in Process*   *Other messages:
Flash Exposure Lock/
Busy/CF Card Full/
CF Card Error/
No CF Card*   *Exposure Level
Indicator/Exposure
Compensation Amount/Flash
Exposure Compensation
Amount/AEB Range/Red-Eye
Reduction Lamp-on Indicator*

- **Auto exposure lock.** Shows that exposure has been locked. This icon also appears when an automatic exposure bracketing sequence is in process.

- **Flash ready indicator.** This icon appears when the flash is fully charged. It also shows when the flash exposure lock has been applied for an inappropriate exposure value.

- **Flash status indicator.** Appears along with the flash ready indicator: the H is shown when high speed (focal plane) flash sync is being used. The * appears when flash exposure lock or a flash exposure bracketing sequence is underway.

- **Flash exposure compensation.** Appears when flash EV changes have been made.

- **Shutter speed/aperture readouts.** Most of the time, these readouts show the current shutter speed and aperture. This pair can also warn you of Compact Flash card conditions (full, error, or missing), ISO speed, flash exposure lock, and a buSY indicator when the camera is busy doing other things (including flash recycling).

- **Exposure level indicator.** This scale shows the current exposure level, with the bottom indicator centered when the exposure is correct as metered. The indicator may also move to the left or right to indicate under- or overexposure (respectively). The scale is also used to show the amount of EV and flash EV adjustments, the number of stops covered by the current automatic exposure bracketing range, and is used as a red-eye reduction lamp indicator.

- **ISO Sensitivity.** New to the EOS 40D is this useful indicator that shows the current ISO setting value. Those who have accidentally taken dozens of shots under bright sunlight at ISO 1600 because they forgot to change the setting back after some indoor shooting will treasure this addition.

- **B/W indicator.** Illuminates when the Monochrome Picture Style is being used. There's no way to restore color when you're shooting JPEGs without RAW, so this indicator is another valuable warning.

- **White balance correction.** Shows that white balance has been tweaked.

- **Maximum burst available.** Changes to a number to indicate the number of frames that can be taken in Continuous mode using the current settings.

- **Focus confirmation.** This green dot appears when the subject covered by the active autofocus zone is in sharp focus.

Underneath Your EOS 40D

There's not a lot going on with the bottom panel of your EOS 40D. You'll find a tripod socket, which secures the camera to a tripod, and is also used to lock on the optional BG-E2N battery grip, which provides more juice to run your camera to take more exposures with a single charge. It also adds a vertically oriented shutter release, Main Dial, AE lock/FE lock, and AF point selection controls for easier vertical shooting. There's a terminal connector under a rubber cover to provide a connection between the 40D and accessories that fasten to the underside.

Figure 2.18

*Extension System
Terminal Cover*

Tripod Socket

*Battery Compartment
Latch*

*Optional Battery/
Grip Mounting Holes*

To mount the grip, slide the battery door latch to open at an angle and lightly pull to remove it. That will let you remove the battery door. Then slide the grip into the battery cavity, aligning the pin on the grip with the small hole on the other side of the tripod socket. Tighten the grip's tripod socket screw to lock the grip onto the bottom of your 40D. Figure 2.18 shows the underside view of the camera, and Figure 2.19 offers a close-up look at the accessory terminal connection.

Figure 2.19

*Extension System
Terminal Connection*

3

Setting Up Your Canon EOS 40D

The Canon EOS 40D is undoubtedly the most customizable, tweakable, fine-tunable camera Canon has offered non-professional users. In fact, this versatility has made the 40D surprisingly popular among professional photographers as well. If your camera doesn't behave in exactly the way you'd like, chances are you can make a small change in the shooting, playback, setup, and custom menus that will tailor the 40D to your needs. In fact, if you don't like the *menus* you can create your own using the clever My Menu system.

This chapter will help you sort out the settings you can make to customize how your Canon EOS 40D uses its features, shoots photos, displays images, and processes the pictures after they've been taken. As I've mentioned before, this book isn't intended to replace the manual you received with your 40D, nor have I any interest in rehashing its contents. You'll still find the original manual useful as a standby reference that lists every possible option in exhaustive (if mind-numbing) detail—without really telling you how to use those options to take better pictures. There is, however, some unavoidable duplication between the Canon manual and this chapter, because I'm going to explain the key menu choices and the options you may have in using them. You should find, though, that this chapter gives you the information you need in a much more helpful format, with plenty of detail on why you should make some settings that are particularly cryptic.

I'm not going to waste a lot of space on some of the more obvious menu choices. For example, you can probably figure out that the Beep option in Shooting Menu 1 deals with the solid-state beeper in your camera that sounds off during various activities (such as the self-timer countdown). You can certainly decipher the import of the two options available for the Beep entry (On and Off). In this chapter, I'll devote no more than a sentence or two to the blatantly obvious settings and concentrate on the more confusing aspects of 40D setup, such as automatic exposure bracketing. I'll start off with an overview of using the 40D's menus themselves.

Anatomy of the EOS 40D's Menus

If you used a Canon EOS 30D before you purchased your EOS 40D, you're in for a pleasant surprise from a menu perspective. The time-consuming scrolling through one endless menu (aided by Jump button leaps to the beginning of each menu section) is gone. The EOS 40D has been brought up to date with nine individually tabbed menus, each with a single screen of options (so you won't need to scroll within a menu to see all the entries). The new menus are much cleaner, too, lacking the color-keyed icons, Jump button reminder, scroll bar with position indicator, and surrounding menu border.

With the revamped system, just press the Menu button, spin the Main Dial to highlight the menu tab you want to access (or press the Jump button to hop from tab to tab), and then scroll up and down within a menu with the Quick Control Dial. What could be easier? Canon's "pro" cameras have had this type of menu system for some time, and even the entry-level Digital Rebels have had tabbed menus. Be thankful that Canon's experiment with a single continuous menu has been dumped.

Tapping the Menu button brings up a typical menu like the one shown in Figure 3.1. (If the camera goes to "sleep" while you're reviewing a menu, you may need to wake it up again by tapping the shutter release button.) There are nine menu tabs: Shooting 1, Shooting 2, Playback 1, Playback 2, Set-Up 1, Set-Up 2, Set-Up 3, Custom, and My Menu. The tabs are color coded: red for Shooting menus, blue for Playback menus, yellow for Set-up menus, orange for the Custom menu, and green for the My Menu tab. The currently selected menu's icon is white within a white border, on a background corresponding to its color code. All the inactive menus are grayed out and the icon and their borders are color coded.

Here are the things to watch for as you navigate the menus:

- **Menu tabs.** In the top row of the menu screen, the menu that is currently active will be highlighted as described earlier. One, two, or three dots in the tab lets you know if you are in, say Set-Up 1, Set-Up 2, or Set-Up 3. Just remember that the two red camera icons stand for shooting options; the two blue right-pointing triangles represent playback options; the three yellow wrench/hammer icons stand for set-up options; the orange camera denotes Custom Functions; and the green star stands for personalized menus defined for the star of the show—you.

- **Selected menu item.** The currently selected menu item will have a black background and will be surrounded by a box the same hue as its color code.

- **Other menu choices.** The other menu items visible on the screen will have a medium or dark gray background (alternating).

- **Current setting.** The current settings for visible menu items are shown in the right-hand column, until one menu item is selected (by pressing the Set key or multi-controller). At that point all the settings vanish from the screen except for those dealing with the active menu choice.

Figure 3.1
The EOS 40D's menus are arranged in a series of nine tabs.

Selected menu

Inactive menus

Selected menu item

Other menu choices

Current setting

When you've moved the menu highlighting to the menu item you want to work with, press the Set button or multi-controller to select it. The current settings for the other menu items in the list will be hidden, and a list of options for the selected menu item (or a submenu screen) will appear. Within the menu choices you can scroll up or down with the Quick Control Dial or multi-controller, press Set or the multi-controller to select the choice you've made, and press the Menu button again to exit.

HYPER MENU NAVIGATION

As I mentioned, you can use the Main Dial or Jump button to move from menu to menu, and the Quick Control Dial to highlight a particular menu entry. Press the Set button to select a menu item. That procedure is probably the best way to start out, because those controls are used to make so many settings with the EOS 40D that they quickly become almost intuitive. The 40D manual uses the Main Dial/Quick Control Dial method in its Menu Setting description. But, there's a better way.

If you have an agile thumb, you can do all your menu navigation with the joystick-like multi-controller:

- Shift the multi-controller left/right to jump from tab to tab.

- Press the multi-controller up/down to move within the menu choices of a given tab.

- Press the multi-controller in to select a menu item and press it again to return to the menu choices.

It gets even better. You can jump from tab to tab even if you've highlighted a particular menu setting on another tab—and the 40D will remember which menu entry you've highlighted when you return to that menu. The memorization works even if you leave the menu system or turn your camera off. The 40D always remembers the last menu entry you used with a particular tab. So, if you generally use the FORMAT command each time you access the Set-up 1 menu, that's the entry that will be highlighted when you choose that tab. The camera remembers which tab was last used, too, so, potentially, formatting your memory card might take just a couple presses (the Menu button, the Set button to select the highlighted FORMAT command, then a click of the Quick Command Dial to choose OK, and another press of Set to start the format process).

Shooting Menu 1/2 Options

The various direct setting buttons on the top panel of the camera, for Autofocus mode, white balance, Drive mode, ISO sensitivity, Metering mode, and flash, along with exposure compensation (EV) adjustments are likely to be the most common settings changes you make, with changes during a particular session fairly common. You'll find that the Shooting menu options are those that you access second-most frequently when you're using your EOS 40D. You might make such adjustments as you begin a shooting session, or when you move from one type of subject to another. Canon makes accessing these changes very easy.

This section explains the options of the two Shooting menus and how to use them. The options you'll find in these red-coded menus include:

- Quality

- Red-Eye On/Off

- Beep

- Shoot w/o card

- Review time

- AEB (Automatic Exposure Bracketing)

- White balance

- Custom WB

- WB Shift/BKT

- Color Space

- Picture Style

- Dust Delete Data

Quality Settings

You can choose the image quality settings used by the 40D to store its files. You have three choices to make:

- **Resolution.** The number of pixels captured determines the absolute resolution of the photos you shoot with your EOS 40D. Your choices range from 10 megapixels (Large or L), measuring $3,888 \times 2,592$ pixels; 5.3 megapixels (Medium or M), measuring $2,816 \times 1,880$ pixels; to 2.5 megapixels (Small or S), $1,936 \times 1,288$ pixels.

- **JPEG compression.** To reduce the size of your image files and allow more photos to be stored on a given Compact Flash card, the 40D uses JPEG compression to squeeze the images down to a smaller size. This compacting reduces the image quality a little, so you're offered your choice of Fine compression and Normal compression. The symbols help you remember that Fine compression (represented by a quarter-circle) provides the smoothest results, while Normal compression (signified by a stair-step icon) provides "jaggier" images.

- **JPEG, RAW/sRAW, or both.** You can elect to store only JPEG versions of the images you shoot, or you can save your photos as uncompressed, loss-free RAW files, which consume more than twice as much space on your memory card. Or, you can store both at once as you shoot. The EOS 40D also can use an sRAW file format that is about 25 percent the resolution of a full-sized RAW file. Many photographers elect to save *both* JPEG and either a RAW or sRAW file, so they'll have a JPEG version that might be usable as-is, as well as the original "digital negative" RAW file in case they want to do some processing of the image later. You'll end up with two different versions of the same file: one with a .jpg extension, and one with the .cr2 extension that signifies a Canon RAW or sRAW file. Note that the L+RAW, M+RAW, or S+RAW save a full-resolution (3,888 × 2,592 pixel) RAW file in addition to the JPEG at the specified Large, Medium, or Small resolutions. Similarly, the JPEG+sRAW option always stores a reduced size (1,926 × 1,288 pixel) sRAW file, regardless of the resolution of the JPEG size you've selected.

To choose the combination you want, access the menus, scroll to **Quality**, and press the **Set** button. A screen similar to the one shown in Figure 3.2 will appear. Use the Quick Control Dial or multi-controller to cycle among the 20 choices. In practice, you'll probably use only the Large-Fine, RAW+Large Fine, or RAW selections.

Why so many choices, then? There are some limited advantages to using the Medium and Small resolution settings, Normal JPEG compression setting, and the sRAW format. They all allow stretching the capacity of your Compact Flash card so you can shoehorn quite a few more pictures onto a single memory card. That can come in useful when on vacation and you're running out of storage, or when you're shooting non-critical work that doesn't require a full eight megapixels of resolution (such as photos taken for real estate listings, web page display, photo ID cards, or similar applications). Some photographers like to record RAW+JPEG Standard so they'll have a moderate quality JPEG file for review only, while retaining access to the original RAW file for serious editing.

For most work, using lower resolution and extra compression is false economy. You never know when you might actually need that extra bit of picture detail. Your best bet is to have enough memory cards to handle all the shooting you want to do until you have the chance to transfer your photos to your computer or a personal storage device.

However, reduced image quality can sometimes be beneficial if you're shooting sequences of photos rapidly, as the 40D is able to hold more of them in its internal memory buffer before transferring to the Compact Flash card. Still, for most sports and other applications, you'd probably rather have better, sharper pictures than longer periods of continuous shooting.

Figure 3.2
Choose your resolution, JPEG compression, and file format from this screen.

JPEG vs. RAW

You'll sometimes be told that RAW files are the "unprocessed" image information your camera produces, before it's been modified. That's nonsense. RAW files are no more unprocessed than your camera film is after it's been through the chemicals to produce a negative or transparency. A lot can happen in the developer that can affect the quality of a film image—positively and negatively—and, similarly, your digital image undergoes a significant amount of processing before it is saved as a RAW file. Canon even applies a name (Digic III) to the digital image processing (DIP) chip used to perform this magic.

A RAW file is more similar to a film camera's processed negative. It contains all the information, captured in 14-bit channels per color (and stored in a 16-bit space), with no compression, no sharpening, no application of any special filters or other settings you might have specified when you took the picture. Those settings are *stored* with the RAW file so they can be applied when the image is converted to a form compatible with your favorite image editor. However, using RAW conversion software such as Adobe Camera RAW or Canon's Digital Photo Professional, you can override those settings and apply settings of your own. You can select essentially the same changes there that you might have specified in your camera's picture-taking options.

RAW exists because sometimes we want to have access to all the information captured by the camera, before the camera's internal logic has processed it and converted the image to a standard file format. RAW doesn't save as much space as JPEG. What it does do is preserve all the information captured by your camera after it's been converted from analog to digital form. Of course, the 40D's sRAW format preserves the *settings* information, but discards some of the resolution to give you that 1,926 × 1,288 small RAW file.

So, why don't we always use RAW? Although some photographers do save only in RAW format, it's more common to use either RAW plus one of the JPEG options, or just shoot JPEG and eschew RAW altogether. While RAW is overwhelmingly helpful when an image needs to be fine-tuned, in other situations working with a RAW file can slow you down significantly. RAW images take longer to store on the Compact Flash card, and require more post-processing effort, whether you elect to go with the default settings in force when the picture was taken, or make minor adjustments.

As a result, those who depend on speedy access to images or who shoot large numbers of photos at once may prefer JPEG over RAW. Wedding photographers, for example, might expose several thousand photos during a bridal affair and offer hundreds to clients as electronic proofs for inclusion in an album. Wedding shooters take the time to make sure that their in-camera settings are correct, minimizing the need to post process photos after the event. Given that their JPEGs are so good, there is little need to get bogged down shooting RAW.

Sports photographers also eschew RAW files. I visited a local Division III college one sunny September afternoon while I was writing this book and managed to cover a football game, trot down a hill to shoot a women's soccer match later that afternoon, and ended up in the adjacent field house shooting a volleyball invitational tournament an hour later. I managed to shoot 1,920 photos, most of them

MANAGING LOTS OF FILES

The only long-term drawback to shooting everything in RAW+JPEG is that it's easy to fill up your computer's hard drive if you are a prolific photographer. Here's what I do. My most recent photos are stored on my working hard drive in a numbered folder, say 40D-01, with subfolders named after the shooting session, such as 080301Trees, for pictures of trees taken on March 1, 2008. An automatic utility copies new and modified photos to a different hard drive for temporary backup four times daily.

When the top-level folder accumulates about 30GB of images, I back it up to DVDs and then move the folder to a 500GB drive dedicated solely for storage of folders that have already been backed up onto DVD. Then I start a new folder, such as 40D-02, on the working hard drive and repeat the process. I always have at least one backup of every image taken, either on another hard drive or on a DVD.

at a 6.5 fps clip, in about four hours. I certainly didn't have any plans to do post-processing on very many of those shots, and firing the 40D at its maximum frame rate didn't allow RAW shooting, so carefully exposed and precisely focused JPEG images were my file format of choice that day.

JPEG was invented as a more compact file format that can store most of the information in a digital image, but in a much smaller size. JPEG predates most digital SLRs, and was initially used to squeeze down files for transmission over slow dialup connections. Even if you were using an early dSLR with 1.3 megapixel files for news photography, you didn't want to send them back to the office over a modem at 1,200 bps.

But, as I noted, JPEG provides smaller files by compressing the information in a way that loses some image data. JPEG remains a viable alternative because it offers several different quality levels. At the highest quality Fine level, you might not be able to tell the difference between the original RAW file and the JPEG version, even though the RAW file occupies, by Canon's estimate, 12.4MB on your memory card, while the Fine JPEG takes up only 3.5MB of space. You've squeezed the image by more than half without losing much visual information at all. If you don't mind losing some quality, you can use more aggressive Standard compression with JPEG to cut the size in half again, to 1.8MB.

In my case, I shoot virtually everything at RAW+JPEG Fine. Most of the time, I'm not concerned about filling up my memory cards, as I usually have a minimum of three 8GB Compact Flash cards with me. If I know I may fill up all those cards, I have a tiny battery-operated personal storage device that can copy an 8GB card in about 15 minutes. As I mentioned earlier, when shooting sports I'll shift to JPEG FINE (with no RAW file) to squeeze a little extra speed out of my 40D's Continuous Shooting mode, and to reduce the need to wade through eight-photo bursts taken in RAW format. On the other hand, on my last trip to Europe, I took only RAW (instead of my customary RAW+JPEG) photos to fit more images onto my 60GB personal storage device, shown in Figure 3.3, as I planned on doing at least some post-processing on many of the images for a travel book I was working on.

Figure 3.3 If RAW storage space is a concern, consider a portable storage device like this one.

Red-Eye Reduction

Your EOS 40D has a fairly effective Red-Eye Reduction flash mode. Unfortunately, your camera is unable, on its own, to *eliminate* the red-eye effects that occur when an electronic flash (or, rarely, illumination from other sources) bounces off the retinas of the eye and into the camera lens. Animals seem to suffer from yellow or green glowing pupils, instead; the effect is equally undesirable. The effect is worst under low-light conditions (exactly when you might be using a flash) as the pupils expand to allow more light to reach the retinas. The best you can hope for is to *reduce* or minimize the red-eye effect.

The best way to truly eliminate red-eye is to raise the flash up off the camera so its illumination approaches the eye from an angle that won't reflect directly back to the retina and into the lens. The extra height of the built-in flash may not be sufficient, however. That alone is a good reason for using an external flash. If you're working with your 40D's built-in flash, your only recourse may be to switch the Red-Eye Reduction feature on with the menu choice shown in Figure 3.4. It causes a lamp on the front of the camera to illuminate with a half-press of the shutter release button, which may cause your subjects' pupils to contract, decreasing the amount of the red-eye effect. (You may have to ask your subject to look at the lamp to gain maximum effect.) Figure 3.5 shows the effects of wider pupils (left) and those that have been contracted using the 40D's Red-Eye Reduction feature.

Figure 3.4
Turn on your camera's Red-Eye Reduction feature to help eliminate demon-red pupils.

Red-eye On/Off   Off
▶On

Figure 3.5 Same pose, same location (but different days) and red-eye is tamed (right), thanks to the EOS 40D's red-eye reduction lamp.

Beep

The EOS 40D's internal beeper provides a helpful chirp to signify various functions, such as the countdown of your camera's self-timer. You can switch it off if you want to avoid the beep because it's annoying, impolite, or distracting (at a concert or museum), or undesired for any other reason. It's one of the few ways to make the 40D a bit quieter, other than Live View's "silent shoot" mode. (I've actually had new dSLR owners ask me how to turn off the "shutter sound" the camera makes; such an option was available in the point-and-shoot camera they'd used previously.) Select **Beep** from the menu, press **Set**, and use the Quick Control Dial to choose On or Off, as you prefer, as shown in Figure 3.6. Press **Set** again to activate your choice.

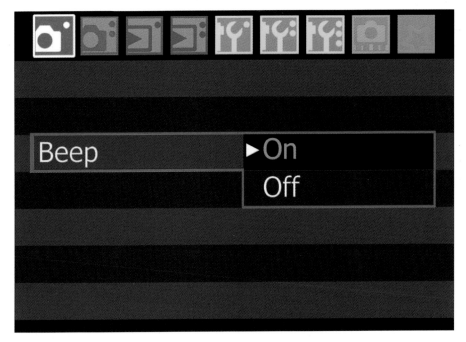

Figure 3.6

Silence your camera's beep when it might prove distracting.

Shoot without a Compact Flash Card Installed

This entry in the Set-up 1 menu (see Figure 3.7) gives you the ability to snap off "pictures" without a Compact Flash card installed—or to lock the camera shutter release if that is the case. It is sometimes called Play mode, because you can experiment with your camera's features or even hand your 40D to a friend to let them fool around, without any danger of pictures actually being taken. Back in our film days, we'd sometimes finish a roll, rewind the film back into its cassette surreptitiously, and then hand the camera to a child to take a few pictures—without actually wasting any film. It's hard to waste digital film, but Shoot Without Card mode is still appreciated by some, especially camera vendors who want to be able to demo a camera at a store or trade show, but don't want to have to equip each and every demonstrator model with a Compact Flash card. Choose this menu item, press **Set**, select **On** or **Off**, and press **Set** again to enable or disable this capability.

Figure 3.7
You can enable triggering the shutter even when no Compact Flash card is present.

Review Time Out

You can adjust the amount of time an image is displayed for review on the LCD after each shot is taken. You can elect to disable this review entirely (Off), or choose display times of 2, 4, or 8 seconds. You can also select Hold, an indefinite display, which will keep your image on the screen until you use one of the other controls, such as the shutter button, Main Dial, or Quick Control Dial. Turning the review display off or choosing a brief duration can help preserve battery power. However, the 40D will always override the review display when the shutter button is partially or fully depressed, so you'll never miss a shot because a previous image was on the screen. Choose **Review Time** from the Shooting 1 menu, and select Off, 2 sec., 4 sec., 8 sec., or Hold, as shown in Figure 3.8. If you want to retain an image on the screen for a longer period, but don't want to use Hold as your default, press the Erase button under the LCD monitor. The image will display until you choose Cancel or Erase from the menu that pops up at the bottom of the screen.

Figure 3.8

Adjust the time an image is displayed on the LCD for review after a picture is taken.

Automatic Exposure Bracketing

The first entry on the Shooting 2 menu is AEB, or automatic exposure bracketing. As you'll learn in Chapter 4, bracketing using the 40D's AEB feature is a way to shoot several consecutive exposures using different settings, to improve the odds that one will be exactly right. Select this menu choice, then use the Quick Control Dial to spread or contract the three dots beneath the –2/+2 scale until you've defined the range you want the bracket to cover, shown as two-thirds-stop jumps in Figure 3.9. When AEB is activated, the three bracketed shots will be exposed in this sequence: metered exposure, decreased exposure, increased exposure (unless you've redefined the bracketing sequence to decreased exposure, metered exposure, increased exposure using C. Fn I -05). You'll find more information about exposure bracketing in Chapter 4.

Figure 3.9

Set the range of the three bracketed exposures.

White Balance

This menu entry allows you to choose one of the white balance preset values from among Auto, Daylight, Shade, Cloudy/Twilight/Sunset, Tungsten, White Fluorescent Light, Flash, or Custom. You'll find more information on choosing the right white balance in Chapters 4 and 7. Once you've selected **White balance** from the Shooting 2 menu, use the Quick Control Dial to choose a setting from the two columns of entries, then press the Set button to lock it in. (See Figure 3.10.) If you choose the "K" entry, you can select an exact color temperature from 2,500K to 10,000K using the Main Dial. Choosing the right white balance can have a dramatic effect on the colors of your image, as you can see in Figure 3.11.

Figure 3.10
White balance presets can be chosen here.

Figure 3.11 Adjusting color temperature can provide different results of the same subject at 3,400K (left), 5,000K (center), and 2,800K (right).

Custom White Balance

If automatic white balance or one of the six preset settings available (Auto, Daylight, Shade, Cloudy/Twilight/Sunset, Tungsten, White Fluorescent, or Flash) aren't suitable, you can set a custom white balance using this menu option. The custom setting you establish will then be applied whenever you select Custom using the White Balance menu entry described earlier.

To set the white balance to an appropriate color temperature under the current ambient lighting conditions, focus manually (with the lens set on MF) on a plain white or gray object, such as a card or wall, making sure the object fills the spot metering circle in the center of the viewfinder. Then, take a photo. Next press the Menu button and select **Custom WB** from the Shooting 2 menu. Use the Quick Control Dial until the reference image you just took appears and press the Set button to store the white balance of the image as your Custom setting.

A WHITE BALANCE LIBRARY

Shoot a selection of blank-card images under a variety of lighting conditions on a spare Compact Flash card. If you want to "recycle" one of the color temperatures you've stored, insert the card and set the Custom white balance to that of one of the images in your white balance library, as described above.

White Balance Shift and Bracketing

White balance shift allows you to dial in a white balance color bias along the Blue/Yellow (Amber) dimensions, and/or Magenta/Green scale. In other words, you can set your color balance so that it is a little bluer or yellower (only), a little more magenta or green (only), or a combination of the two bias dimensions. You can also bracket exposures, taking several consecutive pictures each with a slightly different color balance biased in the directions you specify.

The process is a little easier to visualize if you look at Figure 3.12. The center intersection of lines BA and GM (remember high school geometry!) is the point of zero bias. Move the point at that intersection using the multi-controller joystick to locate it at any point on the graph using the Blue-Yellow (Amber) and Green-Magenta coordinates. The amount of shift will be displayed in the SHIFT box to the right of the graph.

Figure 3.12
Use the Quick Control Dial to specify color balance bracketing using Green-Magenta bias or to specify Blue-Yellow/Amber bias.

White balance bracketing is like white balance shifting, only the bracketed changes occur along the bias axis you specify. The three squares in Figure 3.12 show that the white balance bracketing will occur in two stop steps along the blue-yellow (amber) axis. The amount of the bracketing is shown in the lower box to the right of the graph.

This form of bracketing is similar to exposure bracketing, but with the added dimension of hue. Bias bracketing can be performed in any JPEG-only mode. You can't use RAW, sRAW, RAW+JPEG, or sRAW+JPEG, because the RAW files already contain the information needed to fine-tune the white balance and white balance bias.

When you select WB SHIFT/BKT, the adjustment screen appears. First, you turn the Quick Control Dial to set the range of the shift in either the Green/Magenta dimension (turn the dial to the left to change the vertical separation of the three dots representing the separate exposures), or in the Blue-Yellow/Amber dimension by turning the Quick Control Dial to the right. Use the multi-controller joystick to move the bracket set around within the color space, and outside the Green-Magenta or Blue-Yellow/Amber axes.

Use the multi-controller only after you've accumulated some experience in shifting around the white balance manually. In most cases, it's fairly easy to determine if you want your image to be more green, more magenta, more blue, or more yellow, although judging your current shots on the LCD screen can be tricky unless you view the screen in a darkened location so it will be bright and easy to see. You'll find more about bracketing in Chapter 4.

Color Space

You can select one of two color gamuts (the range of colors available to represent an image) using this menu entry, shown previously among the other menu choices in Figure 3.9. Adobe RGB is an expanded color space useful for commercial and professional printing, and it can reproduce a wider range of colors. Canon recommends against using this color space if your images will be displayed primarily on your computer screen or output by your personal printer. The sRGB setting is recommended for images that will be output locally on the user's own printer, as this color space matches that of the typical inkjet printer fairly closely. Strictly speaking, both color spaces can reproduce the exact same absolute number of colors (16.8 million when reduced to a 24-bit file from the original capture), but Adobe RGB spreads those colors over a larger space. Think of a box of crayons (the jumbo 16.8 million crayon variety). Some of the basic crayons from the original sRGB set have been removed and replaced with new hues not contained in the original box. Your "new" box contains colors that can't be reproduced by your computer monitor, but which work just fine with a commercial printing press.

BEST OF BOTH WORLDS

If you plan to use RAW+JPEG or sRAW+JPEG for most of your photos, go ahead and set sRGB as your color space. You'll end up with JPEGs suitable for output on your own printer, but you can still extract an Adobe RGB version from the RAW file at any time. It's like shooting two different color spaces at once—sRGB and Adobe RGB—and getting the best of both worlds.

Picture Styles

Picture Styles let you choose a combination of sharpness, contrast, color saturation, and color tone settings that you can apply to all the pictures you take using a particular style. The Canon EOS 40D has a "Standard" Picture Style, plus preset styles for Portrait, Landscape, Neutral, and Faithful pictures (which can all be customized with your preferences), plus three user-definable settings you can apply to any sort of shooting situation you want, such as sports, architecture, or baby pictures. There is also a Monochrome Picture Style that allows you to adjust filter effects or add color toning to your black-and-white images.

The Picture Styles feature, introduced to the EOSx0 camera line with the Canon EOS 30D, is one of the most important tools for customizing the way your 40D renders its photos. Picture Styles are extremely flexible. If you don't like one of the predefined styles, you can adjust it to suit your needs. You can also use those three User Definition files to create styles that are all your own. If you want rich, bright colors to emulate Velvia film or the work of legendary photographer Pete Turner, you can build your own color-soaked style. If you want soft, muted colors and less sharpness to create a romantic look, you can do that, too. Perhaps you'd like a setting with extra contrast for shooting outdoors on hazy or cloudy days.

Once your styles are set up, Picture Styles are easy to access. Press the Picture Styles button under the color LCD, and use the Quick Control Dial or multi-controller to scroll through the list of available styles. Press Set or the multi-controller button to activate the style of your choice. You can also select a Picture Style from this menu entry (although it takes a few seconds longer). You'll primarily use this menu item to define or redefine your Picture Styles. (You can also set up Picture Styles using the 40D's Picture Styles Editor, as described in this book's Chapter 8.)

Choose **Picture Styles** from the Shooting 2 menu and press **Set** to produce the menu screen shown in Figure 3.13. Use the Quick Control Dial to rotate among the nine choices (the ones shown, plus User Def. 1, User Def. 2, and User Def. 3) and press **Set** to activate your choice. Then press the Menu button to exit the menu system. You can see that switching among Picture Styles is fast and easy enough to allow you to shift gears as often as you like during a shooting session.

The EOS 40D is smart enough to use Picture Styles on its own. When using one of the Basic Zone modes, the camera selects the Standard Picture Style automatically, except if you select the Portrait or Landscape modes. The Portrait and Landscape Picture Styles will be used (respectively) instead.

Figure 3.13
Nine different Picture
Styles are available;
these six plus three
User Def styles not
shown.

Picture Style	◐, ◑, ⚬, ◓
Standard	3, 0, 0, 0
Portrait	2, 0, 0, 0
Landscape	4, 0, 0, 0
Neutral	0, 0, 0, 0
Faithful	0, 0, 0, 0
Monochrome	3, 0, N, N
INFO. Detail set.	**SET** OK

Defining Picture Styles

Canon makes interpreting current Picture Style settings and applying changes very easy. The current settings are shown as numeric values on the menu screen shown in Figure 3.13. Some camera vendors use word descriptions, like Sharp, Extra Sharp, or Vivid, More Vivid that are difficult to relate to. The 40D's settings, on the other hand, are values on uniform scales, with seven steps (from 1 to 7) for sharpness, and plus/minus four steps clustered around a zero (no change) value for contrast and saturation (so you can change from low contrast/low saturation, –4, to high contrast/high saturation, +4), as well as color tone (–4/reddish to +4/yellowish). (EOS 20D veterans will note that the earlier camera used coarser –2/+2 steps for all these, including sharpness.) The individual icons represent (left to right) Sharpness, Contrast, Saturation, and Color Tone. To change one of the existing Picture Styles, or to define your own, just follow these steps:

1. Access the Picture Style menu (pressing the Picture Style button under the LCD is the fastest way) and use the Quick Command Dial to scroll to the style you'd like to adjust.

2. Press the INFO. button to choose **Detail set.** and produce the screen shown in Figure 3.14. The Quick Command Dial can scroll among the four parameters, plus **Default set.** at the bottom of the screen, which restores the values to the preset numbers.

Figure 3.14
Each parameter can be changed separately.

3. Press **Set** to change the values of one of the four parameters. If you're redefining one of the default presets, the menu screen will look like the figure, which represents the Landscape Picture Style.

4. Use the Quick Command Dial or multi-controller to move the triangle to the value you want to use. Note that the previous value remains on the scale, represented by a gray triangle. This makes it easy to return to the original setting if you want.

5. Press the Set button to lock in that value, then press the Menu button three times to back out of the menu system.

Any Picture Style that has been changed from its defaults will be shown in the Picture Style menu with blue highlighting the altered parameter. You don't have to worry about changing a Picture Style and then forgetting that you've modified it. A quick glance at the Picture Style menu will show you which styles and parameters have been changed.

Making changes in the Monochrome Picture Style is slightly different, as the Saturation and Color Tone parameters are replaced with Filter Effect and Toning Effect options. (Keep in mind that once you've taken a photo using a Monochrome Picture Style, you can't convert the image back to full color.) You can choose from Yellow, Orange, Red, Green filters, or None, and specify Sepia, Blue, Purple or Green toning, or None. You can still set the Sharpness and Contrast parameters that are available with the other Picture Styles. Figure 3.15 shows filter effects being applied to the Monochrome Picture Style.

Figure 3.15
Select from among four color filters in the Monochrome Picture Style.

FILTERS VS. TONING

Although some of the color choices overlap, you'll get very different looks when choosing between Filter Effects and Toning Effects. Filter Effects add no color to the monochrome image. Instead, they reproduce the look of black-and-white film that has been shot through a color filter. That is, Yellow will make the sky darker and the clouds will stand out more, while Orange makes the sky even darker and sunsets more full of detail. The Red filter produces the darkest sky of all and darkens green objects, such as leaves. Human skin may appear lighter than normal. The Green filter has the opposite effect on leaves, making them appear lighter in tone. Figure 3.16 shows the same scene shot with no filter, then Yellow, Green, and Red filters.

The Sepia, Blue, Purple, and Green toning effects, on the other hand, all add a color cast to your monochrome image. Use these when you want an old-time look or a special effect, without bothering to recolor your shots in an image editor.

Figure 3.16 No filter (upper left); yellow filter (upper right); green filter (lower left); and red filter (lower right).

Dust Delete Data

This menu choice lets you "take a picture" of any dust or other particles that may be adhering to your sensor. The 40D will then append information about the location of this dust to your photos, so that the Digital Photo Professional software can use this reference information to identify dust in your images and remove it automatically. You should capture a Dust Delete Data photo from time to time as your final line of defense against sensor dust.

To use this feature, select **Dust Delete Data** to produce the screen shown in Figure 3.17. Select **OK** and press the Set button. The camera will first perform a self-cleaning operation by applying ultrasonic vibration to the low-pass filter that resides on top of the sensor. Then, a screen will appear asking you to press the shutter button. Point the 40D at a solid white card with the lens set on manual focus and rotate the focus ring to infinity. When you press the shutter release, the camera takes a photo of the card using aperture priority and f/22 (which provides enough depth-of-field (actually, in this case *depth-of-focus*) to image the dust sharply. The "picture" is not saved to your Compact Flash card but, rather, is stored in a special memory area in the camera. Finally, a "Data obtained" screen appears.

The Delete Dust Data information is retained in the camera until you update it by taking a new "picture." The 40D adds the information to each image file automatically.

Figure 3.17
Capture updated dust data for your sensor to allow Digital Photo Professional to remove it automatically.

Playback Menu 1/2 Options

The two blue-coded Playback menus are where you select options related to the display, review, transfer, and printing of the photos you've taken. The choices you'll find include:

- Protect images
- Rotate
- Erase images
- Print order
- Transfer order

- Highlight alert
- AF point disp.
- Histogram
- Auto Play

Protect

If you want to keep an image from being accidentally erased (either with the Erase button or by using the Erase menu), you can mark that image for protection. To protect one or more images, press the Menu button and choose **Protect**. Then use the Quick Control Dial to view the image to be protected. Press the **Set** button to apply the protection. A key icon will appear at the upper edge of the information display while still in the protection screen, and when reviewing that image later (see Figure 3.18). To remove protection, repeat the process. You can scroll among the other images on your memory card and protect/unprotect them in the same way. Image protection will not save your images from removal when the card is reformatted.

Figure 3.18
Protected images can be locked against accidental erasure (but not preserved from formatting).

Rotate

While you can set the EOS 40D to automatically rotate images taken in a vertical orientation using the Auto Rotate option in the Set-up menu, you can manually rotate an image during playback using this menu selection. Select **Rotate** from the Playback 1 menu, use the Quick Command Dial to page through the available images on your memory card until the one you want to rotate appears, then press **Set**. The image will appear on the screen rotated 90 degrees, as shown in Figure 3.18. Press **Set** again, and the image will be rotated 270 degrees.

Erase Images

Choose this menu entry and you'll be given two choices: **Select and erase images** and **All images on card.** The former option displays the most recent image. Press **Set** to mark that image for deletion, and then rotate the Quick Command Dial to view other images, using the **Set** button to mark those you want to delete. When finished marking pictures, press the Trash button, and you'll see a screen that says **Erase selected images** with two options, **Cancel** and **OK.** Use the Quick Command Dial to choose **OK**, then press the **Set** button to erase the images, or select **Cancel** and press the **Set** button to return to the selection screen. Press the Menu button to unmark your selections and return to the menu.

The **All images on card** choice removes all the pictures on the card, except for those you've marked with the Protect command, and does not reformat the memory card.

Print Order

The EOS 40D supports the DPOF (Digital Print Order Format) that is now almost universally used by digital cameras to specify which images on your memory card should be printed, and the number of prints desired of each image. This information is recorded on the memory card, and can be interpreted by a compatible printer when the camera is linked to the printer using the USB cable, or when the memory card is inserted into a card reader slot on the printer itself. Photo labs are also equipped to read this data and make prints when you supply your memory card to them.

You can read more about assembling print orders in Chapter 8.

Transfer Order

You can specify which images are to be transferred to your personal computer when the EOS 40D is linked to the computer with the USB cable. Individual images are "marked" using a review and selection system similar to the one used to specify print orders. You'll find more about creating a transfer order in Chapter 8.

Highlight Alert

This menu entry is the first item on the second Playback menu tab and has just two options: Enable and Disable. When set to Enable, overexposed highlight areas in your image will blink during picture review. That's your cue to consider using exposure compensation to reduce exposure, unless a minus-EV setting will cause loss of shadow detail that you want to preserve. You can read more about correcting exposure in Chapter 4.

Autofocus Points Display

The 40D can display the autofocus point (or points) that was active when the picture was taken as a tiny red square when the full information display is chosen for playback. (Some users mistake the red square in the playback thumbnail as a "hot" pixel.) Choose **AF point disp.** in the Playback 2 menu and select **Enable** or **Disable**. There is little reason not to view this information, so most leave this setting switched on at all times. There's more about choosing autofocus points in Chapter 5.

Histogram

The 40D can show either a Brightness histogram or set of three separate Red, Green, and Blue histograms in the full information display during picture review. Brightness histograms give you information about the overall tonal values present in the image. The RGB histograms can show more advanced users valuable data about specific channels that might be "clipped" (details are lost in the shadows or highlights). Select **Histogram** from the Playback 2 menu and choose **Brightness** or **RGB**. You can read more about using histograms in Chapter 4.

Auto Play

Auto Play is a convenient way to review images one after another, without the need to manually switch between them. To activate, just choose **Auto Play** from the Playback 2 menu. During playback, you can press the **Set** button to pause the "slide show" (in case you want to examine an image more closely), or the Info. button to change the amount of information displayed on the screen with each image. For example, you might want to review a set of images and their histograms to judge the exposure of the group of pictures.

Set-up Menu 1/2/3 Options

There are three yellow-coded Set-up menus where you make adjustments on how your camera *behaves* during your shooting session, as differentiated from the Shooting menu, which adjusts how the pictures are actually taken. Your choices include:

- Auto power off
- File numbering
- Auto rotate
- INFO. button
- Format
- LCD brightness
- Date/Time
- Language

- Video system
- Sensor cleaning
- Live View function settings
- Flash control
- Camera user setting
- Clear all camera settings
- Firmware Ver.

Auto Power Off

This setting allows you to determine how long the EOS 40D remains active before shutting itself off. As you can see in Figure 3.19, you can select 1, 2, 4, 8, 15, or 30 minutes or Off, which leaves the camera turned on indefinitely. However, even

Figure 3.19
Select an automatic shut-off period to save battery power.

if the camera has shut itself off, if the power switch remains in the On position, you can bring the camera back to life by pressing the shutter button or, if using a Creative Zone mode, by pressing the * button.

SAVING POWER WITH THE EOS 40D

There are three settings and several techniques you can use to help you stretch the longevity of your 40D's battery. The first setting is the Review Time option described earlier under the Shooting 1 menu. That big 3-inch LCD uses a lot of juice, so reducing the amount of time it is used (either for automatic review or for manually playing back your images) can boost the effectiveness of your battery. Auto Power Off turns off most functions (metering and autofocus shut off by themselves about six seconds after you release the shutter button or take a picture) based on the delay you specify. The third setting is the LCD Brightness adjustment described below. If you're willing to shade the LCD with your hand, you can often get away with lower brightness settings outdoors, which will further increase the useful life of your battery. The techniques? Use the internal flash as little as possible; no flash at all or fill flash use less power than a full blast. Turn off image stabilization if your lens has that feature and you feel you don't need it. When transferring pictures from your 40D to your computer, use a card reader instead of the USB cable. Linking your camera to your computer and transferring images using the cable takes longer and uses a lot more power.

File Numbering

The EOS 40D will automatically apply a file number to each picture you take, using consecutive numbering for all your photos over a long period of time, spanning many different memory cards, starting over from scratch when you insert a new card, or when you manually reset the numbers. Numbers are applied from 0001 to 9999, at which time the camera creates a new folder on the card (100, 101, 102, and so forth), so you can have 0001 to 9999 in folder 100, then numbering will start over in folder 101.

The camera keeps track of the last number used in its internal memory. That can lead to a few quirks you should be aware of. For example, if you insert a memory card that had been used with a different camera, the 40D may start numbering with the next number after the highest number used by the previous camera. (I once had a brand new 40D start numbering files in the 8,000 range.) I'll explain how this can happen next.

On the surface, the numbering system seems simple enough: In the menu, you can choose Continuous, Automatic Reset, or Manual Reset. Here is how each works:

■ **Continuous.** If you're using a blank/reformatted memory card, the 40D will apply a number that is one greater than the number stored in the camera's internal memory. If the card is not blank and contains images, then the next number will be one greater than the highest number on the card *or* in internal memory. (In other words, if you want to use continuous file numbering consistently, you must always use a card that is blank or freshly formatted.) Here are some examples.

*You've taken 4,235 shots with the camera, and you insert a blank/reformatted memory card. The next number assigned will be 4,236, based on the value stored in internal memory.

*You've taken 4,235 shots with the camera, and you insert a memory card with a picture numbered 2,728. The next picture will be numbered 4,236.

*You've taken 4,235 shots with the camera, and you insert a memory card with a picture numbered 8,281. The next picture will be numbered 8,282, and that value will be stored in the camera's menu as the "high" shot number (and will be applied when you next insert a blank card).

■ **Automatic Reset.** If you're using a blank/reformatted memory card, the next photo taken will be numbered 0001. If you use a card that is not blank, the next number will be one greater than the highest number found on the memory card. Each time you insert a memory card, the next number will either be 0001, or one higher than the highest already on the card.

■ **Manual Reset.** The 40D creates a new folder numbered one higher than the last folder created, and restarts the file numbers at 0001. Then, the camera uses the numbering scheme that was previously set, either Continuous or Automatic Reset, each time you subsequently insert a blank or non-blank memory card.

Auto Rotate

You can turn this feature On or Off. When activated, the EOS 40D rotates pictures taken in vertical orientation on the LCD screen so you don't have to turn the camera to view them comfortably. However, this orientation also means that the longest dimension of the image is shown using the shortest dimension of the LCD, so the picture is reduced in size. You have three options, shown in Figure 3.20. The image can be autorotated when viewing in the camera *and* on your computer screen using your image editing/viewing software. The image can be marked

Figure 3.20
Choose autorotation
both in the camera
and on your
computer display
(top); only on your
computer display
(middle); or no
automatic rotation
(bottom).

to autorotate *only* when reviewing your image in your image editor or viewing software. This option allows you to have rotation applied when using your computer, while retaining the ability to maximize the image on your LCD in the camera. The third choice is Off. The image will not be rotated when displayed in the camera or with your computer. Note that if you switch Auto Rotate off, any pictures shot while the feature is disabled will not be automatically rotated when you turn Auto Rotate back on; information embedded in the image file when the photo *is taken* is used to determine whether autorotation is applied.

Info. Button

The Info. button on the back panel of the Canon EOS 40D by default alternates between the Camera Settings and Shooting Functions information displays (see Figure 3.21). If one is shown, press the Info. button to see the other. If you'd rather have only one of those screens shown (and disable the toggling feature), choose **INFO. button** from Set-up Menu 1 (see Figure 3.22) and change from **Normal disp.** to either **Camera set.** or **Shoot. func.**

Figure 3.21
The Info. button toggles between the Camera Settings (top) and Shooting Functions menus (bottom).

Figure 3.22
To view only the information screen you prefer, choose INFO. Button from the Set-up 1 menu.

Format

Use this item to erase everything on your memory card and set up a fresh file system ready for use. When you select **Format**, you'll see a display like Figure 3.23, showing the capacity of the card, how much of that space is currently in use, and two choices at the bottom of the screen to **Cancel** or **OK** (proceed with the format). A blue-green bar appears on the screen to show the progress of the formatting step.

Figure 3.23
You must confirm the format step before the camera will erase a memory card.

LCD Brightness

Choose this menu option, the first on the second Set-up menu tab, and a thumbnail image with a grayscale strip appears on the LCD, as shown in Figure 3.24. Use the multi-controller or the Quick Control Dial to adjust the brightness to a comfortable viewing level. Brighter settings use more battery power, but can allow you to view an image on the LCD outdoors in bright sunlight. When you have the brightness you want, press the Set button to lock it in and return to the menu.

Date/Time

Use this option to set the date and time, which will be embedded in the image file along with exposure information and other data.

Figure 3.24
Adjust LCD brightness for easier viewing under varying ambient lighting conditions.

Language

Choose from 18 languages for menu display, rotating the Quick Command Dial or using the multi-controller joystick until the language you want to select is highlighted. Press the Set button to activate. Your choices include English, German, French, Dutch, Danish, Portuguese, Finnish, Italian, Norwegian, Swedish, Spanish, Greek, Russian, Polish, Simplified Chinese, Traditional Chinese, Korean, and Japanese.

If you accidentally set a language you don't read and find yourself with incomprehensible menus, don't panic. Just choose the third option from the top of the Set-up 2 menu, and select the idioma, sprache, langue, or kieli of your choice.

Video System

This setting controls the output of the 40D through the AV cable when you're displaying images on an external monitor. You can select either NTSC, used in the United States, Canada, Mexico, many Central, South American, and Caribbean countries, much of Asia, and other countries; or PAL, which is used in the UK, much of Europe, Africa, India, China, and parts of the Middle East.

Sensor Cleaning: Auto

One of the Canon EOS 40D's best new features is the automatic sensor cleaning system that reduces or eliminates the need to clean your camera's sensor manually using brushes, swabs, or bulb blowers (you'll find instructions on how to do that in Chapter 9). Canon has applied anti-static coatings to the sensor and other portions of the camera body interior to counter charge build-ups that attract dust. A separate filter over the sensor vibrates ultrasonically each time the 40D is powered on or off, shaking loose any dust, which is captured by a sticky strip beneath the sensor.

Use this menu entry (shown in Figure 3.25) to enable or disable automatic sensor cleaning on power up (select **Auto Cleaning** to choose) to activate automatic cleaning during a shooting session (select **Clean Now**). You can also choose the **Clean manually** option to flip up the mirror and clean the sensor yourself with a blower, brush, or swab, as described in Chapter 9. If the battery level is too low to safely carry out the cleaning operation, the 40D will let you know and refuse to proceed, unless you use the optional AC Adapter Kit ACK-E2.

Figure 3.25
Use this menu choice to activate automatic sensor cleaning or enable/disable it on power up.

Live View Function Settings

Here is where you adjust the EOS 40D's Live View functions, which enable you to work with a real-time LCD display as you preview and compose your image. I'm going to provide detailed instructions for using Live View in Chapter 5, as some functions are controlled here, and some are set in the Custom Functions menus (described later in this chapter). You'll want to review the Live View section of Chapter 5 for detailed information on how to use the four settings you can make from this menu entry.

- **Live View shooting.** Activates Live View. Choose **Disable** to turn the feature off; select **Enable** and Live View will be activated when you press the **Set** button.

- **Grid Display.** Overlays a "rule of thirds" grid on the LCD to help with alignment and composition.

- **Silent Shooting.** Provides a quieter shutter sound when taking pictures using Live View. There are two modes: Mode 1 reduces the noise level of the shutter, but allows taking several shots in succession, including continuous shooting at about 6 fps. Mode 2 reduces the noise even further by delaying the action when you press the shutter release down (only a slight click is heard). When you let up slightly on the shutter release, the shot is taken, producing another soft click. Continuous shooting is not possible in Mode 2. Silent shooting can also be disabled entirely.

- **Metering Timer.** This option turns off the exposure meter after a specified period of time (4, 16, or 30 seconds, plus 1, 10, and 30 minutes).

Flash Control

This multi-level menu entry includes five settings for controlling the Canon EOS 40D's built-in, pop-up electronic flash unit, as well as accessory flash units you can attach to the camera. (See Figure 3.26.) I'll provide in-depth coverage of how you can use these options in Chapter 6, but will list the main options here for reference.

Flash Firing

Use this option to enable or disable the built-in electronic flash. You might want to totally disable the 40D's flash (both built-in and accessory flash) when shooting in sensitive environments, such as concerts, in museums, or during religious ceremonies. When disabled, the flash cannot fire even if you accidentally elevate it, or have an accessory flash attached and turned on.

Figure 3.26
The Flash Control
menu entry has five
setting submenus.

Built-in Flash Function Setting

There are three choices for this menu choice (the Flash mode entry is grayed out and cannot be selected):

- **Shutter sync.** You can choose **1st Curtain sync**, which fires the flash as soon as the shutter is completely open (this is the default mode). Alternatively, you can select **2nd Curtain sync**, which fires the flash as soon as the shutter opens, and then triggers a second flash at the end of the exposure, just before the shutter starts to close. This action allows photographing a blurred trail of light of moving objects with sharp flash exposures at the beginning and the end of the exposure. This type of flash exposure is slightly different from what some other cameras produce using 2nd Curtain sync. I'll explain how it works in Chapter 6.

- **Flash exposure compensation.** If you'd rather adjust flash exposure using a menu than with the ISO/Flash exposure compensation button, you can do that here. Select this option with the Set button, then dial in the amount of flash EV compensation you want using the multi-controller or Quick Control Dial. The EV that was in place before you started to make your adjustment is shown as a blue indicator, so you can return to that value quickly. Press **Set** again to confirm your change, then press the Menu button twice to exit.

- **E-TTL II.** You can choose **Evaluative** (matrix) or **Average metering** modes for the electronic flash exposure meter. Evaluative looks at selected areas in the scene to calculate exposure, while Average calculates flash exposure by reading the entire scene.

External Flash Function Setting

You can access this menu only when you have a compatible electronic flash attached and switched on. The settings available are shown in Figure 3.27. If you press the INFO. button while adjusting flash settings, both the changes made to the settings of an attached external flash and to the built-in flash will be cleared.

- **Flash mode.** This entry allows you to set the flash mode for the external flash, from E-TTL II, A-TTL, or TTL. All three provide through-the lens flash metering, but with different degrees of sophistication. E-TTL (Evaluative Through-The-Lens) uses a preflash just prior to taking the picture to allow the camera's metering sensor to read the flash exposure and compare it with ambient light to provide the best exposure. A-TTL (Advanced Through-The-Lens) metering is an earlier system used with some Canon speedlights to read illumination through the lens, but concentrate sensitivity on the active focus point, also using a preflash. The TTL (Through-The Lens) system is a less sophisticated flash exposure control system used by some flash units. It doesn't use a preflash. You should always choose E-TTL if your flash supports it, or select one of the other systems compatible with the speedlite you are using.

Figure 3.27
External flash units can be controlled from the Canon EOS 40D using this menu.

- **Shutter sync.** As with the 40D's internal flash, you can choose 1st Curtain sync, which fires the flash as soon as the shutter is completely open (this is the default mode). Alternatively, you can select 2nd Curtain sync, which fires the flash as soon as the shutter opens, and then triggers a second flash at the end of the exposure, just before the shutter starts to close.

- **FEB.** Flash Exposure Bracketing (FEB) operates similarly to ordinary exposure bracketing, providing a series of different exposures to improve your chances of getting the exact right exposure, or to provide alternative renditions for creative purposes.

- **Flash exposure compensation.** You can adjust flash exposure using a menu here. Select this option with the Set button, then dial in the amount of flash EV compensation you want using the multi-controller or Quick Control Dial. The EV that was in place before you started to make your adjustment is shown as a blue indicator, so you can return to that value quickly. Press **Set** again to confirm your change, then press the Menu button twice to exit.

- **E-TTL II.** You can choose Evaluative (matrix) or Average metering modes for the electronic flash exposure meter. Evaluative looks at selected areas in the scene to calculate exposure, while Average calculates flash exposure by reading the entire scene.

- **Zoom.** Some flash units can vary their coverage to better match the field of view of your lens at a particular focal length. You can allow the external flash to zoom automatically, based on information provided, or manually, using a zoom button on the flash itself.

External Flash Custom Function Setting

Many external Speedlites from Canon include their own list of Custom Functions, which can be used to specify things like flash metering mode and flash bracketing sequences, as well as more sophisticated features, such as modeling light/flash (if available), use of external power sources (if attached), and functions of any slave unit attached to the external flash. This menu entry allows you to set an external flash unit's Custom Functions from your 40D's menu.

Clear External Flash Custom Function Setting

This entry allows you to zero-out any changes you've made to your external flash's Custom Functions, and return them to their factory default settings.

Camera User Setting

This entry, the first in the third Set-up menu tab, allows you to register your EOS 40D's current camera shooting settings and file them away in the C1, C2, or C3 positions on the Mode Dial. Doing this overwrites any settings previously stored at that Camera User position. You can also clear the settings for any of the three Mode Dial positions individually, returning them to their factory default values.

Clear All Camera Settings

This menu choice resets all the settings to their default values. Regardless of how you've set up your EOS 40D, it will be adjusted for One-Shot AF mode, automatic AF point selection, evaluative metering, JPEG Fine Large image quality, automatic ISO, sRGB color mode, automatic white balance, and Standard Picture Style. Any changes you've made to exposure compensation, flash exposure compensation, and white balance will be canceled, and any bracketing for exposure or white balance nullified. Custom white balances and Dust Delete Data will be erased.

However, Custom Functions and Camera User Settings will *not* be cleared. If you want to cancel those as well, you'll need to use the Camera User Setting option (described previously) and the Custom Functions clearing option, which I'll describe shortly.

Firmware Version

You can see the current firmware release in use in the menu listing. If you want to update to a new firmware version, insert a memory card containing the binary file, and press the Set button to begin the process. You can read more about firmware updates in Chapter 9.

Custom Functions I/II/III/IV

Custom Functions let you customize the behavior of your camera in a variety of different ways, ranging from whether or not the flash fires automatically to the function carried out when the Set button is pressed. If you don't like the default way the camera carries out a particular task, you just may be able to do something about it. You can find the Custom Functions in their own menu, color-coded orange.

We can grudgingly thank Canon for redesigning and partially simplifying setting of Custom Functions when the EOS 40D was created. With this camera's predecessor, the EOS 30D, all 19 functions were crowded onto one screen, with two cryptic rows of settings (from 01 to 10 on the top row, and 11 to 19 on the bottom row), each with a series of numbers beneath the settings row that represented the current value of that Custom Function. So, you could tell at a glance that the numeral 1 underneath Setting 02 meant… uh, that Setting 02, whatever it was, was adjusted to something other than its default value (because 0s represented the defaults). It was hard enough to figure out what a setting meant, and even more difficult to find the setting you wanted to change quickly.

In increasing the number of custom settings from 19 to 24 for the EOS 40D, Canon obviously realized that the old system was unwieldy. Indeed, the number of C. Fn. settings actually increased by more than five; several options that were grouped in the Custom Functions menu with the EOS 30D were moved to other locations (for example, the 30D's flash-related C. Fn 07, 14, and 15 were relocated to the Flash Control entry in the Set-up 2 menu). A few others were deleted entirely: the 30D's C. Fn 11 was used to set whether the first entry in a menu or the last menu item accessed was highlighted when the Menu button was pressed. With the 40D, the last menu item accessed is always highlighted (unless you've specified that the My Menu tab always be displayed first).

So, the Custom Functions options have been cleaned up, reorganized, and expanded. Canon has made adjusting these options only slightly less unwieldy by dividing them into four sub-menus that, at least, give you a fighting chance of finding the Custom Function you want by organizing them by type of feature. The four categories, shown in Figure 3.28, are: Exposure, Image, Auto focus/Drive, Operation/Others. The menu also has an option for clearing all the Custom Functions and returning them to their default values. I'm going to explain each of the categories of Custom Functions separately, but first you need your introduction into the mysteries of Canon's still-cryptic method of setting them.

Each of the Custom Functions is set in exactly the same way, so I'm not going to bog you down with a bunch of illustrations showing how to make this setting or that. One quick run-through using Figure 3.29 should be enough. Here are the key parts of the Custom Function screen:

- **Custom function category.** At the top of the Settings screen is a label that tells you which category that screen represents.

- **Current Function name.** Use the Quick Control Dial to select the function you want to adjust. The name of the function currently selected appears at the top of the screen, and its number is marked with an overscore in the row of numbers at the bottom of the screen. You don't need to memorize the function numbers.

Figure 3.28
The 24 Custom Functions are divided into submenus in four categories.

Figure 3.29
Each C. Fn. screen has from three to seven settings, represented by the numbers at the bottom of the screen.

Available settings

C. Fn. currently selected

Current setting of the Custom Function above

Custom Function category

Name of current Custom Function

Fn currently selected

Scroll bar appears when more than five options are available

- **Function number.** The function number appears in two places. In the upper-right corner you'll find a box with the current function clearly designated. In the lower half of the screen are two lines of numbers, from 1 to 7 (or 1 to 3 with the C. Fn II Image category). The currently selected function will have an orange line above it.

- **Available settings.** Within the alternating medium gray/dark gray blocks appear numbered setting options. The current setting is highlighted in blue. If more than five options are available, a scroll bar appears at the left, and you can use the Quick Control Dial to scroll down to the hidden option. When you've highlighted the setting option you want, press the Set button to select it, then press the Menu button twice to back out of the Custom Functions menus.

- **Current setting.** Underneath each Custom Function is a number from 0 to 5 that represents the current setting for that function.

- **Option selection.** When a function is selected, the currently selected option appears in a highlighted box. As you scroll up and down the option list, the setting in the box changes to indicate an alternate value.

In the listings that follow, I'm going to depart from the sometimes-cryptic labels Canon assigns to each Custom Function in the menu, and instead categorize them by what they actually do. I'm also going to provide you with a great deal more information on each option and what it means to your photography.

Custom Function I (C.Fn. I): Exposure

This is the Custom Function category you can use to set the increments for exposure and ISO, define bracketing parameters, and other settings.

C.Fn I-01: Size of Exposure Adjustments

Exposure level increments. This setting tells the EOS 40D the size of the "jumps" it should use when making exposure adjustments—either one-third or one-half stop. The increment you specify here applies to f/stops, shutter speeds, EV changes, and autoexposure bracketing.

- **0: 1/3 stop.** Choose this setting when you want the finest increments between shutter speeds and/or f/stops. For example, the 40D will use shutter speeds such as 1/60th, 1/80th, 1/100th, and 1/125th second, and f/stops such as f/5.6, f/6.3, f/7.1, and f/8, giving you (and the autoexposure system) maximum control.

■ **1: 1/2 stop.** Use this setting when you want larger and more noticeable changes between increments. The 40D will apply shutter speeds such as 1/60th, 1/125th, 1/250th, and 1/500th second, and f/stops including f/5.6, f/6.7, f/8, f/9.5, and f/11. These coarser adjustments are useful when you want more dramatic changes between different exposures.

C.Fn I-02: Size of ISO Sensitivity Adjustments

ISO speed setting increments. This setting determines the size of the "jumps" it should use when making ISO adjustments—either one-third or one full stop. At the one-third stop setting, typical ISO values would be 100, 125, 160, 200, and so forth. Switch to the one-stop setting, and ISO values would be 100, 200, 400, 800, and so forth. The larger increment can help you leap from one ISO setting to one that's twice (or half) as sensitive with one click.

C.Fn I-03: Whether ISO 3200 Is Available or Disabled

ISO expansion. Ordinarily, only ISO settings from 100 to 1600 are available. The ISO Expansion function is disabled by default to prevent you from unintentionally using ISO settings higher than ISO 1600. If you want to use the ISO 3200 setting, it must be activated using this Custom Function. I've found the noise produced at the ISO 3200 setting on my EOS 40D to be quite acceptable under certain situations. That's particularly so with images of subjects that have a texture of their own that tends to hide or mask the noise. Figure 3.30 is an example of this type of shot. It was taken in the waning light just before dusk, and although there is a fair amount of noise in the brickwork in the building, even at this extreme enlargement the multicolored speckles are not objectionable. (The entire frame is shown in the inset.)

■ **0: Off.** The ISO 3200 setting is locked out and not available when using the ISO button or menu options.

■ **1: On.** The ISO 3200 setting (which shows as H—for High on the status panel) can be selected.

CAUTION

Be aware that if you've activated Highlight Tone Priority (described later), ISO 3200 will not be available even if you have enabled ISO expansion. When viewing the shooting information displays, including on the LCD panel and viewfinder, the 0s in the ISO speed will be shown in a smaller size (for example 16oo instead of 1600) as an indicator that Highlight Tone Priority has been activated.

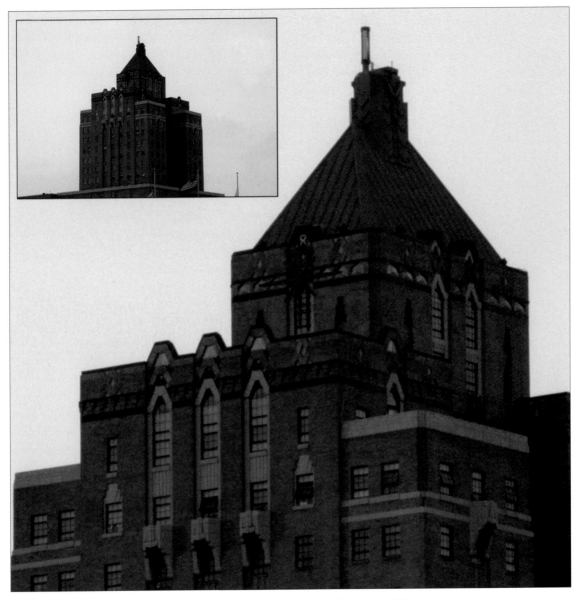

Figure 3.30 This enlargement shows that noise levels can be acceptable even at ISO 3200.

C.Fn I-04: Whether Bracketing Is Cancelled Automatically

Bracketing auto cancel. When Auto Cancel is activated (the default), AEB (Auto Exposure Bracketing) and WB-BKT (White Balance Bracketing) are cancelled when you turn the 40D off, change lenses, use the flash, or change memory cards; when Auto Cancel is deactivated, bracketing remains in effect until you manually turn it off or use the flash. When Auto Cancel is switched off, the AEB and WB-BKT settings will be kept even when the power switch is turned to the OFF position. The flash still cancels auto exposure bracketing, but your settings are retained.

C.Fn I-05: Order in Which Bracketing Changes Are Applied

Bracketing sequence. You can define the sequence in which AEB and WB-BKT series are exposed. For example, if your bias preference is set to Blue/Amber, the white balance sequence when option 0 is selected will be: current WB, more blue, more amber. If your bias preference is set to Magenta/Green, then the sequence for option 0 will be: current WB, more magenta, more green.

- **0:** Exposure sequence is: metered exposure, decreased exposure, increased exposure (0, -, +). White balance sequence is: current WB, more blue/more magenta (depending on how your bias is set), more amber/more green (ditto).

- **1:** The sequence is: decreased exposure, metered exposure, increased exposure (-, 0, +). White balance sequence is: more blue/more magenta, current WB, more amber/more green.

C.Fn I-06: Overriding Your Preference in Aperture Priority or Shutter Priority Modes

Safety shift. Ordinarily, both Aperture Priority and Shutter Priority modes work fine, because you'll select an f/stop or shutter speed that allows the 40D to produce a correct exposure using the other type of setting (shutter speed for Av; aperture for Tv). However, when lighting conditions change, it may not be possible to select an appropriate setting with the available exposure options, and the camera will be unable to take a picture at all.

For example, you might be at a concert shooting the performers and, to increase your chances of getting a sharp image, you've selected Tv mode and a shutter speed of 1/250th second. Under bright lights and with an appropriate ISO setting, the 40D might select f/5.6, f/4, or even f/2.8. Then, in a dramatic moment, the stage lights are dimmed significantly. An exposure of 1/250th second at f/2 is called for, but your lens has an f/2.8 maximum aperture. If you've used this Custom Function to allow the 40D to override your selection, the camera will automatically switch to 1/125th second to allow the picture to be taken at f/2.8.

Safety Shift will make similar adjustments if your scene suddenly becomes too bright; although, in practice, you'll find that the override will be needed most often when using Tv mode. It's easier to "run out of" f/stops, which generally range no smaller than f/22 or f/32, than to deplete the available supply of shutter speeds, which can be as brief as 1/8,000th second. For example, if you're shooting at ISO 400 in Tv mode at 1/1,000th second, an extra-bright beach scene could easily call for an f/stop smaller than f/22, causing overexposure. However, Safety Shift would bump your shutter speed up to 2,000th second with no problem.

On the other hand, if you were shooting under the same illumination in Av mode with the preferred aperture set to f/16, the EOS 40D could use 1/1,000th, 1/2,000th, 1/4,000th, or 1/8,000th second shutter speeds to retain that f/16 aperture under conditions that are 2X, 4X, 8X, or 16X as bright as normal daylight. No Safety Shift would be needed, even if the ISO were (for some unknown reason) set much higher than the ISO 400 used in this example.

- **0: Disable.** Turn off Safety Shift. Your specified shutter speed or f/stop remains locked in, even if conditions are too bright or too dim for an appropriate exposure.

- **1: Enable.** Safety Shift is activated. The 40D will adjust the preferred shutter speed or f/stop to allow a correct exposure.

C.Fn I-07: Flash Synchronization Speed when Using Aperture Priority

Flash sync. Speed in Av mode. You'll find this setting useful when using flash. When you're set to Aperture Priority mode, you select a fixed f/stop and the EOS 40D chooses an appropriate shutter speed. That works fine when you're shooting by available light. However, when you're using flash, the flash itself provides virtually all of the illumination that makes the main exposure, and the shutter speed determines how much, if any, of the ambient light contributes to a second, non-flash exposure. Indeed, if the camera or subject is moving, you can end up with two distinct exposures in the same frame: the sharply defined flash exposure, and a second, blurry "ghost" picture created by the ambient light.

If you *don't* want that second exposure, you should use the highest shutter speed that will synchronize with your flash (that's 1/250th second with the EOS 40D). If you do want the ambient light to contribute to the exposure (say, to allow the background to register in night shots, or to use the ghost image as a special effect), use a slower shutter speed. For brighter backgrounds, you'll need to put the camera on a tripod or other support to avoid the blurry ghosts.

- **0: Auto.** The 40D will vary the shutter speed in Av mode, allowing ambient light to partially illuminate the scene in combination with the flash exposure, as at right in Figure 3.31.

Figure 3.31 At left, a 1/250th second shutter speed eliminated ambient light so only the flash illuminated the scene; at right, a 1/60th second shutter speed let the ambient light supplement the electronic flash.

- **1: 1/250th sec. (fixed).** The camera always uses 1/250th second as its shutter speed in Av mode, reducing the effect of ambient light and, probably, rendering the background dark.

Custom Function II (C.Fn. II): Image

C.Fn II-01: Reducing Noise Effects at Shutter Speeds of One Second or Longer

Long exposure noise reduction. Visual noise is that awful graininess that shows up as multicolored specks in images, and this setting helps you manage it. In some ways, noise is like the excessive grain found in some high-speed photographic films. However, while photographic grain is sometimes used as a special effect, it's rarely desirable in a digital photograph.

The visual noise-producing process is something like listening to a CD in your car, and then rolling down all the windows. You're adding sonic noise to the audio signal, and while increasing the CD player's volume may help a bit, you're still contending with an unfavorable signal to noise ratio that probably mutes tones (especially higher treble notes) that you really want to hear.

The same thing happens when the analog signal is amplified: You're increasing the image information in the signal, but boosting the background fuzziness at the same time. Tune in a very faint or distant AM radio station on your car stereo. Then turn up the volume. After a certain point, turning up the volume further no longer helps you hear better. There's a similar point of diminishing returns for digital sensor ISO increases and signal amplification as well.

These processes create several different kinds of noise. Noise can be produced from high ISO settings. As the captured information is amplified to produce higher ISO sensitivities, some random noise in the signal is amplified along with the photon information. Increasing the ISO setting of your camera raises the threshold of sensitivity so that fewer and fewer photons are needed to register as an exposed pixel. Yet, that also increases the chances of one of those phantom photons being counted among the real-life light particles, too.

Fortunately, the EOS 40D's sensor and its digital processing chip are optimized to produce the low noise levels, so ratings as high as ISO 1600 can be used routinely (although there will be some noise, of course), and even ISO 3200 can generate good results if you've opted for ISO expansion to make that rating available.

A second way noise is created is through longer exposures. Extended exposure times allow more photons to reach the sensor, but increase the likelihood that some photosites will react randomly even though not struck by a particle of light. Moreover, as the sensor remains switched on for the longer exposure, it heats, and this heat can be mistakenly recorded as if it were a barrage of photons. This Custom Function can be used to tailor the amount of noise-canceling performed by the digital signal processor.

- **0: Off.** Disables long exposure noise reduction. Use this setting when you want the maximum amount of detail present in your photograph, even though higher noise levels will result. This setting also eliminates the extra time needed to take a picture caused by the noise reduction process. If you plan to use only lower ISO settings (thereby reducing the noise caused by ISO amplification), the noise levels produced by longer exposures may be acceptable. For example, you might be shooting a waterfall at ISO 100 with the camera mounted on a tripod, using a neutral density filter and long exposure to cause the water to blur, as shown in Figure 3.32. To maximize detail in the non-moving portions of your photos, you can switch off long exposure noise reduction.

■ **1: Auto.** The EOS 40D examines your photo taken with an exposure of one second or longer, and if long exposure noise is detected, a second, blank exposure is made and compared to the first image. Noise found in the "dark frame" image is subtracted from your original picture, and only the noise-corrected image is saved to your memory card. Because the noise-reduction process

Figure 3.32
When lower ISO settings are used, as in this two-second exposure of a waterfall, long exposure noise reduction might not be needed.

effectively doubles the time required to take a picture, this is a good setting to use when you want to avoid this delay when possible, but still have noise reduction applied when appropriate.

- **2: On.** When this setting is activated, the 40D applies dark frame subtraction to all exposures longer than 1 second. You might want to use this option when you're working with high ISO settings (which will already have noise boosted a bit) and want to make sure that any additional noise from long exposures is eliminated, too. Noise reduction will be applied to some exposures that would not have caused it to kick in using the Auto setting.

C.Fn II-02: Eliminating Noise Caused by Higher ISO Sensitivities

High ISO speed noise reduction. This setting applies noise reduction that is especially useful for pictures taken at high ISO sensitivity settings. The default is 0 (Off), but you can specify 1 (On) to apply additional noise reduction at *all* ISO settings. At lower ISO values, noise reduction improves the appearance of shadow areas without affecting highlights; at higher ISO settings, noise reduction is applied to the entire photo. Note that when this function is activated, the maximum number of continuous shots that can be taken will decrease significantly, because of the additional processing time for the images.

- **0: Off.** No additional noise reduction will be applied.
- **1: On.** Activates ISO noise reduction. At lower ISO values, noise reduction is applied primarily to shadow areas; at higher ISO settings, noise reduction affects the entire image.

C.Fn II-03: Improving Detail in Highlights

Highlight Tone priority. This setting concentrates the available tones in an image from the middle grays up to the brightest highlights, in effect expanding the dynamic range of the image at the expense of shadow detail. You'd want to activate this option when shooting subjects in which there is lots of important detail in the highlights, and less detail in shadow areas. Highlight tones will be preserved, while shadows will be allowed to go dark more readily. Bright beach or snow scenes, especially those with few shadows (think high noon, when the shadows are smaller) can benefit from using Highlight Tone priority.

- **0: Off.** The EOS 40D's normal dynamic range is applied.
- **1: On.** Highlight areas are given expanded tonal values, while the tones available for shadow areas are reduced. The ISO 3200 (H) setting is disabled, even if ISO Expansion has been activated.

Custom Function III (C.Fn. III): Autofocus/Drive

Here you'll find the important options for controlling how the Canon EOS 40D's autofocus system operates, along with settings for Live View and mirror lockup.

C.Fn III-01: How the Autofocus System Behaves when Autofocus Fails

Lens drive when AF impossible. This setting controls how the 40D's autofocus system handles hard-to-autofocus (or impossible-to-autofocus) situations. Canon's AF system operates on differences in contrast: When a subject displays the greatest amount of contrast, it is deemed to be in sharp focus. When a scene has little inherent contrast (say, a blank wall or the sky) or if there isn't enough illumination to allow determining contrast accurately (in low light levels, or with lenses having maximum apertures of less than f/5.6) a lens may be unable to achieve autofocus. Very long telephoto lenses suffer from this syndrome because their depth-of-field is so shallow that the correct point of focus may zip past during the AF process before the AF system has a chance to register it.

Use this setting to tell the 40D either to keep trying to focus if AF seems to be impossible or to stop seeking focus.

- **0: Focus search on.** The 40D will keep trying to focus, even if the effort causes the lens to become grossly out of focus. Use this default setting if you'd prefer that the lens keep trying. Sometimes you can point the lens at an object with sufficient contrast at approximately the same distance to let the AF system lock on, then reframe your original subject with the hope that accurate focus will now be achieved.

- **1: Focus search off.** When this option is selected, the camera will stop trying to focus uselessly, allowing you to attempt to manually bring the subject into focus.

C.Fn III-02: Function of the AF Stop Button on Certain Canon Image Stabilized Lenses

Lens AF stop button function. If you have an upper-echelon Canon image-stabilized supertelephoto lens, you might find an interesting button called AF Stop on your lens. (If you don't have such a lens, you can skip this Custom Function entirely.) Normally, the AF Stop button does what its name implies: press the button and autofocus ceases. This can be a useful feature that enables you to lock focus when your fingers are wrapped around the barrel of the lens. However, you can change the behavior of this button using this Custom Function setting, as described next:

- **0: AF stop.** Pressing the AF Stop button on the lens locks the autofocus mechanism.

- **1: AF start.** Pressing the button causes the autofocus mechanism to function only while the AF Stop button is held down.

- **2: AE lock.** Pressing the AF Stop button activates the AE (autoexposure) lock if pressed during metering, making it possible to focus and meter separately.

- **3: AF point: M → Auto/Auto → ctr.** When the camera is set to manual AF point selection, holding down the AF Stop button switches to automatic AF point selection. You'd want to use this option if you find that you sometimes can't choose AF selection points manually fast enough and want the camera to take over. When the 40D is set to automatic AF point selection, hold down the AF Stop button to switch to the center AF point.

- **4: ONE SHOT ← → AI SERVO.** If the camera is set to One Shot autofocus, holding down the button will switch it temporarily to AI Servo autofocus. This is useful when you want to switch back and forth quickly between the two modes.

- **5 IS Start.** Pressing the AF Stop button activates Image Stabilization only while the button is held down (instead of switching it completely on or off using the stabilizer on/off button on the lens).

C.Fn III-03: Controller Used to Select Autofocus Points Manually

AF point selection method. With this setting, you can customize the controls used to choose an autofocus point manually, perhaps making the selection easier or more intuitive for you, or (as is the default) making this process require the use of two controls so that it can't be done accidentally.

- **0: Normal.** To change the AF point that is active, you must press the AF point selection button (to the immediate right of the * button), then press the multi-controller button in the direction you'd like to move the active AF point.

- **1: Multi-controller direct.** When this option is chosen, you can select the active AF point with the multi-controller button alone. You can switch back to auto point selection by pressing the AF point selection button.

- **2: Quick Control Dial direct.** Choose this option if you'd like to change the AF selection point using the Quick Control Dial alone. When this option is active, you can change exposure compensation by pressing the AF point selection button while spinning the Main Dial.

C.Fn III-04: Whether the Autofocus Points Are Highlighted in the Viewfinder

Superimposed display. The C.Fn-10 Superimposed display function controls whether the AF points are illuminated in the viewfinder when autofocus is locked. Some people find the glowing red brackets distracting.

■ **0: On.** One or more focus points glow in red when focus locks.

■ **1: Off.** The focus points are not illuminated unless one is selected manually. Some find this option useful when the constant blinking of the AF point in the viewfinder becomes distracting.

C.Fn III-05: Activation of the Autofocus Assist Lamp

AF-assist beam firing. This setting determines when the AF assist lamp is activated to emit a pulse of light that helps provide enough contrast for the EOS 40D to focus on a subject.

■ **0: Emits.** The AF assist light is emitted by the camera's built-in flash whenever light levels are too low for accurate focusing using the ambient light.

■ **1: Does not emit.** The AF assist illumination is disabled. You might want to use this setting when shooting at concerts, weddings, or darkened locations where the light might prove distracting or discourteous.

■ **2: Only external flash emits.** The built-in AF assist light is disabled, but if a Canon EX dedicated flash unit is attached to the camera, its AF assist feature will be used when needed. Because the flash unit's AF assist is more powerful, you'll find this option useful when you're using flash and are photographing objects in dim light that are more than a few feet away from the camera (and thus not likely to be illuminated usefully by the EOS 40D's built-in light source).

C.Fn III-06: AF During Live View Shooting

AF during Live View shooting. Because the EOS 40D uses a sensor in the viewfinder to autofocus, autofocusing is not possible when you're viewing a Live View image on the LCD screen. (The mirror is flipped up, and no image is available in the viewfinder.) This setting allows interrupting the Live View image long enough to allow autofocusing. Simply press the AF-ON button, and release it to return to Live View.

■ **0: Disable.** Live View is continuous, and focus must be achieved manually.

■ **1: Enable.** Pressing the AF-ON button flips the mirror back down so the 40D can autofocus. Releasing the AF-ON button returns to Live View.

C.Fn III-07: Whether It Is Possible to Lock Up the Viewing Mirror Prior to an Exposure

Mirror lockup. The Mirror lockup function determines whether the reflex viewing mirror will be flipped up out of the way in advance of taking a picture, thereby eliminating any residual blurring effects caused by the minuscule amount of camera shake that can be produced if (as is the case normally) the mirror is automatically flipped up an instant before the actual exposure. When shooting telephoto pictures with a very long lens, or close-up photography at extreme magnifications, even this tiny amount of vibration can have an impact.

You'll want to make this adjustment immediately prior to needing the mirror lockup function, because once it's been enabled, the mirror *always* flips up, and picture taking becomes a two-press operation. That is, you press the shutter release once to lock exposure and focus, and to swing the mirror out of the way. Your viewfinder goes blank (of course, the mirror's blocking it). Press the shutter release a second time to actually take the picture. Because the goal of mirror lockup is to produce the sharpest picture possible, and because of the viewfinder blackout, you can see that the camera should be mounted on a tripod prior to taking the picture, and, to avoid accidentally shaking the camera yourself, using an off-camera shutter release mechanism, such as the Canon Remote Switch RS-80N3 or Timer Remote Controller TC-80N3, is a good idea.

- **0: Disable.** Mirror lockup is not possible.

- **1: Enable.** Mirror lockup is activated and will be used for every shot until disabled.

Canon lists some important warnings and techniques related to using mirror lockup in the EOS 40D manual, and I want to emphasize them here and add a few of my own, even if it means a bit of duplication. Better safe than sorry!

- **Don't use ML for sensor cleaning.** Though locked up, the mirror will flip down again automatically after 30 seconds, which you don't want to happen while you're poking around the sensor with a brush, swab, or air jet. There's a separate menu item—sensor cleaning—for sensor housekeeping. You can find more about this topic in Chapter 9.

- **Avoid long exposure to extra-bright scenes.** The shutter curtain, normally shielded from incoming light by the mirror, is fully exposed to the light being focused on the focal plane by the lens mounted on the 40D. When the mirror is locked up, you certainly don't want to point the camera at the sun, and even beach or snow scenes may be unsafe if the shutter curtain is exposed to their illumination for long periods. (This advice also applies to Live View, of course, because the sensor is similarly exposed while you're previewing the image on the LCD.)

- **ML can't be used in continuous shooting modes.** The EOS 40D will use single shot mode for mirror lockup exposures, regardless of the sequence mode you've selected.

- **Use self-timer to eliminate second button press.** If you've activated the self-timer, the mirror will flip up when you press the shutter button down all the way, and then the picture will be taken two seconds later. This technique can help reduce camera shake further if you don't have a remote release available and have to use a finger to press the shutter button.

Custom Function IV (C.Fn. IV): Operation/Others

Within this category of Custom Functions you'll find seven options for adjusting the behavior of controllers and buttons, specifying the focusing screen in use and other features.

C.Fn IV-01: What Happens when You Partially Depress the Shutter Release/Press the AE Lock Button

Shutter button/AF-ON button. This setting controls the behavior of the shutter release and the AF-ON button. In the option list below, the first action in the pair represents what happens when you press the shutter release; the second action says what happens when the AF-ON button is pressed. Note that if you (like many) would prefer to have the 40D meter and focus when the shutter button is pressed halfway, this is not the default behavior. You must set this Custom Function to option 4 described below.

- **0: Metering/AF Start.** With this option, pressing the shutter release halfway activates metering, and the AF-ON button starts the autofocus process. Use this default setting when you want to control each of these actions separately.

- **1: Metering/AF Start—AF Stop.** Pressing the shutter release halfway activates metering and the AF-ON button starts autofocus. You can press it again to stop the autofocus process.

- **2: Metering Start/Metering+AF Start.** Use this setting with subjects that stop and start moving unexpectedly. Exposure will be measured when the picture is actually taken (you press the shutter release down all the way), but you can press the AF-ON button to activate or halt the AF process as your subject starts and stops. This option is useful when using the continuous-focus AI Servo AF mode.

- **3: AE lock/Metering+AF Start.** Use the AF-ON button to autofocus and read the exposure. Then, if you want to change the exposure to another portion of the picture, reframe and press the shutter release halfway to lock in exposure. Then, return to your original composition and press the shutter release button all the way to take the picture. This capability, although it sounds confusing, is useful when you want to autofocus on one area of the image, then meter using a different area.

- **4: Metering+AF start/Disable.** When this option is selected, both metering and autofocus are activated by pressing the shutter release. The AF-ON button is disabled.

C.Fn IV-02: Swapping the Functions of the AF-ON and AE Lock Buttons

AF-ON/AE lock button switch. Use this option to exchange the functions of the AF-ON and AE Lock (*) buttons.

- **0: Disable.** The AF-ON button turns on autofocus, and the AE Lock button locks exposure.

- **1: Enable.** Pressing the AF-ON button locks exposure; pressing the * button locks autofocus. This setting swaps the action of the two buttons compared to the 0 option.

C.Fn IV-03: Using the Set Button as a Function Key

SET button when shooting. You already know that the Set button is used to select a choice or option when navigating the menus. However, when you're taking photos, it has no function at all. You can easily remedy that with this setting. This setting allows you to assign one of four different actions to the Set key. Because the button is within easy reach of your right thumb, that makes it quite convenient for accessing a frequently used function. When this Custom Function is set to 0, the Set button has no additional function (except to activate Live View when it is turned on), and options 1 through 4 assign an action to the button during shooting.

- **0: Default (no function).** This is the default during shooting. Nothing happens when you press the Set button while in shooting mode.

- **1: Change quality.** Pressing the Set button produces the Quality menu screen on the color LCD. You can cycle among the various quality options by rotating the Quick Control Dial or using the multi-controller. Press **Set** again to lock in your choice.

- **2: Change Picture Style.** The Set button summons the Picture Style menu to the back panel LCD. Use the Quick Control Dial or multi-controller to select the Picture Style you want to use and press **Set** again to activate the style. This option duplicates the action of the Picture Style button under the LCD, but some people find the larger Set button easier to find with their thumb.

CAUTION

One thing to keep in mind when redefining the behavior of controls (including other controls that can be modified within the Custom Functions menus) is that any non-standard customization you do will definitely be confusing to others who use your camera, and may even confuse you if you've forgotten that you've changed a control from its default function.

- **3: Menu display.** Pressing Set produces the 40D's Menu screen on the LCD, with the last menu entry you used highlighted. Press **Set** again to work with that menu normally, or press the Menu button to cancel and back out of the menus. This setting duplicates the Menu button's function, but some find it easier to locate the Set button with their thumb.

- **4: Image display.** Shows the most recent photo taken in Replay mode, so you can view that image or scroll through the other photos you've taken. Using the Set button for this function may be more convenient than pressing the Display key, because you can find the Set button with your thumb more quickly without looking.

C.Fn IV-04: Reverse Dial Direction when Using Shutter Priority or Aperture Priority

Dial direction during Tv/Av. This setting reverses the result when rotating the Quick Control Dial and Main Dial when using Shutter Priority or Aperture Priority (Tv and Av). That is, rotating the Main Dial to the right will decrease the shutter speed rather than increase it; f/stops will become larger rather than smaller. Use this if you find the default rotation scheme in Tv and Av modes are not to your liking. Activating this option also reverses the dial direction in Manual exposure mode. In other shooting modes, only the Main Dial's direction will be reversed.

- **0: Normal.** The Main Dial and Quick Control Dial change shutter speed and aperture normally.

- **1: Reverse direction.** The dials adjust shutter speed and aperture in the reverse direction when rotated.

C.Fn IV-05: Which Focusing Screen Is Installed

Focusing screen. If you exchange the focus screen provided with your EOS 40D for one of the optional focus screens, you need to tell the camera which screen has been installed to insure proper autofocus and exposure metering. Note that this Custom Function is *not* one of the values stored in the Camera User Settings on the theory that a camera owner won't be changing focus screens all the time, and will stick with one screen. (Changing screens is a minor pain, anyway; find one you like and stick with it.)

- **0: EF-A.** The Standard Precision Matte focusing screen is installed.

- **1: EF-D.** The Precision Matte focus screen with alignment grid is installed. (See Figure 3.33.)

- **2: EF-S.** The Super Precision Matte focus screen, optimized for lenses with an f/2.8 or larger maximum aperture (the screen itself has a darker texture, and needs the extra illumination) has been installed.

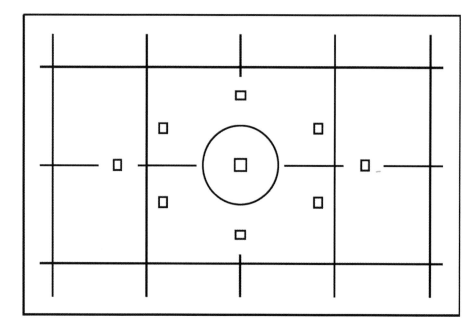

Figure 3.33
The EF-D Precision Matte focus screen has a built-in alignment grid.

C.Fn IV-06: Activating Data Verification Feature

Add original decision data. The EOS 40D has a special feature that allows determining whether a specific image has been modified using a special Canon Data Verification Kit DVK-E2, which consists of a dedicated SM (secure mobile) card reader-writer and verification software that must be used with a computer to verify an image. The C.Fn-19 Add original decision data function determines whether the information needed to verify an image is included in the image file. Data verification is especially useful for law enforcement, legal, and scientific purposes, but not required for everyday shooting (which is why the feature is turned off by default).

- **0: Off.** Data verification information is not added to the image file.

- **1: On.** Data verification information is included in the image file.

C.Fn IV-07: Simulate Current Exposure in Live View Mode

Live View exposure simulation. Use this setting to activate or disable exposure simulation in Live View mode. By default, Live View presents an image optimized for brightness on the LCD: dark scenes will be pumped up in brightness to make them easier to view, while very bright scenes will be dimmed. This overall average image is the most comfortable for viewing and composing. However, you might prefer to have the LCD show how the scene might appear at the current exposure settings. If you enable exposure simulation, underexposed scenes will seem too dark on the LCD, and overexposed subjects too light, allowing you to make corrections before taking the photo.

If you want to see the simulated exposure only some of the time, pressing the depth-of-field button will display the scene with its relative exposure, regardless of how this Custom Function is set.

- **0: Disable.** The LCD adjusts its brightness to present an optimized image regardless of brightness/dimness of the scene. Press the depth-of-field button, and the 40D will show you the simulated exposure even when this feature is disabled.

- **1: Enable.** The real-time image changes in brightness/darkness to indicate whether the current exposure is correct or not. Simulated exposure does not appear when using flash or when the 40D is set for a bulb exposure.

Clear All Custom Func (C. Fn) Settings

This choice, located at the same level as the Custom Function categories, can be used to clear all camera Custom Functions. Press the Set button, then rotate the Quick Control Dial to choose either Cancel or OK. Press the Set button to confirm. All Custom Functions will be reset to their default 0 values.

My Menu

The Canon EOS 40D has a great new feature that allows you to define your own menu, with just the items listed that you want. Remember that the 40D always returns to the last menu and menu entry accessed when you press the Menu button. So you can set up My Menu to include just the items you want, and jump to those items instantly by pressing the Menu button. Or, you can set your camera so that My Menu appears when the Menu button has been pressed, regardless of what other menu entry you accessed last.

To create your own My Menu, you have to *register* the menu items you want to include. Just follow these steps:

1. Press the Menu button and use the Main Dial or multi-controller to select the **My Menu tab**. When you first begin, the personalized menu will be empty except for the My Menu Settings entry. Press the **Set** button to select it. You'll then see a screen like the one shown in Figure 3.34.

2. Rotate the Quick Control Dial to select **Register**, then press the **Set** button.

3. Use the Quick Control Dial to scroll down through the continuous list of menu entries to find one you would like to add. Press **Set**.

4. Confirm your choice by selecting **OK** in the next screen and pressing **Set** again.

5. Continue to select up to six menu entries for My Menu.

6. When you're finished, press the Menu button twice to return to the My Menu screen to see your customized menu, which might look like Figure 3.35.

In addition to registering menu items, you can perform other functions at the My Menu Settings screen:

- **Changing the Order.** Choose **Sort** to reorder the items in My Menu. Select the menu item and press the **Set** button. Rotate the Quick Command Dial to move the item up and down within the menu list. When you've placed it where you'd like it, press the Menu button to lock in your selection and return to the previous screen.

- **Delete/Delete All Items.** Use these to remove an individual menu item or all menu items you've registered in My Menu.

- **Display from My Menu.** As I mentioned earlier, the 40D (almost) always shows the last menu item accessed. That's convenient if you used My Menu last, but if you happen to use another menu, then pressing the Menu button will return to that item instead. If you enable the Display from My Menu option, pressing the Menu button will *always* display My Menu first. You are free to switch to another menu tab if you like, but the next time you press the Menu button, My Menu will come up again. Use this option if you work with My Menu a great deal and make settings with other menu items less frequently.

Figure 3.34
In the My Menu Settings screen you can add menu items, delete them, and specify whether My Menu always pops up when the Menu button is pressed.

My Menu settings

Register

Sort

Delete

Delete all items

Display from My Menu   Disable

MENU

Figure 3.35
You can add one to six menu entries to My Menu. Two entries are shown.

Red-eye On/Off   Off

Format

My Menu Settings

4

Getting the Right Exposure

The Canon EOS 40D gives you complete control over many of the basic functions of the camera. These include exposure, sensitivity (ISO settings), color balance, focus, and image parameters like sharpness and contrast. You can choose to let the camera set any or all of these for you automatically. Or, you can opt to fine-tune how the 40D applies its automatic settings. If you want absolute creative control over any of these functions, you can set them manually, too. That's why the 40D is such a versatile tool for creating images.

This chapter explains the shooting basics of exposure, either as an introduction or as a refresher course, depending on your current level of expertise. When you finish this chapter, you'll understand most of what you need to know to take photographs in a broad range of situations.

Getting a Handle on Exposure

Exposure can make or break your photo. Correct exposure brings out the detail in the areas you want to picture, providing the range of tones and colors you need to create the desired image. Poor exposure can cloak important details in shadow, or wash them out in glare-filled featureless expanses of white. However, getting the perfect exposure can be tricky, because digital sensors can't capture all the tones we are able to see. If the range of tones in an image is extensive, embracing both inky black shadows and bright highlights, we often must settle for an exposure that renders most of those tones—but not all—in a way that best suits the photo we want to produce.

There are four things within our control that affect exposure, listed in "chronological" order (that is, as the light moves from the subject to the sensor):

- **Reflected, transmitted, or emitted light.** We see and photograph objects by light that is reflected from our subjects, transmitted (say, from translucent objects that are lit from behind), or emitted (by a candle or television screen). When more or less light reaches the lens from the subject, we need to adjust the exposure. This part of the equation is under our control to the extent we can increase the amount of light falling on or passing through the subject (by adding extra light sources or using reflectors), or by pumping up the light that's emitted (by increasing the brightness of the glowing object).

- **Light transmitted by the lens.** Not all the illumination that reaches the front of the lens makes it all the way through. Filters can remove some of the light before it enters the lens. Inside the lens barrel is a variable-sized diaphragm called an *aperture* that dilates and contracts to control the amount of light that enters the lens. You, or the 40D's autoexposure system, can control exposure by varying the size of the aperture. The relative size of the aperture is called the *f/stop*.

- **Light passing through the shutter.** Once light passes through the lens, the amount of time the sensor receives it is determined by the 40D's shutter, which can remain open for as long as 30 seconds (or even longer if you use the Bulb setting) or as briefly as 1/8,000th second.

- **Light captured by the sensor.** All the light falling onto the sensor is captured. If the number of photons reaching a particular photosite doesn't pass a set threshold, no information is recorded. Similarly, if too much light illuminates a pixel in the sensor, then the excess isn't recorded or, worse, spills over to contaminate adjacent pixels. We can modify the minimum and maximum number of pixels that contribute to image detail by adjusting the ISO setting. At higher ISOs, the incoming light is amplified to boost the effective sensitivity of the sensor.

These four factors—quantity of light, light passed by the lens, the amount of time the shutter is open, and the sensitivity of the sensor—all work proportionately and reciprocally to produce an exposure. That is, if you double the amount of light, increase the aperture by one stop, make the shutter speed twice as long, or boost the ISO setting 2X, you'll get twice as much exposure. Similarly, you can increase any of these factors while decreasing one of the others by a similar amount to keep the same exposure.

Most commonly, exposure settings are made using the aperture and shutter speed, followed by adjusting the ISO sensitivity if it's not possible to get the preferred exposure (that is, the one that uses the "best" f/stop or shutter speed for the depth-of-field or action-stopping we want). Table 4.1 shows equivalent exposure settings using various shutter speeds and f/stops.

Table 4.1 Equivalent Exposures

Shutter Speed	f/stop
1/30th second	f/22
1/60th second	f/16
1/125th second	f/11
1/250th second	f/8
1/500th second	f/5.6
1/1,000th second	f/4
1/2,000th second	f/2.8
1/4,000th second	f/2
1/8,000th second	f/1.4

When the 40D is set for P mode, the metering system selects the correct exposure for you automatically, but you can change quickly to an equivalent exposure by holding down the shutter release button halfway ("locking" the current exposure), and then spinning the Main Dial until the desired equivalent exposure combination is displayed. This program shift mode does not work when you're using flash.

In Aperture Priority (Av) and Shutter Priority (Tv) modes, you can change to an equivalent exposure, but only by adjusting either the aperture (the camera chooses the shutter speed) or shutter speed (the camera selects the aperture). I'll cover all these exposure modes later in the chapter.

ACTIVATE YOUR QUICK CONTROL DIAL

Throughout this chapter (and throughout this book), if I direct you to use the Quick Control Dial on the back of the camera, you must remember to have activated the dial when you turned on your Canon EOS 40D by rotating the power switch all the way up to the topmost counterclockwise position. Turning it up one position to ON does not activate the Quick Control Dial for functions other than menu navigation. I won't be reminding you to do this every single time, so keep it in mind.

F/STOPS AND SHUTTER SPEEDS

If you're *really* new to more advanced cameras, you might need to know that the lens aperture, or f/stop, is a ratio, much like a fraction, which is why f/2 is larger than f/4, just as 1/2 is larger than 1/4. However, f/2 is actually *four times* as large as f/4. (If you remember your high school geometry, you'll know that to double the area of a circle, you multiply its diameter by the square root of two: 1.4.)

Lenses are usually marked with intermediate f/stops that represent a size that's twice as much/half as much as the previous aperture. So, a lens might be marked:

f/2, f/2.8, f/4, f/5.6, f/8, f/11, f/16, f/22

with each larger number representing an aperture that admits half as much light as the one before, as shown in Figure 4.1.

Shutter speeds are actual fractions (of a second), but the numerator is omitted, so that 60, 125, 250, 500, 1,000, and so forth represent 1/60th, 1/125th, 1/250th, 1/500th, and 1/1,000th second. To avoid confusion, Canon uses quotation marks to signify longer exposures: 2", 2"5, 4", and so forth represent 2.0, 2.5, and 4.0-second exposures, respectively.

Figure 4.1 Top row (left to right): f/2, f/2.8, f/4; bottom row, f/5.6, f/8, f11.

How the EOS 40D Calculates Exposure

Your Canon EOS 40D calculates exposure by measuring the light that passes through the lens and is bounced up by the mirror to sensors located near the focusing surface, using a pattern you can select (more on that later) and based on the assumption that each area being measured reflects about the same amount of light as a neutral gray card with 18 percent reflectance. That assumption is necessary, because different subjects reflect different amounts of light. In a photo containing a white cat and a dark gray cat, the white cat might reflect five times as much light as the gray cat. An exposure based on the white cat will cause the gray cat to appear to be black, while an exposure based only on the gray cat will make the white cat washed out. Light-measuring devices handle this by assuming that the areas measured average a standard value of 18 percent gray, a figure that's been used as a rough standard (not all vendors calibrate their metering for exactly 18 percent gray) for many years.

You could, in many cases, arrive at a reasonable exposure by pointing your 40D at an evenly lit object, such as an actual gray card or the palm of your hand (the backside of the hand is too variable). You'll need to increase the exposure by one stop in the latter case, because the human palm—of any ethnic group—reflects about twice as much light as a gray card. It's more practical though, to use your 40D's system to meter the actual scene, using the options available to you when using one of the Creative Zone modes (P, Tv, Av, M, and A-DEP). (In Basic Zone modes, the metering decisions are handled by the camera's programming.) (See Figure 4.2.)

Figure 4.2
Creative Zone and Basic Zone modes.

Creative Zone modes

Camera User Settings

Basic Zone modes

F/STOPS VERSUS STOPS

In photography parlance, *f/stop* always means the aperture or lens opening. However, for lack of a current commonly used word for one exposure increment, the term *stop* is often used. (In the past, EV served this purpose, but Exposure Value and its abbreviation has been inextricably intertwined with its use in describing Exposure Compensation.) In this book, when I say "stop" by itself (no *f*), I mean one whole unit of exposure, and am not necessarily referring to an actual f/stop or lens aperture. So, adjusting the exposure by "one stop" can mean both changing to the next shutter speed increment (say, from 1/125th second to 1/250th second) or the next aperture (such as f/4 to f/5.6). Similarly, 1/3 stop or 1/2 stop increments can mean either shutter speed or aperture changes, depending on the context. Be forewarned.

In most cases, your camera's light meter will do a good job of calculating the right exposure, especially if you use the exposure tips in the next section. But if you want to double-check, or feel that exposure is especially critical, take the light reading off an object of known reflectance. Photographers sometimes carry around an 18 percent gray card (available from any camera store) and, for critical exposures, actually use that card, placed in the subject area, to measure exposure (or to set a custom white balance if needed).

To meter properly in the Creative Zone, you'll want to choose both the *metering method* (how light is evaluated) and *exposure method* (how the appropriate shutter speeds and apertures are chosen). I'll describe both in the following sections.

Choosing a Metering Method

The 40D has four different schemes for evaluating the light received by its exposure sensors. You can choose among them by pressing the Metering Mode Selection button on the top panel, and using the Main Dial until the icon for the mode you want appears in the status LCD.

- **Evaluative.** The 40D slices up the frame into 35 different zones, shown in Figure 4.3 (the status LCD icon is shown in the upper-left corner). The zones used are linked to the autofocus system. The camera evaluates the measurements, giving extra emphasis to the metering zones that indicate sharp focus, to make an educated guess about what kind of picture you're taking, based on examination of thousands of different real-world photos. For example, if the top sections of a picture are much lighter than the bottom portions, the algorithm can assume that the scene is a landscape photo with lots of sky. This mode is the best all-purpose metering method for most pictures. I'll explain how to choose an autofocus/exposure zone in the section on autofocus operation later in this chapter.

■ **Partial.** This is a *faux* Spot mode, using roughly nine percent of the image area to calculate exposure, which, as you can see in Figure 4.4, is a rather large spot. The status LCD icon is shown in the upper-left corner. One of the improvements brought by the introduction of the 40D's predecessor, the EOS 30D, was a true Spot mode, described later. Use this mode if the background is much brighter or darker than the subject.

■ **Spot.** This mode confines the reading to a limited area in the center of the viewfinder, as shown in Figure 4.5, making up only 3.8 percent of the image (slightly larger than the 3.5 percent Spot used in the 30D). This mode is useful when you want to base exposure on a small area in the frame. If that area is in the center of the frame, so much the better. If not, you'll have to make your meter reading and then lock exposure by pressing the shutter release halfway, or by pressing the AE-Lock button.

Figure 4.3
Evaluative metering uses 35 zones, linked to the autofocus points shown as red brackets.

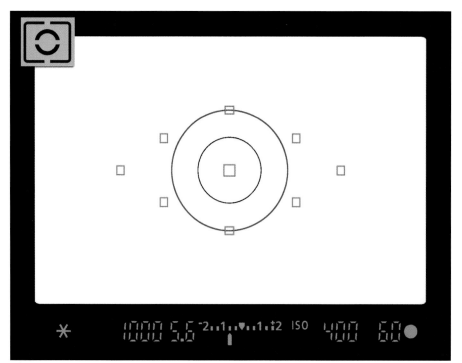

Figure 4.4
Partial metering uses a center spot that's roughly nine percent of the frame area.

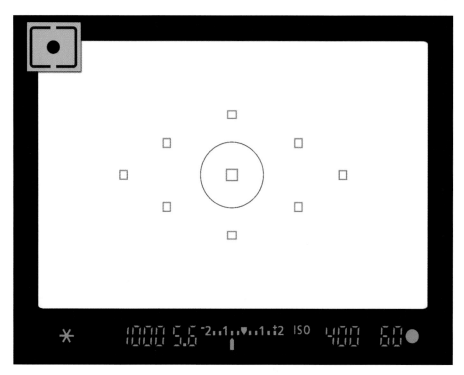

Figure 4.5
Spot metering calculates exposure based on a center spot that's only 3.5 percent of the image area.

■ **Center-Weighted.** In this mode, the exposure meter emphasizes a zone in the center of the frame to calculate exposure, as shown in Figure 4.6, on the theory that, for most pictures, the main subject will be located in the center. Center-weighting works best for portraits, architectural photos, and other pictures in which the most important subject is located in the middle of the frame. As the name suggests, the light reading is *weighted* towards the central portion, but information is also used from the rest of the frame. If your main subject is surrounded by very bright or very dark areas, the exposure might not be exactly right. However, this scheme works well in many situations if you don't want to use one of the other modes.

Figure 4.6
Center-Weighted metering calculates exposure based on the full frame, but emphasizes the center area.

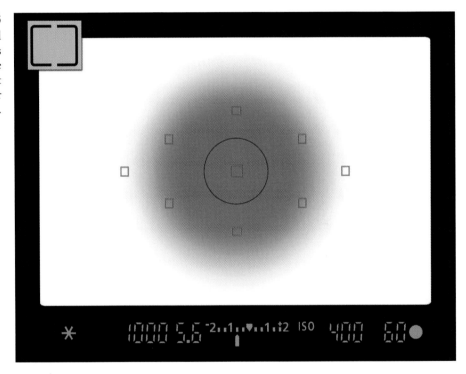

Choosing a Creative Zone Exposure Method

You'll find five methods for choosing the appropriate shutter speed and aperture within the Creative Zone settings. Just spin the Mode Dial to choose the method you want to use. Your choice of which is best for a given shooting situation will depend on things like your need for lots of (or less) depth-of-field, a desire to freeze action or allow motion blur, or how much noise you find acceptable in an image. Each of the EOS 40D's exposure methods emphasizes one aspect of image capture or another. This section introduces you to all five.

A-DEP

The Automatic Depth-of-Field exposure mode is a handy method to use when you want to maximize the range of sharpness in your image. The camera actually selects an f/stop that will allow as much of the subject matter you've framed as possible to be in sharp focus, and then applies the shutter speed necessary to provide a good exposure at that aperture. The disadvantage of this mode is that you relinquish control over shutter speed, f/stop, and focus distance (which makes A-DEP a bit more like a Basic Zone scene mode than a true Creative Zone mode). You might end up with the required depth-of-field, but a blurry photo because the 40D has selected a shutter speed that's too slow for hand-holding!

A-DEP performs its magic by examining the nine autofocus points in the viewfinder to discover the nearest and farthest objects in the frame. Then, it chooses an aperture and focus point that supplies the required DOF (if possible) and sets the appropriate shutter speed. The focus zones that can be rendered in sharp focus will flash red; other zones that can't be included in the focus range remain black, as shown in Figure 4.7. Press the DOF button on the front of the camera to check the range of focus, if you want. This mode won't work under all

Figure 4.7
A-DEP mode can provide automatic depth-of-field for many types of subjects.

conditions, for example, with flash or if you're using manual focus. The viewfinder provides you with status information:

- **Flashing red AF points.** Shows the subjects covered by the DOF range set.

- **Blinking aperture indicator in viewfinder.** The desired DOF range cannot be set because the subjects are separated too widely for sufficient depth-of-field at the smallest available aperture.

- **Blinking 30 shutter speed in viewfinder.** Illumination is too dim to provide requested DOF at the current ISO setting.

- **Blinking 8,000 shutter speed in viewfinder.** Illumination is too bright to provide requested DOF at the current ISO setting.

Because of the limitations of A-DEP mode, I don't favor it. However, it's fun to play with and may come in handy in certain situations, especially when you're shooting quickly and don't have time to manipulate depth-of-field manually.

Aperture Priority

In Av mode, you specify the lens opening used, and the 40D selects the shutter speed. Aperture Priority is especially good when you want to use a particular lens opening to achieve a desired effect. Perhaps you'd like to use the smallest f/stop possible to maximize depth-of-field in a close-up picture. Or, you might want to use a large f/stop to throw everything except your main subject out of focus, as in Figure 4.8. Maybe you'd just like to "lock in" a particular f/stop because it's the sharpest available aperture with that lens. Or, you might prefer to use, say, f/2.8 on a lens with a maximum aperture of f/1.4, because you want the best compromise between speed and sharpness.

Aperture priority can even be used to specify a *range* of shutter speeds you want to use under varying lighting conditions, which seems almost contradictory. But think about it. You're shooting a soccer game outdoors with a telephoto lens and want a relatively high shutter speed, but you don't care if the speed changes a little should the sun duck behind a cloud. Set your 40D to Av, and adjust the aperture until a shutter speed of, say, 1/1,000th second is selected at your current ISO setting. (In bright sunlight at ISO 400, that aperture is likely to be around f/11.) Then, go ahead and shoot, knowing that your 40D will maintain that f/11 aperture (for sufficient DOF as the soccer players move about the field), but will drop down to 1/750th or 1/500th second if necessary should the lighting change a little.

A blinking **30** or **8,000** shutter speed in the viewfinder indicates that the 40D is unable to select an appropriate shutter speed at the selected aperture and that over- and underexposure will occur at the current ISO setting. That's the major pitfall of using Av: you might select an f/stop that is too small or too large to allow an optimal exposure with the available shutter speeds. For example, if you choose f/2.8 as your aperture and the illumination is quite bright (say, at the beach or in snow), even your camera's fastest shutter speed might not be able to cut down the amount of light reaching the sensor to provide the right exposure. Or, if you select f/8 in a dimly lit room, you might find yourself shooting with a very slow shutter speed that can cause blurring from subject movement or camera shake. Aperture Priority is best used by those with a bit of experience in choosing settings. Many seasoned photographers leave their 40D set on Av all the time.

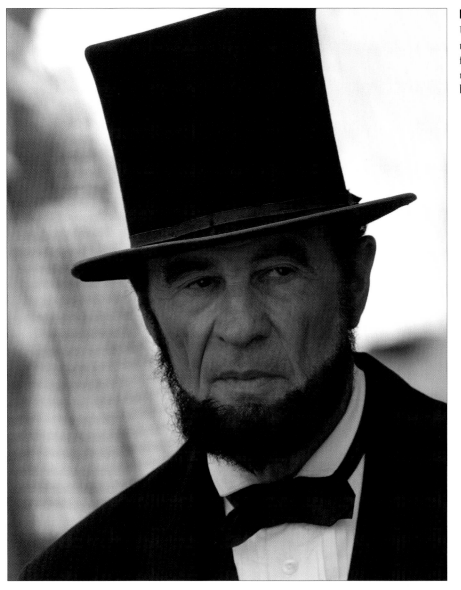

Figure 4.8
Use Aperture Priority to "lock in" a large f/stop when you want to blur the background.

Shutter Priority

Shutter priority (Tv) is the inverse of aperture priority: you choose the shutter speed you'd like to use, and the camera's metering system selects the appropriate f/stop. Perhaps you're shooting action photos and you want to use the absolute fastest shutter speed available with your camera; in other cases you might want to use a slow shutter speed to add some blur to a sports photo that would be mundane if the action were completely frozen. (See Figure 4.9.) Shutter Priority mode gives you some control over how much action-freezing capability your digital camera brings to bear in a particular situation.

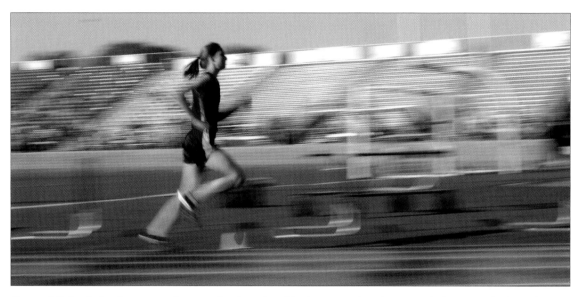

Figure 4.9 Lock the shutter at a slow speed to introduce blur into an action shot, as with this panned image of a distance runner.

You'll also encounter the same problem as with aperture priority when you select a shutter speed that's too long or too short for correct exposure under some conditions. I've shot outdoor soccer games on sunny Fall evenings and used Shutter Priority mode to lock in a 1/1,000th second shutter speed, only to find my 40D refused to shoot when the sun dipped behind some trees and there was no longer enough light to shoot at that speed, even with the lens wide open.

Like Av mode, it's possible to choose an inappropriate shutter speed. If that's the case, the maximum aperture of your lens (to indicate underexposure) or the minimum aperture (to indicate overexposure) will blink.

SAFETY SHIFT

The EOS 40D has a function called Safety Shift that operates in both Shutter Priority and Aperture Priority modes to help prevent bad exposures if the brightness of your subject changes abruptly so much that your selected shutter speed or f/stop no longer can be used to produce a good exposure. Perhaps you're photographing someone on stage and a spotlight is thrown on them at a critical moment, producing six or eight times as much illumination as you'd anticipated. Or, maybe the spotlight is turned off when you weren't expecting it. When Safety Shift is activated (through C. Fn.I-06), the 40D will change your specified shutter speed (in Tv mode) or aperture (in Av mode) to compensate.

Program Mode

Program mode (P) uses the 40D's built-in smarts to select the correct f/stop and shutter speed using a database of picture information that tells it which combination of shutter speed and aperture will work best for a particular photo. If the correct exposure cannot be achieved at the current ISO setting, the shutter speed indicator in the viewfinder will blink **30** or **8,000**, indicating under- or overexposure (respectively). You can then boost or reduce the ISO to increase or decrease sensitivity.

The 40D's recommended exposure can be overridden if you want. Use the EV setting feature (described later, because it also applies to Tv and Av modes) to add or subtract exposure from the metered value. And, as I mentioned earlier in this chapter, you can change from the recommended setting to an equivalent setting (as shown in Table 4.1) that produces the same exposure, but using a different combination of f/stop and shutter speed. To accomplish this:

1. Press the shutter release halfway to lock in the current base exposure, or press the AE-Lock button (*) on the back of the camera (in which case the * indicator will illuminate in the viewfinder to show that the exposure has been locked).

2. Spin the Main Dial to change the shutter speed (the 40D will adjust the f/stop to match).

Your adjustment remains in force for a single exposure; if you want to change from the recommended settings for the next exposure, you'll need to repeat those steps.

MAKING EV CHANGES

Sometimes you'll want more or less exposure than indicated by the EOS 40D's metering system. Perhaps you want to underexpose to create a silhouette effect, or overexpose to produce a high key look. It's easy to use the 40D's Exposure Compensation system to override the exposure recommendations. Press the shutter release halfway or press the AE-Lock button (*). You don't need to hold it down if you make your EV change within four seconds of depressing either button. Then rotate the Quick Control Dial clockwise to add exposure, and counterclockwise to subtract exposure. The exposure scale in the viewfinder and on the status LCD indicates the EV change you've made. The EV change you've made remains for the exposures that follow, until you manually zero out the EV setting with the Quick Control Dial. (As always, remember to activate the Quick Control Dial by turning the power switch all the way up to the second mark.) EV changes are ignored when using M (manual exposure) or any of the Basic Zone modes.

Manual Exposure

Part of being an experienced photographer comes from knowing when to rely on your EOS 40D's automation (including P mode and Basic Zone settings), when to go semiautomatic (with Tv or Av), and when to set exposure manually (using M). Some photographers actually prefer to set their exposure manually, as the 40D will be happy to provide an indication of when its metering system judges your manual settings provide the proper exposure, using the analog exposure scale at the bottom of the viewfinder and on the status LCD.

Manual exposure can come in handy in some situations. You might be taking a silhouette photo and find that none of the exposure modes or EV correction features give you exactly the effect you want. Set the exposure manually to use the exact shutter speed and f/stop you need. Or, you might be working in a studio environment using multiple flash units. The additional flash are triggered by slave devices (gadgets that set off the flash when they sense the light from another flash, or, perhaps from a radio or infrared remote control). Your camera's exposure meter doesn't compensate for the extra illumination, so you need to set the aperture manually.

Because, depending on your proclivities, you might not need to set exposure manually very often, you should still make sure you understand how it works. Fortunately, the EOS 40D makes setting exposure manually very easy. Just set the Mode Dial to M, turn the Main Dial to set the shutter speed, and the Quick Control Dial to adjust the aperture. Press the shutter release halfway or press the AE-Lock button, and the exposure scale in the viewfinder shows you how far your chosen setting diverges from the metered exposure.

Selecting an Autofocus/Exposure Zone Manually

If you're using P, Av, Tv, or M shooting modes and Evaluative Metering, you can select the autofocus zone manually (and thus the zone linked to the metering system). As I mentioned in Chapter 1, the EOS 40D uses nine different focus points to calculate correct focus. In A-DEP, or any of the Basic Zone shooting modes, the focus point is selected automatically by the camera. In the other Creative Zone modes, you can allow the camera to select the focus point automatically, or you can specify which focus point should be used.

There are several methods to set the focus point manually. You can press the AF point selection button on the back of the camera (with the icon representing focus points), look through the viewfinder, and use the multi-controller knob (to the right and below the viewfinder window) to move the focus point to the zone you want to use, as shown in Figure 4.10. Press the multi-controller knob straight up or down, and the top or bottom focus points are selected. To the left or right, and the side points are selected. Movements to the two o'clock, four o'clock, seven o'clock, or ten o'clock positions choose the in-between focus sensors. Press the multi-controller knob in, and the center focus point becomes active.

Figure 4.10

Select an autofocus point manually, and the 40D's exposure meter will link to that point in Evaluative mode.

You can also choose a focus point by pressing the AF point selection button and then rotating the Main Dial. The focus point will cycle among the edge points counterclockwise (if you turn the Main Dial to the left) or clockwise (if you spin the Main Dial to the right), ending/starting with the center focus point/all nine focus points. You can also use the Quick Control Dial to adjust focus points.

Adjusting Exposure with ISO Settings

Another way of adjusting exposures is by changing the ISO sensitivity setting. Sometimes photographers forget about this option, because the common practice is to set the ISO once for a particular shooting session (say, at ISO 100 or 200 for bright sunlight outdoors, or ISO 800 when shooting indoors) and then forget about ISO. The reason for that is that ISOs higher than ISO 100 or 200 are seen as "bad" or "necessary evils." However, changing the ISO is a valid way of adjusting exposure settings, particularly with the Canon EOS 40D, which produces good results at ISO settings that create grainy, unusable pictures with some other camera models.

Indeed, I find myself using ISO adjustment as a convenient alternate way of adding or subtracting EV when shooting in Manual mode, and as a quick way of choosing equivalent exposures when in Automatic or Semiautomatic modes. For example, I've selected a manual exposure with both f/stop and shutter speed suitable for my image using, say, ISO 200. I can change the exposure in 1/3 stop increments by tapping the ISO-Flash Exposure Compensation button and spinning the Main Dial one click at a time. The difference in image quality/noise at the base setting of ISO 200 is negligible if I dial in ISO 160 or 125 to reduce exposure a little, or change to ISO 250 or 320 to increase exposure. I keep my preferred f/stop and shutter speed, but still adjust the exposure.

Or, perhaps, I am using Tv mode and the metered exposure at ISO 200 is 1/500th second at f/11. If I decide on the spur of the moment I'd rather use 1/500th second at f/8, I can tap the ISO-Flash Exposure Compensation button and spin the Main Dial three clicks counterclockwise to switch to ISO 100. Of course, it's a good idea to monitor your ISO changes, so you don't end up at ISO 1,600 (or higher, if ISO Expansion is enabled) accidentally.

ISO settings can, of course, also be used to boost or reduce sensitivity in particular shooting situations. The EOS 40D can use ISO settings from ISO 100 up to 1,600 (or ISO 3,200 if you've set C. Fn. I-03 to 1).

The camera can adjust the ISO automatically as appropriate for various lighting conditions. In Basic Zone modes, ISO is normally set between ISO 100-800. When you choose the Auto ISO setting, the 40D adjusts the sensitivity dynamically to suit the subject matter. In Basic Zone Auto, Landscape, Close-Up, Night

Portrait, and Flash Off modes, the 40D adjusts ISO between ISO 100-800 as required. In Sports mode, ISO is set between ISO 400-800. In Portrait mode, ISO is fixed at ISO 100, because the 40D attempts to use larger f/stops to blur the background, and the lower ISO setting lends itself to those larger stops.

When Auto ISO is chosen when using Creative Zone modes, sensitivity will be generally set to ISO 400-800 in Program, Av, and A-DEP modes, except when ISO 400 would produce overexposure, and a lower speed (down to ISO 100) will be used instead. In Tv mode, Auto ISO normally produces an ISO 400 setting, but for very bright or dark subjects the 40D will change the ISO in the range ISO 100-800. In Manual exposure mode, Auto ISO is fixed at ISO 400.

When using flash, Auto ISO produces a setting of ISO 400 automatically, except when overexposure would occur (as when shooting subjects very close to the camera), in which case a lower setting (down to ISO 100) will be used. Remember that if the Auto ISO ranges aren't suitable for you, individual ISO values can also be selected in any of the Creative Zone modes.

Bracketing

Bracketing is a method for shooting several consecutive exposures using different settings, as a way of improving the odds that one will be exactly right. Before digital cameras took over the universe, it was common to bracket exposures, shooting, say, a series of three photos at 1/125th second, but varying the f/stop from f/8 to f/11 to f/16. In practice, smaller than whole-stop increments were used for greater precision. Plus, it was just as common to keep the same aperture and vary the shutter speed, although in the days before electronic shutters, film cameras often had only whole increment shutter speeds available.

Today, cameras like the 40D can bracket exposures much more precisely, and bracket white balance as well. While WB bracketing is sometimes used when getting color absolutely correct in the camera is important, auto exposure bracketing (AEB) is used much more often. When this feature is activated, the 40D takes three consecutive photos: one at the metered "correct" exposure, one with less exposure, and one with more exposure, using an increment of your choice up to plus 2/minus 2 stops. (Choose between increments by setting Custom Function I-01 to 0 [1/3 stop] or 1 [1/2 stop].) In Av mode, the aperture will change, while in Tv mode, the shutter speed will change.

Using AEB is trickier than it needs to be, but you can follow these steps:

1. Press the Menu button and use the Main Dial to select the Shooting 2 tab, and then rotate the Quick Control Dial to the AEB position and press the Set button. A dot is centered on the plus/minus scale.

2. Rotate the Quick Control Dial to spread out or contract the three dots to include the desired range you want to cover. For example, with the dots clustered tightly together, the three bracketed exposures will be spread out over a single stop. Separating the cluster produces a wider range and larger exposure change between the three shots in the bracket set, as shown in Figure 4.11.

Figure 4.11
Rotate the Quick Control Dial to set the increment between bracketed shots.

3. Press the Set button to enter the settings and then Menu button to exit the menu system.

4. Take your three photos. You can use single shooting mode to take the trio of pictures yourself, use the self-timer (which will expose all three pictures after the delay), or switch to Continuous Shooting mode to take the three pictures in a burst.

5. As the shots are taken, three indicators will appear on the exposure scale in the viewfinder, with one of them flashing for each bracketed photo, showing when the base exposure, underexposure, and overexposure are taken.

6. Bracketing remains in effect when the set is taken so you can continue shooting bracketed exposures until you use the electronic flash, or return to the menu to cancel bracketing (or if Auto Cancel has been specified in the C. Fn. I-04 setting).

Fine-Tuning Exposure Bracketing

As mentioned in Chapter 3, in C. Fn I-05, adjust the order in which bracketed shots are taken. Press the Menu button, use the Main Dial to choose the Custom Function tab, and select C. Fn I: Exposure. Scroll to Bracketing Sequence with the Quick Command Dial and press the Set button. Choose C. Fn. 05, and select one of the options described below. Press the Set button to activate your choice.

You can define the sequence in which both AEB and WB-BKT series are exposed. If your bias preference is set to blue/amber, the white balance sequence when option 0 is selected will be: current WB, more blue, more amber. If your bias preference is set to magenta/green, then the sequence for option 0 will be: current WB, more magenta, more green.

- **0:** Exposure sequence is: metered exposure, decreased exposure, increased exposure (0, -, +). White balance sequence is: current WB, more blue/more magenta (depending on how your bias is set), more amber/more green (ditto).

- **1:** The sequence is: decreased exposure, metered exposure, increased exposure (-, 0, +). White balance sequence is: more blue/more magenta, current WB, more amber/more green.

When automatic cancel is activated, bracketing remains in effect until you turn the camera off, change lenses, use the flash, or swap memory cards.

Dealing with Noise

Image noise is that random grainy effect that some like to use as a visual effect, but which, most of the time, is objectionable because it robs your image of detail even as it adds that "interesting" texture. Noise is caused by two different phenomena: high ISO settings and long exposures.

High ISO noise commonly appears when you raise your camera's sensitivity setting above ISO 400. With Canon cameras, which are renown for their good ISO noise characteristics, noise may become visible at ISO 800, and is usually fairly noticeable at ISO 1,600. At ISO 3,200 noise is usually quite bothersome, which is why that lofty sensitivity rating is disabled by default and must be activated with ISO expansion using Custom Function 08. This kind of noise appears as a result of the amplification needed to increase the sensitivity of the sensor. While higher ISOs do pull details out of dark areas, they also amplify non-signal information randomly, creating noise.

A similar noisy phenomenon occurs during long time exposures, which allow more photons to reach the sensor, increasing your ability to capture a picture under low-light conditions. However, the longer exposures also increase the likelihood that some pixels will register random phantom photons, often because the longer an imager is "hot" the warmer it gets, and that heat can be mistaken for photons. There's also a special kind of noise that CMOS sensors like the one used in the 40D are potentially susceptible to. With a CCD, the entire signal is conveyed off the chip and funneled through a single amplifier and analog-to-digital conversion circuit. Any noise introduced there is, at least, consistent. CMOS imagers, on the other hand, contain millions of individual amplifiers and A/D converters, all working in unison. Because all these circuits don't necessarily all process in precisely the same way all the time, they can introduce something called fixed-pattern noise into the image data.

Fortunately, Canon's electronics geniuses have done an exceptional job minimizing noise from all causes in the 40D. Even so, you might still want to apply the optional long exposure noise reduction that can be activated using Custom Function 02. This type of noise reduction involves the 40D taking a second, blank exposure, and comparing the random pixels in that image with the photograph you just took. Pixels that coincide in the two represent noise and can safely be suppressed. This noise reduction system, called *dark frame subtraction*, effectively doubles the amount of time required to take a picture, and is used only for exposures longer than one second. Noise reduction can reduce the amount of detail in your picture, as some image information may be removed along with the noise. So, you might want to use this feature with moderation.

To activate your 40D's long exposure noise reduction features, go to the Custom Function menu, choose C. Fn. II: Image, and select either C. Fn. II-01 (Long exposure noise reduction) or C. Fn. II-02 (High ISO noise reduction) as explained in Chapter 3.

You can also apply noise reduction to a lesser extent using Photoshop, and when converting RAW and sRAW files to some other format, using your favorite RAW converter, or an industrial-strength product like Noise Ninja (www.picture-code.com) to wipe out noise after you've already taken the picture.

Fixing Exposures with Histograms

While you can often recover poorly exposed photos in your image editor, your best bet is to arrive at the correct exposure in the camera, minimizing the tweaks that you have to make in post-processing. However, you can't always judge exposure just by viewing the image on your 40D's LCD after the shot is made. Nor can you get a 100 percent accurately exposed picture by using the 40D's Live View "exposure simulation" feature described in Chapter 3. Ambient light may make the LCD difficult to see, and the brightness level you've set can affect the appearance of the playback image.

Instead, you can use a histogram, which is a chart displayed on the EOS 40D's LCD that shows the number of tones being captured at each brightness level. You can use the information to provide correction for the next shot you take. The 40D offers two histogram variations: one that shows overall brightness levels for an image and an alternate version that separates the red, green, and blue channels of your image into separate histograms.

DISPLAYING HISTOGRAMS

To view histograms on your screen, press the Info button while an image is shown on the LCD. Keep pressing the button until the histogram(s) are shown. The display will cycle between several levels of information, including flashing highlights and two histograms. One histogram shows overall brightness levels, while the second type of histogram screen shows both brightness levels and levels for each of the red, green, and blue channels. During histogram display, you'll also see a thumbnail at the left side of the screen with your image displayed. Overexposed areas (shown in black in Figure 4.12) will blink, which is your prompt to use negative exposure compensation. (See Making EV Changes, above.) To change your default histogram type from Brightness to RGB, use the Histogram setting in the Playback 2 menu.

Figure 4.12
A histogram shows the relationship of tones in an image.

Both types are charts that include a representation of up to 256 vertical lines on a horizontal axis that show the number of pixels in the image at each brightness level, from 0 (black) on the left side to 255 (white) on the right. (The 3-inch LCD doesn't have enough pixels to show each and every one of the 256 lines, but, instead provides a representation of the shape of the curve formed.) The more pixels at a given level, the taller the bar at that position. If no bar appears at a particular position on the scale from left to right, there are no pixels at that particular brightness level.

A typical histogram produces a mountain-like shape, with most of the pixels bunched in the middle tones, with fewer pixels at the dark and light ends of the scale. Ideally, though, there will be at least some pixels at either extreme, so that your image has both a true black and a true white representing some details. Learn to spot histograms that represent over- and underexposure, and add or subtract exposure using an EV modification to compensate.

For example, Figure 4.13 shows the histogram for an image that is badly underexposed. You can guess from the shape of the histogram that many of the dark tones to the left of the graph have been clipped off. There's plenty of room on the

Figure 4.13 This histogram shows an underexposed image.

right side for additional pixels to reside without having them become overexposed. Or, a histogram might look like Figure 4.14, which is overexposed. In either case, you can increase or decrease the exposure (either by changing the f/stop or shutter speed in Manual mode or by adding or subtracting an EV value in Autoexposure mode) to produce the corrected histogram shown in Figure 4.15, in which the tones "hug" the right side of the histogram to produce as many highlight details as possible. See "Making EV Changes," above for information on dialing in exposure compensation.

The histogram can also be used to aid in fixing the contrast of an image, although gauging incorrect contrast is more difficult. For example, if the histogram shows all the tones bunched up in one place in the image, the photo will be low in contrast. If the tones are spread out more or less evenly, the image is probably high in contrast. In either case, your best bet may be to switch to RAW (if you're not already using that format) so you can adjust contrast in post processing. However, you can also change to a user-defined picture style (User Def. 1, User Def. 2, or User Def. 3 in the Picture Style menu) with contrast set lower (–1 to –4) or higher (+1 to +4) as required. You'll find more about using picture styles in Chapter 5.

Figure 4.14 This histogram reveals that the image is overexposed.

Figure 4.15 A histogram for a properly exposed image should look like this.

Basic Zone Modes

Your Canon EOS 40D includes seven Basic Zone shooting modes that can automatically make all the basic settings needed for certain types of shooting situations, such as portraits, landscapes, close-ups, sports, night portraits, and "no-flash zone" pictures. They are especially useful when you suddenly encounter a picture-taking opportunity and don't have time to decide exactly which Creative Zone mode you want to use. Instead, you can spin the Mode Dial to the appropriate Basic Zone mode and fire away, knowing that, at least, you have a fighting chance of getting a good or usable photo.

Basic Zone modes are also helpful when you're just learning to use your 40D. Once you've learned how to operate your camera, you'll probably prefer one of the Creative Zone modes that provide more control over shooting options. The Basic Zone scene modes may give you a few options or none at all. The AF mode, drive mode, and metering mode are all set for you.

Here are the modes available:

- **Full Auto.** This is the mode to use when you hand your camera to a total stranger and ask him or her to take your picture posing in front of the Eiffel Tower. All the photographer has to do is press the shutter release button. Every other decision is made by the camera's electronics.

- **Portrait.** This mode tends to use wider f/stops and faster shutter speeds, providing blurred backgrounds and images with no camera shake. If you hold the shutter release down, the 40D will take a continuous sequence of photos, which can be useful in capturing fleeting expressions in portrait situations.

- **Landscape.** The 40D tries to use smaller f/stops for more depth-of-field, and boosts saturation slightly for richer colors.

- **Close-up.** This mode is similar to the Portrait setting, with wider f/stops to isolate your close-up subjects, and high shutter speeds to eliminate the camera shake that's accentuated at close focusing distances. However, if you have your camera mounted on a tripod or are using an image-stabilized (IS) lens, you might want to use the Creative Zone Aperture Priority (Av) mode instead, so you can specify a smaller f/stop with additional depth-of-field.

- **Sports.** In this mode, the 40D tries to use high shutter speeds to freeze action, switches to high-speed continuous drive to allow taking a quick sequence of pictures with one press of the shutter release, and uses AI Servo AF to continually refocus as your subject moves around in the frame. You can find more information on autofocus options in Chapter 5.

- **Night Portrait.** Combines flash with ambient light to produce an image that is mainly illuminated by the flash, but the background is exposed by the available light. This mode uses longer exposures, so a tripod, monopod, or IS lens is a must.

- **Flash Off.** Absolutely prevents the flash from flipping up and firing, which you might want in some situations, such as religious ceremonies, museums, classical music concerts, and your double-naught spy activities.

5

Advanced Shooting with Your Canon EOS 40D

Getting the right exposure is one of the foundations of a great photograph, but a lot more goes into a compelling shot than good tonal values. A sharp image, proper white balance, good color, and other factors all can help elevate your image from good to exceptional. So, now that you've got a good understanding of exposure tucked away, you'll want to learn how to work with some additional exposure options, use the automatic and manual focusing controls available with the Canon EOS 40D, and master some of the many ways you can fine-tune your images.

More Exposure Options

In Chapter 4, you learned techniques for getting the *right* exposure, but I haven't explained all your exposure options just yet. You'll want to know about the *kind* of exposure settings that are available to you with the Canon EOS 40D. There are options that let you control when the exposure is made, or even how to make an exposure that's out of the ordinary in terms of length (time or bulb exposures). The sections that follow explain your camera's special exposure features, and even discuss a few it does not have (and why it doesn't).

A Tiny Slice of Time

Exposures that seem impossibly brief can reveal a world we didn't know existed. In the 1930s, Dr. Harold Edgerton, a professor of electrical engineering at MIT, pioneered high-speed photography using a repeating electronic flash unit he patented called the *stroboscope*. As the inventor of the electronic flash, he popularized its use to freeze objects in motion, and you've probably seen his photographs of bullets piercing balloons and drops of milk forming a coronet-shaped splash.

Electronic flash freezes action by virtue of its extremely short duration—as brief as 1/50,000th second or less. Although the EOS 40D's built-in flash unit can give you these ultra-quick glimpses of moving subjects, an external flash, such as one of the Canon Speedlites, offers even more versatility. You can read more about using electronic flash to stop action in Chapter 7.

Of course, the 40D is fully capable of immobilizing all but the fastest movement using only its shutter speeds, which range all the way up to an astonishing 1/8,000th second. Indeed, you'll rarely have need for such a brief shutter speed in ordinary shooting. If you wanted to use an aperture of f/1.8 at ISO 100 outdoors in bright sunlight, for some reason, a shutter speed of 1/8,000th second would more than do the job. You'd need a faster shutter speed only if you moved the ISO setting to a higher sensitivity (but why would you do that?). Under less than full sunlight, 1/8,000th second is more than fast enough for any conditions you're likely to encounter.

Most sports action can be frozen at 1/2,000th second or slower, and for many sports a slower shutter speed is actually preferable—for example, to allow the wheels of a racing automobile or motorcycle, or the propeller on a classic aircraft to blur realistically. Figure 5.1 is another example. The 1/500 second shutter speed effectively stopped the soccer players in mid-stride, but allowed the fast-moving soccer ball to blur slightly. If the ball were perfectly sharp, it might look on first glance as if it had been glued to the player's leg. The blur tells us that this shot wasn't faked.

But if you want to do some exotic action-freezing photography without resorting to electronic flash, the 40D's top shutter speed is at your disposal. Here are some things to think about when exploring this type of high-speed photography:

- **You'll need a lot of light.** High shutter speeds cut very fine slices of time and sharply reduce the amount of illumination that reaches your sensor. To use 1/8,000th second at an aperture of f/6.3, you'd need an ISO setting of 1,600—even in full daylight. To use an f/stop smaller than f/6.3 or an ISO setting lower than 1,600, you'd need *more* light than full daylight provides. (That's why electronic flash units work so well for high-speed photography when used as the sole illumination; they provide both the effect of a brief shutter speed and the high levels of illumination needed.)

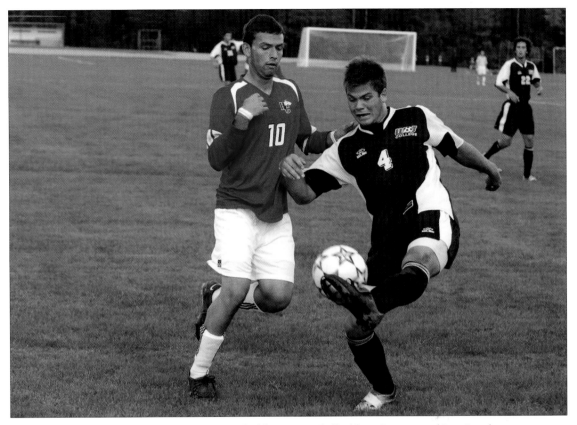

Figure 5.1 A little blur can be a good thing, as the blurry soccer ball adds excitement to this action shot.

■ **Forget about reciprocity failure.** If you're an old-time film shooter, you might recall that very brief shutter speeds (as well as very high light levels and very *long* exposures) produced an effect called *reciprocity failure,* in which given exposures ended up providing less than the calculated value because of the way film responded to very short, very intense, or very long exposures of light. Solid-state sensors don't suffer from this defect, so you don't need to make an adjustment when using high shutter speeds (or brief flash bursts).

■ **No elongation effect.** This is another old bugaboo that has largely been solved through modern technology, but I wanted to bring it to your attention anyway. In olden times, cameras used shutters that traveled horizontally. To achieve faster shutter speeds, focal plane shutters (located just in front of the plane of the sensor) open only a smaller-than-frame-sized slit so that, even though the shutter is already traveling at its highest rate of speed, the film/sensor is exposed for a briefer period of time as the slit moves across the surface.

At very short shutter speeds, and with subjects moving horizontally at very fast velocities, it was possible for the subject to partially "keep up" with the shutter if it were traveling in the same direction as the slit, producing an elongated effect. Conversely, subjects moving in the opposite direction of shutter motion could be compressed. Today, shutters like those in the 40D move vertically and at a higher maximum rate of speed. So, unless you're photographing a rocket blasting into space, and holding the camera horizontally to boot (or shooting a racing car in vertical orientation), it's almost impossible to produce unwanted elongation/compression.

- **Don't combine high shutter speeds with electronic flash.** You might be tempted to use an electronic flash with a high shutter speed. Perhaps you want to stop some action in daylight with a brief shutter speed and use electronic flash only as supplemental illumination to fill in the shadows. Unfortunately, under most conditions you can't use flash in subdued illumination with your 40D at any shutter speed faster than 1/250th second. That's the fastest speed at which the camera's focal plane shutter is fully open: at shorter speeds, the "slit" described above comes into play, so that the flash will expose only the small portion of the sensor exposed by the slit during its duration. (Check out "High Speed Sync" in Chapter 7 if you want to see how you *can* use shutter speeds shorter than 1/250th second with certain Canon Speedlites, albeit at much-reduced effective power levels.)

Working with Short Exposures

You can have a lot of fun exploring the kinds of pictures you can take using very brief exposure times, whether you decide to take advantage of the action-stopping capabilities of your built-in or external electronic flash or work with the Canon EOS 40D's faster shutter speeds. Here are a few ideas to get you started:

- **Take revealing images.** Fast shutter speeds can help you reveal the real subject behind the façade, by freezing constant motion to capture an enlightening moment in time. Legendary fashion/portrait photographer Philippe Halsman used leaping photos of famous people, such as the Duke and Duchess of Windsor, Richard Nixon, and Salvador Dali to illuminate their real selves. Halsman said, "*When you ask a person to jump, his attention is mostly directed toward the act of jumping and the mask falls so that the real person appears.*" Try some high-speed portraits of people you know in motion to see how they appear when concentrating on something other than the portrait.

■ **Create unreal images.** High-speed photography can also produce photographs that show your subjects in ways that are quite unreal. A helicopter in mid-air with its rotors frozen or a motocross cyclist leaping over a ramp, but with all motion stopped so that the rider and machine look as if they were frozen in mid-air, make for an unusual picture. (See Figure 5.2.) When we're accustomed to seeing subjects in motion, seeing them stopped in time can verge on the surreal.

Figure 5.2 Freezing a leaping motocross rider in mid-air makes for an image that verges on the surreal.

■ **Capture unseen perspectives.** Some things are *never* seen in real life, except when viewed in a stop-action photograph. Edgerton's balloon bursts were only a starting point. Freeze a hummingbird in flight for a view of wings that never seem to stop. Or, capture the splashes as liquid falls into a bowl, as shown in Figure 5.3. No electronic flash was required for this image (and wouldn't have illuminated the water in the bowl as evenly). Instead, a clutch of high intensity lamps and an ISO setting of 1,600 allowed the EOS 40D to capture this image at 1/2,000th second.

Figure 5.3 A large amount of artificial illumination and an ISO 1,600 sensitivity setting allowed capturing this shot at 1/2,000th second without use of an electronic flash.

- **Vanquish camera shake and gain new angles.** Here's an idea that's so obvious it isn't always explored to its fullest extent. A high enough shutter speed can free you from the tyranny of a tripod, making it easier to capture new angles, or to shoot quickly while moving around, especially with longer lenses. I tend to use a monopod or tripod for almost everything when I'm not using an image-stabilized lens, and I end up missing some shots because of a reluctance to adjust my camera support to get a higher, lower, or different angle. If you have enough light and can use an f/stop wide enough to permit a high shutter speed, you'll find a new freedom to choose your shots. I have a favored 170mm-500mm lens that I use for sports and wildlife photography, almost invariably with a tripod, as I don't find the "reciprocal of the focal length" rule particularly helpful in most cases. (I would *not* handhold this hefty lens at its 500mm setting with a 1/500th second shutter speed under most circumstances.) However, at 1/2,000th second or faster, it's entirely possible for a steady hand to use this lens without a tripod or monopod's extra support, and I've found that my whole approach to shooting animals and other elusive subjects changes in high-speed mode. Selective focus allows dramatically isolating my prey wide open at f/6.3, too.

Long Exposures

Longer exposures are a doorway into another world, showing us how even familiar scenes can look much different when photographed over periods measured in seconds. At night, long exposures produce streaks of light from moving, illuminated subjects like automobiles or amusement park rides. Extra-long exposures of seemingly pitch-dark subjects can reveal interesting views using light levels barely bright enough to see by. At any time of day, including daytime (in which case you'll often need the help of neutral density filters to make the long exposure practical), long exposures can cause moving objects to vanish entirely, because they don't remain stationary long enough to register in a photograph.

Three Ways to Take Long Exposures

There are actually three common types of lengthy exposures: *timed exposures, bulb exposures,* and *time exposures.* The EOS 40D offers only the first two, but once you understand all three, you'll see why Canon made the choices it did. Because of the length of the exposure, all of the following techniques should be used with a tripod to hold the camera steady.

- **Timed exposures.** These are long exposures from 1 second to 30 seconds, measured by the camera itself. To take a picture in this range, simply use Manual or Tv modes and use the Main Dial to set the shutter speed to the length of time you want, choosing from preset speeds of 1.0, 1.5, 2.0, 3.0, 4.0, 6.0, 8.0, 10.0, 15.0, 20.0, or 30.0 seconds (if you've specified 1/2 stop increments for exposure adjustments), or 1.0, 1.3, 1.6, 2.0, 2.5, 3.2, 4.0, 5.0, 6.0, 8.0, 10.0, 13.0, 15.0, 20.0, 25.0, and 30.0 seconds (if you're using 1/3 stop increments). The advantage of timed exposures is that the camera does all the calculating for you. There's no need for a stop-watch. If you review your image on the LCD and decide to try again with the exposure doubled or halved, you can dial in the correct exposure with precision. The disadvantage of timed exposures is that you can't take a photo for longer than 30 seconds.

- **Bulb exposures.** This type of exposure is so-called because in the olden days the photographer squeezed and held an air bulb attached to a tube that provided the force necessary to keep the shutter open. Traditionally, a bulb exposure is one that lasts as long as the shutter release button is pressed; when you release the button, the exposure ends. To make a bulb exposure with the 40D, set the camera on Manual mode and use the Main Dial to select the shutter speed immediately after 30 seconds—buLB. Then, press the shutter to start the exposure, and press it again to close the shutter. If you'd like to simulate a time exposure (described below), you can use the Canon RS-80N3 or TC-80N3 remote releases that attach to the terminal on the left side of the camera under the rubber cover. Both have a shutter release lock that can be used to keep the shutter open, and the TC-80N3 includes a timer that can expose a picture for any length from 1 second to 99 hours, 59 minutes, and 59 seconds. Or, if you have a lot of money to spend and can find one, you can use the LC-4 infrared wireless transmitter and receiver.

■ **Time exposures.** This is a setting found on some cameras to produce longer exposures. With cameras that implement this option, the shutter opens when you press the shutter release button, and remains open until you press the button again. Usually, you'll be able to close the shutter using a mechanical cable release or, more commonly, an electronic release cable. The advantage of this approach is that you can take an exposure of virtually any duration without the need for special equipment (the tethered release is optional). You can press the shutter release button, go off for a few minutes, and come back to close the shutter (assuming your camera is still there). The disadvantages of this mode are exposures must be timed manually, and with shorter exposures it's possible for the vibration of manually opening and closing the shutter to register in the photo. For longer exposures, the period of vibration is relatively brief and not usually a problem—and there is always the release cable option to eliminate photographer-caused camera shake entirely. While the 40D does not have a built-in time exposure capability, you can simulate it with the bulb exposure technique, described previously.

Working with Long Exposures

Because the EOS 40D produces such good images at longer exposures, and there are so many creative things you can do with long-exposure techniques, you'll want to do some experimenting. Get yourself a tripod or another firm support and take some test shots with long exposure noise reduction both enabled and disabled (to see whether you prefer low noise or high detail) and get started. Here are some things to try:

■ **Make people invisible.** One very cool thing about long exposures is that objects that move rapidly enough won't register at all in a photograph, while the subjects that remain stationary are portrayed in the normal way. That makes it easy to produce people-free landscape photos and architectural photos at night or, even, in full daylight if you use a neutral density filter (or two) (or three) to allow an exposure of at least a few seconds. At ISO 100, f/22, and a pair of 8X (three-stop) neutral density filters you can use exposures of nearly two seconds; overcast days and/or even more neutral density filtration would work even better if daylight people-vanishing is your goal. They'll have to be walking *very* briskly and across the field of view (rather than directly toward the camera) for this to work. At night, it's much easier to achieve this effect with the 20- to 30-second exposures that are possible, as you can see in Figures 5.4 and 5.5.

Figure 5.4
This alleyway is thronged with people, as you can see in this two-second exposure using only the available illumination.

Figure 5.5
With the camera still on a tripod, a 30-second exposure rendered the passersby almost invisible.

■ **Create streaks.** If you aren't shooting for total invisibility, long exposures with the camera on a tripod can produce some interesting streaky effects. Even a single 8X ND filter will let you shoot at f/22 and 1/6th second in daylight, giving you results as shown in Figure 5.6.

Figure 5.6 The busses passing by this public square moved quickly enough to be shown only as a blur at 1/6th second in this tripod-mounted shot in full daylight, with an 8X neutral density filter allowing the long exposure.

■ **Produce light trails.** At night, car headlights and taillights and other moving sources of illumination can generate interesting light trails, as shown in Figure 5.7. Your camera doesn't even need to be mounted on a tripod; handholding the 40D for longer exposures adds movement and patterns to your trails. If you're shooting fireworks, a longer exposure may allow you to combine several bursts into one picture.

■ **Blur waterfalls, etc.** You'll find that waterfalls and other sources of moving liquid produce a special type of long-exposure blur, because the water merges into a fantasy-like veil that looks different at different exposure times, and with different waterfalls. Cascades with turbulent flow produce a rougher look at a given longer exposure than falls that flow smoothly. Although blurred waterfalls have become almost a cliché, there are still plenty of variations for a creative photographer to explore.

Figure 5.7 Long exposures can transform the most mundane nighttime subjects, such as this amusement park ride, into an interesting light-trails display.

■ **Show total darkness in new ways.** Even on the darkest, moonless nights, there is enough starlight or glow from distant illumination sources to see by, and, if you use a long exposure, there is enough light to take a picture, too. I was visiting a lakeside park after dark and saw that the dim light from the lamps in the parking lot provided sufficient light to see a distant stand of trees. A 30-second exposure with the lens almost wide open revealed the scene shown in Figure 5.8, even though in real life, there was barely enough light to make out the closest tree. Although the photo appears as if it were taken at twilight or sunset, in fact the shot was made at 11 p.m. It was a new moon that night, so the main illumination was starlight, spill light from the parking lot, and a distant city (which added a sunset-like effect to the sky at the horizon that shows at the far side of the lake).

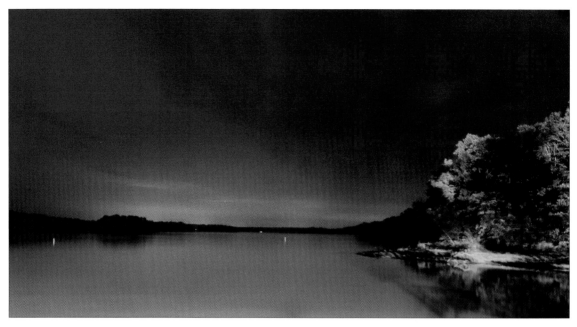

Figure 5.8 A 30-second exposure on a dark night revealed this lakeside setting, illuminated only by starlight, spill light from a parking lot adjacent to the shore, and distant city lights.

Delayed Exposures

Sometimes it's desirable to have a delay of some sort before a picture is actually taken. Perhaps you'd like to get in the picture yourself, and would appreciate it if the camera waited 10 seconds after you press the shutter release to actually take the picture. Maybe you want to give a tripod-mounted camera time to settle down and damp any residual vibration after the release is pressed to improve sharpness for an exposure with a relatively slow shutter speed. It's possible you want to explore the world of time-lapse photography. The next sections present your delayed exposure options.

Self-Timer

The EOS 40D has a built-in self-timer with 10-second and 2-second delays. Activate the timer by pressing the AF-DRIVE and spinning the Quick Command Dial until either of the two self-timer clock icons appear on the LCD status panel. Press the shutter release button halfway to lock in focus on your subjects (if you're taking a self-portrait, focus on an object at a similar distance and use focus lock). When you're ready to take the photo, continue pressing the shutter release the rest of the way. The lamp on the front of the camera will blink slowly for eight seconds (when using the 10-second timer) and the beeper will chirp (if you haven't disabled it in the Shooting menu, as described in Chapter 3). During the final two seconds, the beeper sounds more rapidly and the lamp remains on until the picture is taken. The top-panel LCD displays a countdown while all this is going on.

Another way to use the self-timer is with the mirror lockup feature (C.Fn-III-07). This is something you might want to do if you're shooting close-ups, landscapes, or other types of pictures using the self-timer only to trip the shutter in the most vibration-free way possible. Forget to bring along your tripod, but still want to take a close-up picture with a precise focus setting? Set your digital camera to the self-timer function, then put the camera on any reasonably steady support, such as a fence post or a rock. When you're ready to take the picture, press the shutter release. The camera might teeter back and forth for a second or two, but it will settle back to its original position before the self-timer activates the shutter. The self-timer remains active until you turn it off—even if you power down the 40D.

Remote Control

As outlined in the "Bulb Exposure" description earlier, your Canon EOS 40D can be triggered using a plug-in remote control with an electronic or infrared connection. For example, the Remote Switch RS-80N3 allows triggering a camera attached to the end of its cable. More versatile is the Canon TC-80N3, a remote switch with a 2.6-foot cord (you can add a 33-foot extension cable) and includes a more flexible self-timer that can be set to trip the camera after a delay of anywhere from 1 second to 99 hours, 59 minutes, and 59 seconds (in other words, one second less than 100 hours). It has an LCD display that makes it easy to make and view settings.

Time-Lapse/Interval Photography

Who hasn't marveled at a time-lapse photograph of a flower opening, a series of shots of the moon marching across the sky, or one of those extreme time-lapse picture sets showing something that takes a very, very long time, such as a building under construction.

You probably won't be shooting such construction shots, unless you have a spare 40D you don't need for a few months (or are willing to go through the rigmarole of figuring out how to set up your camera in precisely the same position using the same lens settings to shoot a series of pictures at intervals). However, other kinds of time-lapse photography are entirely within reach.

Although the EOS 40D can't take time-lapse/interval photographs all by itself, if you're willing to tether the camera to a computer (a laptop will do) using the USB cable, you can take time-lapse photos using the Digital Photo Professional software furnished with your camera. There's more information on using this software in Chapter 8.

If you want freedom to shoot anywhere, the TC-80N3 is an affordable add-on (around $135) with much more than the self-timer and remote control features mentioned previously. In fact, it has 15 different modes with an interesting array of delay/interval combinations. For example, you can set the self-timer for a specific period of time, then take a specified number of exposures at one-second intervals. Or, you can set a delay period that must elapse before the 40D begins a long exposure. Finally, you can choose to shoot a set number of pictures at intervals from 1 second to 99 hours, 59 minutes, and 59 seconds.

Here are some tips for effective time-lapse photography:

- **Use AC power.** If you're shooting a long sequence, consider connecting your camera to an AC adapter, as leaving the 40D on for long periods of time will rapidly deplete the battery.

- **Make sure you have enough storage space.** Unless your memory card has enough capacity to hold all the images you'll be taking, you might want to change to a higher compression rate or reduced resolution to maximize the image count.

- **Make a movie.** While time-lapse stills are interesting, you can increase your fun factor by compiling all your shots into a motion picture using your favorite desktop movie-making software.

- **Protect your camera.** If your camera will be set up for an extended period of time (longer than an hour or two), make sure it's protected from weather, earthquakes, animals, young children, innocent bystanders, and theft.

- **Vary intervals.** Experiment with different time intervals. You don't want to take pictures too often or less often than necessary to capture the changes you hope to image.

Getting into Focus

Learning to use the Canon EOS 40D's autofocus system is easy, but you do need to fully understand how the system works to get the most benefit from it. Once you're comfortable with autofocus, you'll know when it's appropriate to use the manual focus option, too. The important thing to remember is that focus isn't absolute. For example, some things that look in sharp focus at a given viewing size and distance might not be in focus at a larger size and/or closer distance. In addition, the goal of optimum focus isn't always to make things look sharp. Not all of an image will be or should be sharp. Controlling exactly what is sharp and what is not is part of your creative palette. Use of depth-of-field characteristics to throw part of an image out of focus while other parts are sharply focused is one of the most valuable tools available to a photographer. But selective focus works only when the desired areas of an image are in focus properly. For the digital SLR photographer, correct focus can be one of the trickiest parts of the technical and creative process.

To make your job easier, the EOS 40D has a precision nine-point autofocus system that uses a separate CMOS sensor in the viewing system to measure the contrast of the image. When the contrast is highest at the active autofocus point(s), that part of the image is in sharp focus. These points are of the advanced "cross" type (that is, they measure in both horizontal and vertical directions) and can be selected automatically by the camera, or manually by you, the photographer. They're represented by the nine sets of brackets visible in the viewfinder (see Figure 5.9).

Your camera's autofocus sensors require a minimum amount of light to operate, which is why autofocus capabilities are possible only with lenses having an f/5.6 or larger maximum aperture. If necessary, the AF assist beam built into the 40D and Canon's dedicated flash units provide additional light that helps assure enough illumination for autofocus.

Figure 5.9

Any of the nine autofocus points can be selected by the photographer manually or by the camera automatically.

Improved Cross-Type Focus Points

One improvement that new Canon EOS 40D owners sometimes overlook is the upgrade to cross-type focus points at all nine focus zone positions (with lenses having that f/5.6 or larger maximum aperture), plus a center cross-type focus point that is extra sensitive when used with lenses having a maximum f/stop of f/2.8 or better. Why is this important? It helps to review exactly how the 40D determines focus.

The camera looks for contrast between adjacent pixels to determine relative sharpness—specifically, the transitions between those groups of pixels that determine the edges in a subject. At top in the extreme enlargement shown in Figure 5.10,

Figure 5.10

Focus sensors detect the increase in contrast in the edges of subjects, starting with a blurry image (top) and producing a sharp, contrasty image (bottom).

the transitions between pixels are soft and blurred. Even the boundary between the bright leaf and its dark background is smudged. When the image is brought into focus (bottom), the transitions are sharp and clear. You can see by the bright pixels around the edge of the leaf that it is backlit, and even some of the veins in the leaf at middle right show up. Although this example is a bit exaggerated so you can see the results on the printed page, it's easy to understand that when the EOS 40D detects maximum contrast in a subject being evaluated by the focus sensor, it is deemed to be in sharp focus.

The value of cross-type focus sensors, which can interpret contrast in both horizontal and vertical directions, can be seen in Figure 5.11. The two upper photos show a horizontal-type sensor evaluating a subject, which happens to be a piece of aged wood siding heavily creased with horizontal lines. At upper left, the sensor sees blurry lines, which become sharper when the wood is brought into focus.

Figure 5.11 Horizontal (and vertical) focus sensors can interpret image contrast in only one direction (top), while cross-type sensors can evaluate contrast in both horizontal and vertical directions.

This type of subject is of average difficulty for a horizontal sensor: easier to interpret than an image with no pattern at all, and harder to focus than, say, vertical lines, which would stand out more clearly. You can see that a horizontal focus sensor does a good job but has some weaknesses. (A vertical-only focus sensor would have the same reduced performance with vertical lines and better focusing with horizontal lines.)

At the bottom of the figure you'll see the same subject being evaluated by a cross-type sensor. The horizontal lines are still more difficult to interpret with the horizontal arm of the cross, but they stand out in sharp contrast (even in the blurry version at lower left) and allow the camera to snap the image into focus easily, as you can see at lower right. In this example, both the horizontal and cross-type sensors were able to produce an equally sharp focus (upper and lower right), but the cross-type sensor probably focused the image a tad faster. And, in lower light levels, with subjects that were moving, or with subjects that have no pattern and less contrast to begin with, the cross-type sensor not only works faster but can focus subjects that a horizontal- or vertical-only sensor can't handle at all.

So, you can see that having nine cross-type focus sensors and one extra-sensitive center cross sensor (with faster lenses) is a definite advantage.

Focus Modes

The 40D has three AF modes: One Shot AF (also known as Single Autofocus), AI Servo (Continuous Autofocus), and AI Focus AF (which switches between the two as appropriate). I'll explain all of these in more detail later in this section.

MANUAL FOCUS

With manual focus activated by sliding the switch on the lens, your 40D lets you set the focus yourself. There are some advantages and disadvantages to this approach. While your batteries will last longer in manual focus mode, it will take you longer to focus the camera for each photo, a process that can be difficult. Modern digital cameras, even dSLRs, depend so much on autofocus that the viewfinders of models that have less than full-frame-sized sensors are no longer designed for optimum manual focus. Pick up any film camera and you'll see a bigger, brighter viewfinder with a focusing screen that's a joy to focus on manually. Until the EOS 40D was introduced, you really needed to use a full-frame digital camera, like the Canon EOS 5D, to get such a bright view and easy manual focus. However, you can now swap the 40D's focus screen—great for viewing and autofocus—and use the EF-S Super Precision Matte screen, which is optimized for manual focus.

Focus Pocus

Although Canon added autofocus capabilities in the 1980s, back in the day of film cameras, prior to that focusing was always done manually. Honest. Even though viewfinders were bigger and brighter than they are today, special focusing screens, magnifiers, and other gadgets were often used to help the photographer achieve correct focus. Imagine what it must have been like to focus manually under demanding, fast-moving conditions such as sports photography.

Focusing was problematic because our eyes and brains have poor memory for correct focus, which is why your eye doctor must shift back and forth between sets of lenses and ask "Does that look sharper—or was it sharper before?" in determining your correct prescription. Similarly, manual focusing involves jogging the focus ring back and forth as you go from almost in focus, to sharp focus, to almost focused again. The little clockwise and counterclockwise arcs decrease in size until you've zeroed in on the point of correct focus. As I mentioned earlier in this chapter, what you're looking for is the image with the most contrast between the edges of elements in the image.

The 40D's autofocus mechanism, like all such systems found in SLR cameras, also evaluates these increases and decreases in sharpness, but it is able to remember the progression perfectly, so that autofocus can lock in much more quickly and, with an image that has sufficient contrast, more precisely. Unfortunately, while the 40D's focus system finds it easy to measure degrees of apparent focus at each of the focus points in the viewfinder, it doesn't really know with any certainty *which* object should be in sharpest focus. Is it the closest object? The subject in the center? Something lurking *behind* the closest subject? A person standing over at the side of the picture? Many of the techniques for using autofocus effectively involve telling the EOS 40D exactly what it should be focusing on.

Adding Circles of Confusion

But there are other factors in play, as well. You know that increased depth-of-field brings more of your subject into focus. But more depth-of-field also makes auto-focusing (or manual focusing) more difficult because the contrast is lower between objects at different distances. So, autofocus with a 200mm lens (or zoom setting) may be easier than at a 28mm focal length (or zoom setting) because the longer lens has less apparent depth-of-field. By the same token, a lens with a maximum aperture of f/1.8 will be easier to autofocus (or manually focus) than one of the same focal length with an f/4 maximum aperture, because the f/4 lens has more depth-of-field *and* a dimmer view. That's why lenses with a maximum aperture smaller than f/5.6 can give your 40D's autofocus system fits.

To make things even more complicated, many subjects aren't polite enough to remain still. They move around in the frame, so that even if the 40D is sharply focused on your main subject, it may change position and require refocusing. An intervening subject may pop into the frame and pass between you and the subject you meant to photograph. You (or the 40D) have to decide whether to lock focus on this new subject, or remain focused on the original subject. Finally, there are some kinds of subjects that are difficult to bring into sharp focus because they lack enough contrast to allow the 40D's AF system (or our eyes) to lock in. Blank walls, a clear blue sky, or other subject matter may make focusing difficult.

If you find all these focus factors confusing, you're on the right track. Focus is, in fact, measured using something called a *circle of confusion*. An ideal image consists of zillions of tiny little points, which, like all points, theoretically have no height or width. There is perfect contrast between the point and its surroundings. You can think of each point as a pinpoint of light in a darkened room. When a given point is out of focus, its edges decrease in contrast and it changes from a perfect point to a tiny disc with blurry edges (remember, blur is the lack of contrast between boundaries in an image). (See Figure 5.12.)

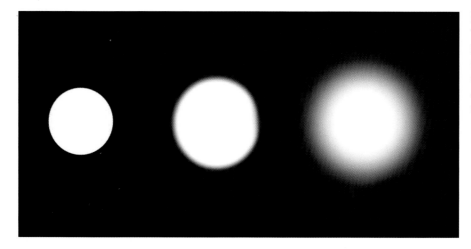

Figure 5.12
When a pinpoint of light (left) goes out of focus, its blurry edges form a circle of confusion (center and right).

If this blurry disc—the circle of confusion—is small enough, our eye still perceives it as a point. It's only when the disc grows large enough that we can see it as a blur rather than a sharp point that a given point is viewed as out of focus. You can see, then, that enlarging an image, either by displaying it larger on your computer monitor or by making a large print, also enlarges the size of each circle of confusion. Moving closer to the image does the same thing. So, parts of an image that may look perfectly sharp in a 5 × 7-inch print viewed at arm's length, might appear blurry when blown up to 11 × 14 and examined at the same distance. Take a few steps back, however, and it may look sharp again.

To a lesser extent, the viewer also affects the apparent size of these circles of confusion. Some people see details better at a given distance and may perceive smaller circles of confusion than someone standing next to them. For the most part, however, such differences are small. Truly blurry images will look blurry to just about everyone under the same conditions.

Technically, there is just one plane within your picture area, parallel to the back of the camera (or sensor, in the case of a digital camera), that is in sharp focus. That's the plane in which the points of the image are rendered as precise points. At every other plane in front of or behind the focus plane, the points show up as discs that range from slightly blurry to extremely blurry (see Figure 5.13). In practice, the

Figure 5.13

Only the blossoms in the foreground are in focus—the area behind them appears blurry because the depth-of-field is limited.

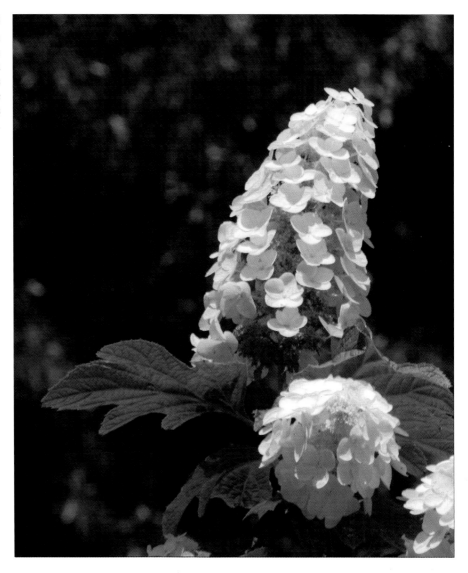

discs in many of these planes will still be so small that we see them as points, and that's where we get depth-of-field. Depth-of-field is just the range of planes that include discs that we perceive as points rather than blurred splotches. The size of this range increases as the aperture is reduced in size and is allocated roughly one-third in front of the plane of sharpest focus, and two-thirds behind it. The range of sharp focus is always greater behind your subject than in front of it.

Making Sense of Sensors

The number and type of autofocus sensors can affect how well the system operates. As I mentioned, the Canon EOS 40D has nine AF points. The new Digital Rebel XTi has nine, too. The original Digital Rebel and Digital Rebel XT had seven autofocus points, and Canon's high-end cameras, like the 21MP Canon EOS-1Ds Mark III has a whopping 45 autofocus points. These focus sensors can consist of vertical or horizontal lines of pixels, cross-shapes, and often a mixture of these types within a single camera, although, as I mentioned, the EOS 40D includes cross-type sensors at all positions. The more AF points available, the more easily the camera can differentiate among areas of the frame, and the more precisely you can specify the area you want to be in focus if you're manually choosing a focus spot.

As the camera collects contrast information from the sensors, it then evaluates it to determine whether the desired sharp focus has been achieved. The calculations may include whether the subject is moving, and whether the camera needs to "predict" where the subject will be when the shutter release button is fully depressed and the picture is taken. The speed with which the camera is able to evaluate focus and then move the lens elements into the proper position to achieve the sharpest focus determines how fast the autofocus mechanism is. Although your 40D will almost always focus more quickly than a human, there are types of shooting situations where that's not fast enough. For example, if you're having problems shooting sports because the 40D's autofocus system manically follows each moving subject, a better choice might be to switch autofocus modes or shift into manual and prefocus on a spot where you anticipate the action will be, such as a goal line or soccer net. At night football games, for example, when I am shooting with a telephoto lens almost wide open, I often focus manually on one of the referees who happens to be standing where I expect the action to be taking place (say, a halfback run or a pass reception). When I am less sure about what is going to happen, I may switch to AI Servo autofocus and let the camera decide.

Your Autofocus Mode Options

Choosing the right autofocus mode and the way in which focus points are selected is your key to success. Using the wrong mode for a particular type of photography can lead to a series of pictures that are all sharply focused—on the wrong subject. When I first started shooting sports with an autofocus SLR (back in the film camera days), I covered one game alternating between shots of base runners and outfielders with pictures of a promising young pitcher, all from a position next to the third base dugout. The base runner and outfielder photos were great, because their backgrounds didn't distract the autofocus mechanism. But all my photos of the pitcher had the focus tightly zeroed in on the fans in the stands behind him. Because I was shooting film instead of a digital camera, I didn't know about my gaffe until the film was developed. A simple change, such as locking in focus or focus zone manually, or even manually focusing, would have done the trick.

To save battery power, your 40D doesn't start to focus the lens until you partially depress the shutter release. But, autofocus isn't some mindless beast out there snapping your pictures in and out of focus with no feedback from you after you press that button. There are several settings you can modify that return at least a modicum of control to you. Your first decision should be whether you set the 40D to One Shot, AI Servo AF, or AI Focus AF. With the camera set for one of the Creative Zone modes, press the AF-DRIVE button and spin the Main Dial until the choice you want is displayed on the LCD status panel (see Figure 5.14). (The AF/M switch on the lens must be set to AF before you can change autofocus mode.)

Figure 5.14

Rotate the Main Dial until the AF choice you want becomes visible (all three choices are never visible simultaneously, as in this illustration).

One Shot AF

In this mode, also called *Single Autofocus*, focus is set once and remains at that setting until the button is fully depressed, taking the picture, or until you release the shutter button without taking a shot. For non-action photography, this setting is usually your best choice, as it minimizes out-of-focus pictures (at the expense of spontaneity). The drawback here is that you might not be able to take a picture at all while the camera is seeking focus; you're locked out until the autofocus mechanism is happy with the current setting. One Shot AF/Single Autofocus is sometimes referred to as *focus priority* for that reason. Because of the small delay while the camera zeroes in on correct focus, you might experience slightly more shutter lag. This mode uses less battery power.

When sharp focus is achieved, the selected focus point will flash red in the viewfinder, and the focus confirmation light at the lower right will flash green. If you're using Evaluative metering, the exposure will be locked at the same time. By keeping the shutter button depressed halfway, you'll find you can reframe the image while retaining the focus (and exposure) that's been set.

AI Servo AF

This mode, also known as *Continuous Autofocus* is the mode to use for sports and other fast-moving subjects. In this mode, once the shutter release is partially depressed, the camera sets the focus but continues to monitor the subject, so that if it moves or you move, the lens will be refocused to suit. Focus and exposure aren't really locked until you press the shutter release down all the way to take the picture. You'll often see Continuous Autofocus referred to as *release priority*. If you press the shutter release down all the way while the system is refining focus, the camera will go ahead and take a picture, even if the image is slightly out of focus. You'll find that AI Servo AF produces the least amount of shutter lag of any autofocus mode: press the button and the camera fires. It also uses the most battery power, because the autofocus system operates as long as the shutter release button is partially depressed.

AI Servo AF uses a technology called *predictive AF*, which allows the 40D to calculate the correct focus if the subject is moving toward or away from the camera at a constant rate. It uses either the automatically selected AF point or the point you select manually to set focus.

AI Focus AF

This setting is actually a combination of the first two. When selected, the camera focuses using One Shot AF and locks in the focus setting. But, if the subject begins moving, it will switch automatically to AI Servo AF and change the focus to keep the subject sharp. AI Focus AF is a good choice when you're shooting a mixture of action pictures and less dynamic shots and want to use One Shot AF when possible. The camera will default to that mode, yet switch automatically to AI Servo AF when it would be useful for subjects that might begin moving unexpectedly.

Setting AF Point

You can change which of the nine focus points the Canon EOS 40D uses to calculate correct focus, or allow the camera to select the point for you. As I mentioned in Chapter 1, in A-DEP, or any of the Basic Zone shooting modes, the focus point is always selected automatically by the camera. In the other Creative Zone modes, you can allow the camera to select the focus point automatically, or you can specify which focus point should be used.

To review, there are several methods to set the focus point manually. You can press the AF point selection button on the back of the camera, look through the viewfinder, and use the multi-controller knob (to the right and below the viewfinder window) to move the focus point to the zone you want to use. For example, press the multi-controller straight up or down, and the top or bottom focus points are selected. To the left or right, and the side points are selected. Movements to the two o'clock, four o'clock, seven o'clock, or ten o'clock positions choose the in-between focus sensors. Press the multi-controller in, and the center focus point becomes active.

You can also choose a focus point by pressing the AF point selection button and then rotating the Main Dial as in Figure 5.15. The focus point will cycle among the edge points counterclockwise (if you turn the Main Dial to the left) or clockwise (if you spin the Main Dial to the right). At each end of the cycle the center focus point and then all nine focus points will be active. When all nine are "live," auto point selection will be switched back on.

Figure 5.15
When selecting focus points manually, rotate the Main Dial to select specific points. Continue rotating until all nine points are visible, and the 40D switches back to automatic AF point selection mode.

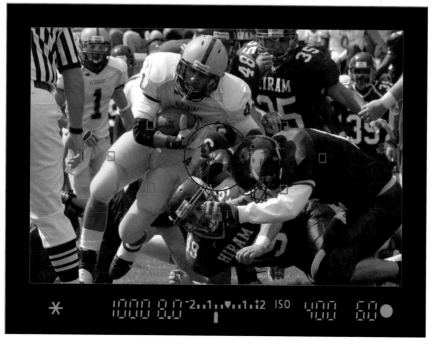

Continuous Shooting

The Canon EOS 40D's pair of Continuous Shooting modes remind me how far digital photography has brought us. The first accessory I purchased when I worked as a sports photographer some years ago was a motor drive for my film SLR. It enabled me to snap off a series of shots in rapid succession, which came in very handy when a fullback broke through the line and headed for the end zone. Even a seasoned action photographer can miss the decisive instant when a crucial block is made, or a baseball superstar's bat shatters and pieces of cork fly out. Continuous shooting simplifies taking a series of pictures, either to ensure that one has more or less the exact moment you want to capture or to capture a sequence that is interesting as a collection of successive images.

The 40D's "motor drive" capabilities are, in many ways, much superior to what you get with a film camera. For one thing, a motor-driven film camera can eat up film at an incredible pace, which is why many of them are used with cassettes that hold hundreds of feet of film stock. At three frames per second (typical of film cameras), a short burst of a few seconds can burn up as much as half of an ordinary 36 exposure roll of film. Digital cameras, in contrast, have reusable "film," so if you waste a few dozen shots on non-decisive moments, you can erase them and shoot more.

The increased capacity of digital film cards gives you a prodigious number of frames to work with. At a baseball game I covered earlier this year, I took more than 1,000 images in a couple hours. Yet, even shooting RAW+JPEG Fine I could fit more than 200 images on a single 4GB Compact Flash card. If I'd switched to JPEG, I could have taken about 900 different images without switching cards. Even at the top speed of 6.5 frames per second that the 40D is capable of, that's a lot of shooting. Given an average burst of about eight frames per sequence (nobody really takes 15-20 shots or more of one play in a baseball game), I was able to capture 32 different sequences before I needed to swap cards.

On the other hand, at a football game I covered later in the same month (there are some weird sports overlaps in early September!), the longer bursts came in handy, because running and passing plays often lasted 5 to 10 seconds, and changed in character as the action switched from the quarterback dropping back to pass or hand off the ball, then the receiver or running back trying to gain as much yardage as possible. Even simple plays, like a punt, seemed more exciting when captured in a sequence of shots, as in Figure 5.16.

Figure 5.16
Continuous shooting
allows you to capture
an entire sequence of
exciting moments as
they unfold.

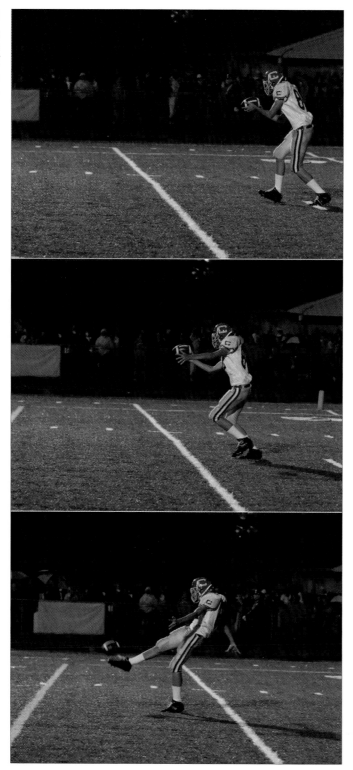

To use the 40D's Continuous Shooting modes, press the AF-Drive button. Spin the Quick Control Dial until either the High-Speed Continuous Shooting (6.5 frames per second) or Low-Speed Continuous Shooting (3 fps) icons appear in the status LCD (see Figure 5.17). When you partially depress the shutter button, the viewfinder will display a number representing the maximum number of shots you can take at the current quality settings. (If your battery is low, this figure will be lower.) The larger buffer in the 40D will generally allow you to take as many as 75 JPEG shots in a single burst, or 17 RAW photos.

Figure 5.17
Press the AF-Drive button and spin the Quick Control Dial until the High-Speed Continuous Shooting or Low-Speed Continuous Shooting icons appear.

To increase this number, reduce the image-quality setting by switching to JPEG only (from JPEG+RAW), to a lower JPEG quality setting, or by reducing the 40D's resolution from L to M or S. The reason the size of your bursts is limited is that continuous images are first shuttled into the 40D's internal memory buffer, then doled out to the Compact Flash card as quickly as they can be written to the card. Technically, the 40D takes the RAW data received from the digital image processor and converts it to the output format you've selected—either .jpg or .cr2 (raw)—and deposits it in the buffer ready to store on the card.

This internal "smart" buffer can suck up photos much more quickly than the CF card and, indeed, some memory cards are significantly faster or slower than others. When the buffer fills, you can't take any more continuous shots (a buSY indicator appears in the viewfinder and LCD status panel) until the 40D has written some of them to the card, making more room in the buffer. (You should keep in mind that faster CF cards write images more quickly, freeing up buffer space faster.)

Setting Image Parameters

You can fine-tune the images that you take in several different ways. For example, if you don't want to choose a predefined white balance or use white balance bracketing (both discussed earlier in this book), you can set a custom white balance based on the illumination of the site where you'll be taking photos, or choose a white balance based on color temperature. With the Picture Styles options, you can set up customized sharpening, tone, color, saturation, and hue for various types of pictures, plus three personal sets of settings that you can recall at any time. This section shows you how to use the available image parameters.

Customizing White Balance

Back in the film days, color films were standardized, or balanced, for a particular "color" of light. Digital cameras like the EOS 40D use a particular "white balance" matched to the color of light used to expose your photograph. The right white balance is measured using a scale called *color temperature.* Color temperatures were assigned by heating a mythical "black body radiator" and recording the spectrum of light it emitted at a given temperature in degrees Kelvin. So, daylight at noon has a color temperature in the 5,500 to 6,000 degree range. Indoor illumination is around 3,400 degrees. Hotter temperatures produce bluer images (think blue-white hot) while cooler temperatures produce redder images (think of a dull-red glowing ember). Because of human nature, though, bluer images are actually called "cool" (think wintry day) and redder images are called "warm," (think ruddy sunset) even though their color temperatures are reversed.

If a photograph is exposed indoors under warm illumination with a digital camera sensor balanced for cooler daylight, the image will appear much too reddish (see Figure 5.18). An image exposed outdoors with the white balance set for incandescent illumination will seem much too blue (see Figure 5.19). These color casts may be too strong to remove in an image editor from JPEG files, although if you shoot RAW or sRAW you can change the WB setting to the correct value when you import the image into your editor.

The Auto White Balance (AWB) setting, available by pressing the Metering-WB button and spinning the Quick Control Dial, examines your scene and chooses an appropriate value. However, the 40D's selection process is far from foolproof. Under bright lighting conditions, it may evaluate the colors in the image and still assume the light source is daylight and balance the picture accordingly, even though, in fact, you may be shooting under extremely bright incandescent illumination. In dimmer light, the camera's electronics may assume that the illumination is tungsten, and color balance for that. Fortunately, some electronic flash

Figure 5.18 An image exposed indoors with the WB set for daylight will appear too reddish.

Figure 5.19 An image exposed outdoors with the WB set for tungsten illumination will appear too blue.

units, such as the Canon Speedlite 580EX, can report to the camera the particular white balance that they are outputting, since a flash's color temperature can vary depending on how brief the flash exposure is.

The other presets in the WB list apply specific color temperatures. For example, the Daylight setting sets WB to 5,200K, while the Shade setting uses a much bluer 7,000K. The chief difference between direct daylight and shade or even tungsten light sources is nothing more than the proportion of red and blue light. The spectrum of colors is continuous, but is biased toward one end or the other.

However, some types of fluorescent lights produce illumination that has a severe deficit in certain colors, such as only *particular* shades of red. If you looked at the spectrum or rainbow of colors encompassed by such a light source, it would have black bands in it, representing particular wavelengths of light that are absent. You can't compensate for this deficiency by adding all tones of red. That's why the White Fluorescent Light setting of your 40D may provide less than satisfactory results with other kinds of fluorescent bulbs. If you take many photographs under a particular kind of non-compatible fluorescent light, you might want to investigate specialized fluorescent light filters for your lenses, available from camera stores.

However, you might also get acceptable results using the final two choices on the WB list. Custom and Color Temperature allow you to use specific white balances you've set yourself using the Custom WB and Color temp choices in the Shooting menu. As I described in Chapter 3, to set a custom white balance you'll need to focus manually (with the lens set on MF) on a plain white or gray object, such as a card or wall, making sure the object fills the spot metering circle in the center of the viewfinder. Then, take a photo under the lighting conditions you want to use as your custom white balance.

Then, press the Menu button and select **Custom WB**. Rotate the Quick Control Dial until the reference image you just took appears and press the **Set** button to store the white balance of the image as your Custom setting. The setting will remain in your 40D's memory. To activate it, just press the Metering-WB button and spin the Quick Control Dial until the **Custom** setting is selected.

As I mentioned in Chapter 3, if you already know the color temperature of your illumination, you can set an exact value in degrees Kelvin using the **Color Temp.** entry in the **White Balance** menu in the **Shooting 1** tab. Select this menu entry, press **Set**, and then turn the Main Dial until the color temperature you want, from 2,800K to 10,000K (in 100K increments) is dialed in. (See Figure 5.20.) Then, you can use this setting by pressing the Metering-WB button, and spinning the Quick Control Dial until the Color Temperature choice (the **K** icon) is selected.

Finally, as I described in Chapter 3, you can *shift* the 40D's standard color temperature that is used as a basis for all its corrections, changing the default temperature to a new value with a bias towards the green, magenta, blue, or amber directions, which correspond to movements along the central axes of the chart shown in Figure 5.21 in the up (green), down (magenta), blue (left), or amber/yellow (right) directions. You can also combine biases of adjacent hues by moving the cursor diagonally towards the upper left (more blue and more green), upper right (more green and more amber), lower right (more amber and more magenta), and lower left (more magenta and more blue).

Figure 5.20
If you know the specific color temperature of your light source, you can dial it in.

Figure 5.21
The standard white balance setting can be biased in a direction of your choosing.

Image Parameters in Picture Styles

As I outlined in Chapter 3, you can redefine the amount of sharpening, contrast, color saturation, and color tone for any of the five preset Picture Styles (Standard, Portrait, Landscape, Neutral, and Faithful) or create your own styles in User Def 1, User Def 2, and User Def 3 (see Figure 5.22). In addition, you can modify the Filter Effect and Toning Effect options in the Monochrome Picture Style. You can learn how to make these changes in Chapter 3, but here is a summary of how the key parameters affect your images.

- **Sharpness.** Increases or decreases the contrast of the edge outlines in your image, making the photo appear more or less sharp, depending on whether you've selected 0 (no sharpening) to +7 (extreme sharpening). Remember that boosting sharpness also increases the overall contrast of an image, so you'll want to use this parameter in conjunction with the contrast parameter with caution.

- **Contrast.** Compresses the range of tones in an image (increase contrast from 0 to +4) or expands the range of tones (from 0 to –4) to decrease contrast. Higher contrast images tend to lose detail in both shadows and highlights, while lower contrast images retain the detail but appear more flat and have less snap.

Figure 5.22
You can customize the sharpness, contrast, color saturation, or tone of the standard Picture Styles, as well as any of the three User Def styles.

- **Color saturation.** You can adjust the richness of the color from low saturation (0 to –4) to high saturation (0 to +4). Lower saturation produces a muted look that can be more realistic for certain kinds of subjects, such as humans. Higher saturation produces a more vibrant appearance, but can be garish and unrealistic if carried too far. Boost your saturation if you want a vivid image, or to brighten up pictures taken on overcast days.

- **Color tone.** This parameter changes the bias of the image toward the red or yellow ends of the scale, with settings from 0 to –4 producing ruddier skin tones, and 0 to +4 creating more yellowish skin tones.

Working with Live View

Live View is one of those features that experienced SLR users (especially those dating from the film era) sometimes think they don't need—until they try it. It's also one of those features (like truly "silent" shooting, without any shutter click) that point-and-shoot refugees are surprised that digital SLRs (until recently) have lacked. As I noted earlier, SLRs have actual, mechanical shutters that can't be completely silenced, as can be done with point-and-shoot cameras. I've fielded almost as many queries from those who want to know how to preview their images on the LCD—just as they did with their point-and-shoot cameras. Indeed, many P & S models don't even *have* optical viewfinders, engendering a whole generation of amateur photographers who think the only way to frame and compose an image is to hold the camera out at arm's length so the back panel LCD can be viewed more easily.

While dSLR veterans didn't really miss what we've come to know as Live View, it was at least, in part, because they didn't have it and couldn't miss what they never had. After all, why would you eschew a big, bright, magnified through-the-lens optical view that showed depth-of-field fairly well, and which was easily visible under virtually all ambient light conditions? LCD displays, after all, were small, tended to wash out in bright light, and didn't really provide you with an accurate view of what your picture was going to look like.

There were technical problems, as well. Real-time previews theoretically disabled a dSLR's autofocus system, as focus was achieved by measuring contrast through the optical viewfinder, which is blocked when the mirror is flipped up for a live view. Extensive previewing had the same effect on the sensor as long exposures: the sensor heated up, producing excess noise. Pointing the camera at a bright light source when using a real-time view could damage the sensor. The list of potential problems goes on and on.

That was then. This is now.

The Canon EOS 40D has a gorgeous 3-inch LCD that can be viewed under a variety of lighting conditions and from wide-ranging angles, so you don't have to be exactly behind the display to see it clearly. (See Figure 5.23.) It offers a 100 percent view of the sensor's capture area (the optical viewfinder shows just 95 percent of the sensor's field of view). It's large enough to allow manual focusing—but if you want to use automatic focus, there's an option that allows briefly flipping the mirror back down for autofocusing, interrupting Live View, and then restoring the sensor preview image after focus is achieved. You still have to avoid pointing your 40D at bright light sources (especially the Sun) when using Live View, but the real-time preview can be used for fairly long periods without frying the sensor. (Image quality can degrade, but the camera issues a warning when the sensor starts to overheat.)

Unlike some of the previous attempts at a Live View-type mode by other sensors (and including Canon with its EOS 20Da), the 40D's Live View works. No beam-splitting prisms that divert some light to the sensor, no grainy black-and-white real-time preview, no need for a spare sensor to provide a simulated Live View. Canon's system works just like you'd want it to: the mirror flips up, the shutter opens, and what the sensor sees is displayed in full color on the LCD on the back of the camera.

Figure 5.23
Live View really shines on the Canon EOS 40D's large 3-inch LCD.

What You Can/Cannot Do with Live View

You may not have considered just what you can do with Live View, because the capability is so novel. But once you've played with it, you'll discover dozens of applications for this capability, as well as a few things that you can't do. Here's a list of Live View Do's/Don'ts/Cans/Can'ts.

- **Preview your images on a TV.** Connect your EOS 40D to a television using the video cable, and you can preview your image on a large screen.

- **Preview remotely.** Extend the cable between the camera and TV screen, and you can preview your images some distance away from the camera.

- **Shoot from your computer.** Canon gives you the software you need to control your camera from your computer, so you can preview images and take pictures without physically touching the EOS 40D.

- **Continuous shooting.** You can shoot bursts of images using Live View, but all shots will use the focus and exposure setting established for the first picture in the series.

- **Shoot from tripod or handheld.** Of course, holding the camera out at arms length to preview an image is poor technique, and will introduce a lot of camera shake. If you want to use Live View for handheld images, use an image-stabilized lens and/or a high shutter speed. A tripod is a better choice if you can use one.

- **Watch your power.** Live View uses a lot of juice and will deplete your battery rapidly. Canon estimates that you can get 130-170 shots per battery when using Live View, depending on the temperature. The optional AC adapter is a useful accessory.

- **MicroDrives not recommended.** Because they use up a lot of power on their own, mini hard drives are not recommended as a storage medium for Live View sessions. Use a Compact Flash card instead.

- **Watch for the warning icon.** A "thermometer" icon appears in the viewfinder when the camera starts to overheat. Image quality will begin degrading at this time (expect increased noise in your images). However, the EOS 40D will turn itself off automatically before the sensor temperature reaches the danger point, and will keep the camera shut down until the high temperature subsides.

Enabling Live View

You need to take some steps before using Live View. This workflow prevents you from accidentally using Live View when you don't mean to, thus potentially losing a shot, and it also helps ensure that you've made all the settings necessary to successfully use the feature efficiently. Here are the steps to follow:

1. **Set focus to Manual.** It's a good idea to set the lens focus switch to the MF position, because most Live View pictures are taken using manual focus. Take this step now so you won't forget that you'll be doing the focusing yourself.

2. **Choose a shooting mode.** Select a Creative Zone shooting mode. Live View doesn't work with any of the Basic Zone modes. You can choose A-DEP, but the 40D will behave as if you selected P, instead, and A-DEP's automatic focus point selection (like all autofocus features) will be disabled.

3. **Enable Live View.** You'll need to activate Live View by choosing **Live View function settings** from the Set-up 2 menu. Select **Enable** and press the Menu button to exit.

OTHER LIVE VIEW FUNCTION SETTINGS

Three other Live View functions can be set from the Shooting 2 menu. You can choose Grid Display (On or Off) to enable or disable a Rule of Thirds grid display that can help you compose and align your images on the LCD. Silent Shoot modes 1 and 2 can be enabled or disabled (as described Chapter 3). You can also set a Metering Timer, which determines how long the 40D continues to measure exposure when you switch to Live View mode. You can also access C.Fn.IV-07 to switch from LCD illumination auto adjust (which keeps the LCD at the same brightness, regardless of exposure) to the Simulates Exposure setting, which uses the brightness of the LCD to emulate the exposure you'd get using the current shutter speed and aperture. If you want to interrupt Live View to use autofocus, you'll need to set C.Fn.III-06 to **AF during Live View Shooting.** I'll explain how to use this feature later in this chapter.

Activating Live View

Once you've enabled Live View, you can continue taking pictures normally through the 40D's viewfinder. When you're ready to activate Live View, press the Set button. The mirror will flip up, and the sensor image will appear on the LCD.

Here are some things you should keep in mind when Live View is active:

- **Manual focus.** You must focus manually, unless you use the optional Live View interrupt/autofocus feature. Later in this section, I'll provide instructions for using MF with Live View.

- **Exposure lag.** If you reframe your photo, there is a lag before the exposure is set properly for the new composition. If you take a picture before the exposure has been re-calculated, you may get an under- or overexposed photo.

- **Metering mode cannot be changed.** Evaluative metering linked to the focus frame is used. You cannot change to Partial, Spot, or Center-Weighted metering when Live View is active.

- **Press DOF button to check exposure.** If you press the depth-of-field button while using Live View, the lens will stop down to the taking aperture and you'll see the effective exposure that has been set, even if Simulate Exposure has not been selected in the Custom Functions menu.

- **Flash OK.** You can use flash when working with Live View, but the FE (flash exposure) lock, modeling flash, and test firing of the flash are not possible. In addition, to change the speedlite's own custom functions, you'll need to use the camera's menus in the Flash Control section of the Set-up 2 menu. The flash's own Custom Function setting capability is disabled.

- **Live View continues.** When you press the shutter release, the 40D will take a photo, then display the image you just shot for review, as normal. When picture review is finished, the camera returns to Live View mode. You can take as many consecutive shots using Live View as you like, barring sensor overheating. To exit Live View entirely, press the Set button.

- **Shooting functions interrupt.** If you change shooting functions, such as EV compensation, white balance, or ISO settings while using Live View, then Live View will quit. Continue making your changes, then press the Set button to activate Live View once more.

- **Information display.** During Live View, useful information is shown on the screen, such as battery status, Picture Style, and most of the shooting information (shutter speed, f/stop, ISO setting, number of exposures remaining) you'd see through the viewfinder. Press the Info. button to change the amount of information shown. Figure 5.24 shows a typical display as seen on the LCD, including the optional Rule of Thirds grid.

Figure 5.24
The information display includes the focus frame that's in the center of the screen, but which can be moved using the multi-controller.

Manual Focusing

Focusing manually on an LCD screen isn't as difficult as you might think, but Canon has made the process even easier by providing a magnified view. Just follow these steps to focus manually.

1. Make sure the focus switch on the lens is set to MF.

2. Use the multi-controller to move the focus frame that's superimposed on the screen to the location where you want to focus. You can press the multi-controller to center the focus frame in the middle of the screen.

3. Press the Zoom button. The area of the image inside the focus frame will be magnified 5X. (See Figure 5.25.) Press the Zoom button again to increase the magnification to 10X. A third press will return you to the full-frame view. The enlarged area is artificially sharpened to make it easier for you to see the contrast changes, and simplify focusing. When zoomed in, the current shutter speed and aperture are shown in orange.

4. Use the focus ring on the lens to focus the image. When you're satisfied, you can zoom back out.

Figure 5.25
You can manually focus the center area, which can be zoomed in 5X or 10X.

Using Autofocus with Live View

You can temporarily interrupt Live View mode to allow the EOS 40D to use autofocus. Because the step takes a few seconds, you're better off using autofocus when the camera is mounted on a tripod. If you handhold the 40D, you may displace the point of focus achieved by the autofocus system. Canon also recommends that you use One Shot focus and center the focus point. You can use AI-Servo and automatic or manual focus point selection, but if the focus point doesn't coincide with the subject you want to focus on, you'll end up with an out-of-focus image. Just follow these steps.

1. Make sure the focus switch on the lens is set to AF.

2. Activate autofocus using C. Fn. III-06 **AF During Live View Shooting**. Choose 1 to enable this feature.

3. Press the AF-DRIVE button and use the Main Dial to make sure the autofocus mode has been set to One Shot.

4. Press the AF-ON button. The mirror will flip down, interrupting the Live View display.

5. When the autofocus system has achieved sharp focus, you'll hear a beep. If you are handholding the 40D, you may hear several beeps as the AF system focuses and refocuses with each camera movement. Release the AF-ON button to return to Live View.

Using Simulated Exposure

You can use C. Fn. IV-07 to activate **Simulate Exposure**, so that the LCD won't maintain a constant brightness level under varying ambient lighting conditions but will instead brighten or dim to emulate the correct exposure or over-/under-exposure you'll get with the current settings.

Enabling this feature also activates the histogram, which you can use to judge exposure (as explained in Chapter 4). If the histogram is not visible on the Live View screen, press the Info. button until it appears. The histogram may not display properly under very low or very high light levels, and is not available at all when you're using flash or exposures with the Bulb setting.

Silent Shooting

Although silent shooting is far from a stealth photography mode, it does produce a quieter shutter noise than what you get when not in Live View mode. That's because the mirror has already been flipped out of the way, so the sound produced primarily comes from the opening and closing of the shutter. You can activate silent shooting from the Live View Function settings entry in the Shooting 2 menu. You have three choices:

- **Mode 1:** This mode reduces the noise level of the shutter, but allows taking several shots in succession, including continuous shooting at about 6 fps.

- **Mode 2:** This mode reduces the noise even further by delaying the action when you press the shutter release down (only a slight click is heard). When you let up slightly on the shutter release, the shot is taken, producing another soft click. Continuous shooting is not possible in Mode 2.

- **Disable:** Turns off the feature, producing the normal shutter noise sounds.

6

Working with Lenses

If Canon has one advantage over many of the other vendors of digital SLRs (other than making great, affordable cameras), it's the mind-bending assortment of high quality lenses available to enhance the capabilities of cameras like the Canon EOS 40D. Thousands of current and older lenses introduced by Canon and third-party vendors since 1987 can be used to give you a wider view, bring distant subjects closer, let you focus closer, shoot under lower light conditions, or provide a more detailed, sharper image for critical work. Other than the sensor itself, the lens you choose for your dSLR is the most important component in determining image quality and perspective of your images.

This chapter explains how to select the best lenses for the kinds of photography you want to do.

But First, a Word from Our Sensor

One pervasive consideration that will trip us up in this chapter (and throughout this book) is the omnipresent *lens crop factor*. If the sensor is smaller than the standard 35mm film frame (24mm × 36mm), then any given lens will produce a field of view that's *cropped* from that full frame. To express the "real" field of view in 35mm terms, you must multiply a lens's focal length by the crop factor, which in the case of the EOS 40D is 1.6X. Canon also sells dSLRs with 1.3X and 1X (full-frame) sensors, which provide the fields of view shown in Figure 6.1. At this writing, Canon's camera line includes the Canon EOS-1Ds Mark III and Canon EOS 5D, which both provide a full-frame, 1X crop (or non-crop) of the image, compared to a film camera. The Canon EOS-1D Mark III offers a 1.3X crop, while the Canon EOS 40D and the Digital Rebel models use a 1.6X crop of the full-frame sensor area.

Figure 6.1
Canon offers digital SLRs with full-frame (1X) crops, as well as 1.3X and 1.6X crops.

If you're accustomed to using full-frame film cameras, you might find it helpful to use the crop factor "multiplier" to translate a lens's real focal length into the full-frame equivalent, even though nothing is actually being multiplied. Throughout most of this book I've been using actual focal lengths and not equivalents, except when referring to specific wide-angle or telephoto focal length ranges and their fields of view.

Your First Lens

Some Canon dSLRs are almost always purchased with a lens. The Digital Rebel and Digital Rebel XT/XTi, for example, are often bought as entry-level cameras, frequently by first-time SLR or dSLR owners who find the Canon EF-S 18-55mm f/3.5-5.6 autofocus lens an irresistible bargain at about $100 over the cost of the camera body alone. Other Canon models, including the EOS 1D, EOS 1Ds, and EOS 5D, are generally purchased without a lens by veteran Canon photographers who already have a complement of optics to use with their cameras.

The Canon EOS 40D falls somewhere in between. I bought mine as a body-only, because I already had a collection of lenses. But you might have purchased your 40D with a lens, because it's an excellent first Canon camera for photographers experienced with another camera line, or for ambitious beginners. That makes an economical "kit" lens very attractive. However, you'll also find many purchasers who, like me, fall into one of the following categories: Those who are upgrading from the Digital Rebel models or an EOS 10D/20D/30D; from a Canon film camera; or who are buying the 40D as a second camera body to complement their Canon EOS 1D, or even as an adjunct to their full-frame 1Ds or 5D cameras. These owners, too, generally have lenses they can use with their new 40D.

So, depending on which category you fall into, you'll need to make a decision about what kit lens to buy, or decide what other kind of lenses you need to fill out your complement of Canon optics. This section will cover "first lens" concerns, while later in the chapter we'll look at "add-on lens" considerations.

When deciding on a first lens, there are several factors you'll want to consider:

- **Cost.** You might have stretched your budget a bit to purchase your EOS 40D, so you might want to keep the cost of your first lens fairly low. Fortunately, there are excellent lenses available that will add from $100 to $300 to the price of your camera if purchased at the same time.

- **Zoom range.** If you have only one lens, you'll want a fairly long zoom range to provide as much flexibility as possible. Fortunately, the two most popular basic lenses for the 40D have 3X to 5X zoom ranges, extending from moderate wide-angle/normal out to medium telephoto. Either are fine for everyday shooting, portraits, and some types of sports.

- **Adequate maximum aperture.** You'll want an f/stop of at least f/3.5 to f/4 for shooting under fairly low light conditions. The thing to watch for is the maximum aperture when the lens is zoomed to its telephoto end. You may end up with no better than an f/5.6 maximum aperture. That's not great, but you can often live with it.

- **Image quality.** Your starter lens should have good image quality, because that's one of the primary factors that will be used to judge your photos. Even at a low price, the several different lenses sold with the 40D as a kit include extra-low dispersion glass and aspherical elements that minimize distortion and chromatic aberration; they are sharp enough for most applications. If you read the user evaluations in the online photography forums, you know that owners of the kit lenses have been very pleased with its image quality.

- **Size matters.** A good walking-around lens is compact in size and light in weight.

- **Fast/close focusing.** Your first lens should have a speedy autofocus system (which is where the ultrasonic motor/USM found in all but the bargain basement lenses is an advantage). Close focusing (to 12 inches or closer) will let you use your basic lens for some types of macro photography.

You can find comparisons of the lenses discussed in the next section, as well as third-party lenses from Sigma, Tokina, Tamron, and other vendors, in online groups and websites. I'll provide my recommendations, but more information is always helpful.

Buy Now, Expand Later

The 40D is commonly available with several good, basic lenses that can serve you well as a "walk-around" lens (one you keep on the camera most of the time, especially when you're out and about without your camera bag). The number of options available to you is actually quite amazing, even if your budget is limited to about $100-$350 for your first lens. One other vendor, for example, offers only 18mm-70mm and 18mm-55mm kit lenses in that price range, plus a 24mm-85mm zoom. Two of the most popular starter lenses Canon offers are shown in Figure 6.2. Canon's best-bet first lenses are:

- **Canon EF-S 18-55mm f/3.5-5.6 Autofocus Lens.** This is the least expensive option, which, depending on where you buy your camera, may add only about $100 to the purchase price of the body alone. This medium-wide to short telephoto lens (29mm-88mm full-frame equivalent) is the standard lens found on Digital Rebel models, and it is frequently sold as the basic kit lens for the EOS 40D for those on a budget. It is designed exclusively for Canon

Figure 6.2
The Canon EF-S 18-55mm f/3.5-5.6 Autofocus lens (left) and Canon EF-S 17-85mm f/4-5.6 IS USM Autofocus lens (right), are two of the most popular starter lenses for the EOS 40D.

dSLRs with a 1.6X crop factor, and it shouldn't be used on full-frame cameras (more on this later). A maximum aperture of f/5.6 at 55mm makes this a relatively slow lens that's not great for low-light shooting. You can often find the 18-55mm lens available separately for $100-$140.

- **Canon EF-S 18-55mm f/3.5-5.6 IS Autofocus Lens.** This new lens, introduced at the same time as the EOS 40D, is worth the slight extra premium, because it adds image stabilization that can counter camera shake by providing the vibration-stopping capabilities of a shutter speed four stops faster than the one you've dialed it. That is, with image stabilization activated, you can shoot at 1/30 second and eliminate camera shake as if you were using a shutter speed of 1/250th second. (At least, that's what Canon claims; I usually have slightly less impressive results.) Of course, IS doesn't freeze subject motion—that basketball player driving for a lay-up will still be blurry at 1/30 second, even though the effects of camera shake will be effectively nullified. But this lens is an all-around good choice.

- **Canon EF-S 17-85mm f/4-5.6 IS USM Autofocus Lens.** This lens smashes through the arbitrary $350 price barrier I set earlier, but I'm making an exception because the 17-85mm lens is probably the most popular "basic" lens sold with the 40D, despite its $500-plus price tag. The allure here is the built-in image stabilization, which allows you to shoot rock-solid photos at shutter speeds that are at least two or three notches slower than you'd need normally (say, 1/8th second instead of 1/30th or 1/60th second), as long as your subject isn't moving. It also has a quiet, fast, reliable ultrasonic motor (more on that later, too). This is another lens designed for the 1.6X crop factor; all the remaining lenses in this list can also be used on full-frame cameras. (I'll tell you why later in this chapter.)

- **Canon EF 55-200mm f/4.5-5.6 II USM Autofocus Lightweight Compact Telephoto Zoom Lens.** If you bought the 18-55mm kit lens, this one picks up where that one leaves off, going from short telephoto to medium long (88mm-320mm full-frame equivalent). It's actually faster at 55mm than the basic kit lens and features a desirable ultrasonic motor. Best of all, it's very affordable at around $225. If you can afford only two lenses, the 18-55mm and this one make a good basic set.

- **EF-S 55-250mm f/4-5.6 IS Telephoto Zoom Lens.** This is an image-stabilized EF-S lens (which means it can't be used with Canon's 1.3X and 1.0X crop-factor pro cameras), providing the longest focal range in the EF-S range to date, and that 4-stop Image Stabilizer. Again, it's more money than the older, non-stabilized EF version, but it's worth the extra cost.

- **Canon EF 24-85mm f/3.5-4.5 USM Auto Focus Wide-Angle Telephoto Zoom Lens.** If you can get by with normal focal length to medium telephoto range, Canon offers four affordable lenses, plus one more expensive killer lens that's worth the extra expenditure. All of them can be used on full-frame or cropped-frame digital Canons, which is why they include "wide angle" in their product names. They're really wide-angle lenses only when mounted on a full-frame camera. This one, priced in the $300 range, offers a useful range of focal lengths, extending from the equivalent of 38mm to 136mm.

- **Canon EF 28-105mm f/3.5-4.5 II USM Autofocus Wide-Angle Telephoto Zoom Lens.** If you want to save about $100 and gain a little reach, this 45mm-168mm (equivalent lens) might be what you are looking for.

- **Canon EF 28-135mm f/3.5-5.6 IS USM Image-Stabilized Autofocus Wide-Angle Telephoto Zoom Lens.** Image stabilization is especially useful at longer focal lengths, which makes this 45mm-216mm (equivalent) lens worth its $400-plus price tag. Several retailers are packing this lens with the 40D as a kit.

- **Canon EF 28-200mm f/3.5-5.6 USM Autofocus Wide-Angle Telephoto Zoom Lens.** If you want one lens to do everything except wide-angle photography, this 7X zoom lens costs less than $400 and takes you from the equivalent of 45mm out to a long 320mm.

- **Canon Zoom Wide-Angle-Telephoto EF 24-70mm f/2.8L USM Autofocus Lens.** I couldn't leave this premium lens out of the mix, even though it costs well over $1,000. As part of Canon's L-series (Luxury) lens line, it offers the best sharpness over its focal range than any of the other lenses in this list. Best of all, it's fast (for a zoom), with an f/2.8 maximum aperture that *doesn't change* as you zoom out. Unlike the other lenses, which may offer only an f/5.6 maximum f/stop at their longest zoom setting, this is a *constant aperture* lens, which retains its maximum f/stop. The added sharpness, constant aperture, and ultra-smooth USM motor are what you're paying for with this lens.

What Lenses Can You Use?

The previous section helped you sort out what lens you need to buy with your 40D (assuming you already didn't own any Canon lenses). Now, you're probably wondering what lenses can be added to your growing collection (trust me, it will grow). You need to know which lenses are suitable and, most importantly, which lenses are fully compatible with your EOS 40D.

With the Canon 40D, the compatibility issue is a simple one: It accepts any lens with the EF or EF-S designation, with full availability of all autofocus, autoaperture, autoexposure, and image-stabilization features (if present). It's comforting to know that any EF (for full-frame or cropped sensors) or EF-S (for cropped sensor cameras only) will work as designed with your camera.

But wait, there's more. You can also attach Nikon F mount, Leica R, Olympus OM, and M42 ("Pentax screw mount") lenses with a simple adapter, if you don't mind losing automatic focus and aperture control. If you use one of these lenses, you'll need to focus manually (even if the lens operates in autofocus mode on the camera it was designed for), and adjust the f/stop to the aperture you want to use to take the picture. That means that lenses that don't have an aperture ring (such as Nikon G-series lenses) must be used only at their maximum aperture. Because of these limitations, you probably won't want to make extensive use of "foreign" lenses on your 40D, but an adapter can help you when you really, really need to use a particular focal length but don't have a suitable Canon-compatible lens. For example, I occasionally use an older 400mm lens that was originally designed for the Nikon line on my 40D. The lens needs to be mounted on a tripod for steadiness, anyway, so its slower operation isn't a major pain. Another good match is the 105mm Micro-Nikkor I sometimes use with my Canon 40D. Macro photos, too, are most often taken with the camera mounted on a tripod, and manual focus makes a lot of sense for fine-tuning focus and depth-of-field. Because of the contemplative nature of close-up photography, it's not much of an inconvenience to stop down to the taking aperture just before exposure.

The limitations on use of lenses within Canon's own product line (as well as lenses produced for earlier Canon SLRs by third-party vendors) is fairly clear-cut. The EOS 40D cannot be used with any of Canon's earlier lens mounting schemes for its film cameras, including the immediate predecessor to the EF mount, the FD mount (introduced with the Canon F1 in 1964 and used until the Canon T60 in 1990), FL (1964-1971), or the original Canon R mount (1959-1964). That's really all you need to know. While you'll find FD-to-EF adapters for about $40, you'll lose so many functions that it's rarely worth the bother.

In retrospect, the switch to the EF mount seems like a very good idea, as the initial EOS film cameras can now be seen as the beginning of Canon's rise to eventually become the leader in film and (later) digital SLR cameras. By completely revamping its lens mounting system, the company was able to take advantage of the latest advances in technology without compromise.

For example, when the original EF bayonet mount was introduced in 1987, the system incorporated new autofocus technology (EF actually stands for "electro focus") in a more rugged and less complicated form. A tiny motor was built into the lens itself, eliminating the need for mechanical linkages with the camera.

WHY SO MANY LENS MOUNTS?

Four different lens mounts in 40-plus years might seem like a lot of different mounting systems, especially when compared to the Nikon F mount of 1959, which retained quite a bit of compatibility with that company's film and digital camera bodies during that same span. However, in digital photography terms, the EF mount itself is positively ancient, having remained reasonably stable for almost two decades. Lenses designed for the EF system work reliably with every EOS film and digital camera ever produced.

However, at the time, yet another lens mount switch, especially a change from the traditional breech system to a more conventional bayonet-type mount, was indeed a daring move by Canon. One of the reasons for staying with a particular lens type is to "lock" current users into a specific camera system. By introducing the EF mount, Canon in effect cut loose every photographer in its existing user base. If they chose to upgrade, they were free to choose another vendor's products and lenses. Only satisfaction with the previous Canon product line and the promise of the new system would keep them in the fold.

Instead, electrical contacts are used to send power and the required focusing information to the motor. That's a much more robust and resilient system that made it easier for Canon to design faster and more accurate autofocus mechanisms just by redesigning the lenses.

EF vs. EF-S

Today, in addition to its EF lenses, Canon offers lenses that use the EF-S (the S stands for "short back focus") mount, with the chief difference being (as you might expect) lens components that extend farther back into the camera body of some of Canon's latest digital cameras (specifically those with smaller than full-frame sensors), such as the 40D and Digital Rebels. As I'll explain next, this refinement allows designing more compact, less-expensive lenses especially for those cameras, but not for models like the EOS 5D, 1Ds Mark III, or 1D Mark III (even though the latter camera does have a sensor that is smaller than full frame).

Canon's EF-S lens mount variation was born in 2003, when the company virtually invented the consumer-oriented digital SLR category by introducing the original EOS 300D/Digital Rebel, a dSLR that cost less than $1,000 *with lens* at a time when all other interchangeable lens digital cameras (including the 40D's "grandparent," the original EOS 10D) were priced closer to $2,000 with a basic lens. Like the EOS 10D introduced earlier that same year, the Digital Rebel featured a smaller than full-frame sensor with a 1.6X crop factor (Canon calls this format APS-C).

But the Digital Rebel accepted lenses that took advantage of the shorter mirror found in APS-C cameras, with elements of shorter focal length lenses (wide angles) that extended *into* the camera, space that was off limits in other models because the mirror passed through that territory as it flipped up to expose the shutter and sensor. (Canon even calls its flip-up reflector a "half mirror.")

In short (so to speak), the EF-S mount made it easier to design less-expensive wide-angle lenses that could be used *only* with 1.6X-crop cameras, and featured a simpler design and reduced coverage area suitable for those non-full-frame models. The new mount made it possible to produce lenses like the ultra-wide EF-S 10-22mm f/3.5-4.5 USM lens, which has the equivalent field of view as a 16mm-35mm zoom on a full-frame camera.

Suitable cameras for EF-S lenses include the Digital Rebel, the newer Canon EOS 350D/Digital Rebel XT/XTi, the Canon EOS 20D/30D, and, today, the EOS 40D. The EF-S lenses cannot be used on the EOS 10D, the 1D Mark II N/Mark III (which have a 28.7mm × 19.1mm APS-H sensor with a 1.3X crop factor), or any of the full-frame digital or film EOS models. It's easy to tell an EF lens from an EF-S lens: The latter incorporate EF-S into their name! Plus, EF lenses have a raised red dot on the barrel that is used to align the lens with a matching dot on the camera when attaching the lens. EF-S lenses and compatible bodies use a white square instead. EF-S lenses also have a rubber ring at the attachment end that provides a bit of weather/dust sealing and protects the back components of the lens if a user attempts to mount it on a camera that is not EF-S compatible.

Ingredients of Canon's Alphanumeric Soup

The actual product names of individual Canon lenses are fairly easy to decipher; they'll include either the EF or EF-S designation, the focal length or focal length range of the lens, its maximum aperture, and some other information. Additional data may be engraved on the barrel or ring surrounding the front element of the lens, as shown in Figure 6.3. Here's a decoding of what the individual designations mean:

- **EF/EF-S.** If the lens is marked EF, it can safely be used on any Canon EOS camera, film or digital. If it is an EF-S lens, it should be used only on an EF-S compatible camera, such as the Digital Rebels, EOS 20D/30D/40D, and any newer APS-C cameras introduced after the publication of this book.

- **Focal length.** Given in millimeters or a millimeter range, such as *60mm* in the case of a popular Canon macro lens, or *17-55mm*, used to describe a medium-wide to short-telephoto zoom.

■ **Maximum aperture.** The largest f/stop available with a particular lens is given in a string of numbers that might seem confusing at first glance. For example, you might see *1:1.8* for a fixed-focal length (prime) lens, and *1:4.5-5.6* for a zoom. The initial 1: signifies that the f/stop given is actually a ratio or fraction (in regular notation, f/ replaces the 1:), which is why a 1:2 (or f/2) aperture is larger than an 1:4 (or f/4) aperture—just as 1/2 is larger than 1/4. With most zoom lenses, the maximum aperture changes as the lens is zoomed to the telephoto position, so a range is given instead: 1:4.5-5.6. (Some zooms, called *constant aperture* lenses, keep the same maximum aperture throughout their range.)

Figure 6.3 Most of the key specifications of the lens are engraved in the ring around the front element.

■ **Autofocus type.** Most newer Canon lenses that aren't of the bargain-basement type use Canon's *ultrasonic motor* autofocus system (more on that later) and are given the USM designation. If USM does not appear on the lens or its model name, the lens uses the less sophisticated AFD (arc-form drive) autofocus system or the micromotor (MM) drive mechanism.

■ **Series.** Canon adds a Roman numeral to many of its products to represent an updated model with the same focal length or focal length range, so some lenses will have a II or III added to their name.

■ **Pro quality.** Canon's more expensive lenses with more rugged construction and higher optical quality, intended for professional use, include the letter L (for "luxury") in their product name. You can further differentiate these lenses visually by a red ring around the lens barrel and the off-white color of the metal barrel itself in virtually all telephoto L-series lenses. (Some L-series lenses have shiny or textured black plastic exterior barrels.) Internally, every L lens includes at least one lens element that is built of ultra-low dispersion glass, is constructed of expensive fluorite crystal, or uses an expensive ground (not molded) aspheric (non-spherical) lens component.

■ **Filter size.** You'll find the front lens filter thread diameter in millimeters included on the lens, preceded by a Ø symbol, as in Ø67 or Ø72.

■ **Special-purpose lenses.** Some Canon lenses are designed for specific types of work, and they include appropriate designations in their names. For example, close-focusing lenses such as the Canon EF-S 60mm f/2.8 Macro USM lens incorporate the word *Macro* into their name. Lenses with perspective control features preface the lens name with T-S (for tilt-shift). Lenses with built-in image-stabilization features, such as the nifty EF 28-300mm f/3.5-5.6L IS USM Telephoto Zoom include *IS* in their product names.

SORTING THE MOTOR DRIVES

Incorporating the autofocus motor inside the lens was an innovative move by Canon, and this allowed the company to produce better and more sophisticated lenses as technology became available to upgrade the focusing system. As a result, you'll find four different types of motors in Canon-designed lenses, each with cost and practical considerations.

■ **AFD (Arc-form drive)** and **Micromotor (MM)** drives are built around tiny versions of electromagnetic motors, which generally use gear trains to produce the motion needed to adjust the focus of the lens. Both are slow, noisy, and not particularly effective with larger lenses. Manual focus adjustments are possible only when the motor drive is disengaged.

- **Micromotor ultrasonic motor (USM)** drives use high-frequency vibration to produce the motion used to drive the gear train, resulting in a quieter operating system at a cost that's not much more than that of electromagnetic motor drives. With the exception of a couple lenses that have a slipping clutch mechanism, manual focus with this kind of system is possible only when the motor drive is switched off and the lens set in Manual mode. This is the kind of USM system you'll find in lower cost lenses.

- **Ring ultrasonic motor (USM)** drives, available in two different types (*electronic focus ring USM* and *ring USM*), also use high-frequency movement, but generate motion using a pair of vibrating metal rings to adjust focus. Both variations allow a feature called Full Time Manual (FTM) focus, which lets you make manual adjustments to the lens's focus even when the autofocus mechanism is engaged. With electronic focus ring USM, manual focus is possible only when the lens is mounted on the camera and the camera is turned on; the focus ring of lenses with ring USM can be turned at any time.

Your Second (and Third...) Lens

There are really only two advantages to owning just a single lens. One of them is creative. Keeping one set of optics mounted on your 40D all the time forces you to be especially imaginative in your approach to your subjects. I once visited Europe with only a single camera body and a 35mm f/2 lens. The experience was actually quite exciting, because I had to use a variety of techniques to allow that one lens to serve for landscapes, available light photos, action, close-ups, portraits, and other kinds of images. Canon makes an excellent 35mm f/2 lens (which focuses down to 9.6 inches) that's perfect for that kind of experiment, although, today, my personal choice would be the sublime Canon Wide-Angle EF 35mm f/1.4L USM Autofocus lens.

Of course, it's more likely that your "single" lens is actually a zoom, which is, in truth, many lenses in one, taking you from, say, 17mm to 85mm (or some other range) with a rapid twist of the zoom lever. You'll still find some creative challenges when you stick to a single zoom lens's focal lengths.

The second advantage of the unilens camera is only a marginal technical benefit since the introduction of the EOS 40D. If you don't exchange lenses, the chances of dust and dirt getting inside your 40D and settling on the sensor is reduced (but *not* eliminated entirely). Although I've known some photographers who minimized the number of lens changes they made for this very reason, reducing the number of lenses you work with is not a productive or rewarding approach for most of us. The 40D's automatic sensor cleaning feature has made this "advantage" much less significant than it was in the past.

It's more likely that you'll succumb to the malady known as *Lens Lust,* which is defined as an incurable disease marked by a significant yen for newer, better, longer, faster, sharper, anything-er optics for your camera. (And, it must be noted, this disease can *cost* you significant yen—or dollars, or whatever currency you use.) In its worst manifestations, sufferers find themselves with lenses that have overlapping zoom ranges or capabilities, because one or the other offers a slight margin in performance or suitability for specific tasks. When you find yourself already lusting after a new lens before you've really had a chance to put your latest purchase to the test, you'll know the disease has reached the terminal phase.

What Lenses Can Do for You

A saner approach to expanding your lens collection is to consider what each of your options can do for you and then choosing the type of lens that will really boost your creative opportunities. Here's a general guide to the sort of capabilities you can gain by adding a lens to your repertoire.

- **Wider perspective.** Your 18-55mm f/3.5-5.6 or 17-85mm f/4-5.6 lens has served you well for moderate wide-angle shots. Now you find your back is up against a wall and you *can't* take a step backwards to take in more subject matter. Perhaps you're standing on the rim of the Grand Canyon, and you want to take in as much of the breathtaking view as you can. You might find yourself just behind the baseline at a high school basketball game and want an interesting shot with a little perspective distortion tossed in the mix. There's a lens out there that will provide you with what you need, such as the EF-S 10-22mm f/3.5-4.5 USM Zoom. If you want to stay in the sub-$600 price category, you'll need something like the Sigma Super Wide-Angle 10-20mm f/4-5.6 EX DC HSM Autofocus lens. The two lenses provide the equivalent of a 16mm to 32/35mm wide-angle view. For a distorted view, there is the Canon Fisheye EF 15mm f/2.8 Autofocus, with a similar lens available from Sigma, which offers an extra-wide circular fisheye, and the Sigma Fisheye 8mm f/3.5 EX DG Circular Fisheye. Your extra-wide choices may not be abundant, but they are there. Figure 6.4 shows the perspective you get from an ultra-wide-angle lens.

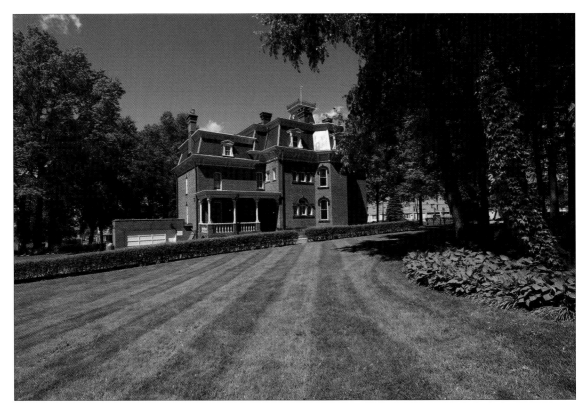

Figure 6.4 An ultra-wide-angle lens provided this view of an Italianate mansion.

- **Bring objects closer.** A long lens brings distant subjects closer to you, offers better control over depth-of-field, and avoids the perspective distortion that wide-angle lenses provide. They compress the apparent distance between objects in your frame. In the telephoto realm, Canon is second to none, with a dozen or more offerings in the sub-$600 range, including the Canon EF 100-300mm f/4.5-5.6 USM Autofocus and Canon EF 70-300mm f/4-5.6 IS USM Autofocus Telephoto Zoom lenses, and a broad array of zooms and fixed-focal length optics if you're willing to spend up to $1,000 or a bit more. Don't forget that the EOS 40D's crop factor narrows the field of view of all these lenses, so your 70-300mm lens looks more like a 112mm-480mm zoom through the viewfinder. Figures 6.5 and 6.6 were taken from the same position as Figure 6.4, but with an 85mm and 500mm lens, respectively.

Figure 6.5 This photo, taken from roughly the same distance (but off the left side), shows the view using a short telephoto lens.

- **Bring your camera closer.** Macro lenses allow you to focus to within an inch or two of your subject. Canon's best close-up lenses are all fixed focal length optics in the 50mm to 180mm range (including the well-regarded Canon EF-S 60mm f/2.8 Compact and Canon EF 100mm f/2.8 USM Macro Autofocus lenses). But you'll find macro zooms available from Sigma and others. They don't tend to focus quite as close, but they provide a bit of flexibility when you want to vary your subject distance (say, to avoid spooking a skittish creature).

- **Look sharp.** Many lenses, particularly Canon's luxury "L" line, are prized for their sharpness and overall image quality. While your run-of-the-mill lens is likely to be plenty sharp for most applications, the very best optics are even better over their entire field of view (which means no fuzzy corners), are sharper at a wider range of focal lengths (in the case of zooms), and have better correction for various types of distortion. That's why the Canon EF 28-105mm f/3.5-4.5 II USM Zoom lens costs a couple hundred dollars, while the "similar" (in zoom range only) Canon EF 24-105mm f/4L IS USM Zoom is priced $1,000 higher.

Figure 6.6 A longer telephoto lens captured this close-up view of the mansion from approximately the same shooting position.

- **More speed.** Your Canon EF 100-300mm f/4.5-5.6 Telephoto Zoom lens might have the perfect focal length and sharpness for sports photography, but the maximum aperture won't cut it for night baseball or football games, or, even, any sports shooting in daylight if the weather is cloudy or you need to use some ungodly fast shutter speed, such as 1/4,000th second. You might be happier with the Canon EF 100mm f/2 Medium Telephoto for close-range stuff, or even the pricier Canon EF 135mm f/2L. If money is no object, you can spring for Canon's 400mm f/2.8 and 600mm f/4 L-series lenses (both with image stabilization and priced in the $6,500-and-up stratosphere). Or, maybe you just need the speed and can benefit from an f/1.8 or f/1.4 lens in the 20mm-85mm range. They're all available in Canon mounts (there's even an 85mm f/1.2 and 50mm f/1.2 for the real speed demons). With any of these lenses you can continue photographing under the dimmest of lighting conditions without the need for a tripod or flash.

■ **Special features.** Accessory lenses give you special features, such as tilt/shift capabilities to correct for perspective distortion in architectural shots. Canon offers three of these TS-E lenses in 24mm, 45mm, and 90mm focal lengths, at a little over $1,000 each. You'll also find macro lenses, including the MP-E 65mm f/2.8 1-5x macro photo lens, which shoots *only* in the 1X to 5X life-size range. If you want diffused images, check out the EF 135mm f/2.8 with two soft-focus settings. The fisheye lenses mentioned earlier, and all IS (image-stabilized) lenses also count as special-feature optics.

Zoom or Prime?

Zoom lenses have changed the way serious photographers take pictures. One of the reasons that I own 12 SLR film bodies is that in ancient times it was common to mount a different fixed focal length prime lens on various cameras and take pictures with two or three cameras around your neck (or tucked in a camera case) so you'd be ready to take a long shot or an intimate close-up or wide-angle view on a moment's notice, without the need to switch lenses. It made sense (at the time) to have a half-dozen or so bodies (two to use, one in the shop, one in transit, and a couple backups). Zoom lenses of the time had a limited zoom range, were heavy, and not very sharp (especially when you tried to wield one of those monsters handheld).

That's all changed today. Lenses like the razor-sharp Canon EF 28-300mm f/3.5-5.6L IS USM can boast 10X or longer zoom ranges, in a package that's about 7-inches long, and while not petite at 3.7 pounds, quite usable handheld (especially with IS switched on). Although such a lens might seem expensive at $2,200-plus, it's actually much less costly than the six or so lenses it replaces.

When selecting between zoom and prime lenses, there are several considerations to ponder. Here's a checklist of the most important factors. I already mentioned image quality and maximum aperture earlier, but those aspects take on additional meaning when comparing zooms and primes.

■ **Logistics.** As prime lenses offer just a single focal length, you'll need more of them to encompass the full range offered by a single zoom. More lenses mean additional slots in your camera bag, and extra weight to carry. Just within Canon's line alone you can select from about a dozen general purpose prime lenses in 28mm, 35mm, 50mm, 85mm, 100mm, 135mm, 200mm, and 300mm focal lengths, all of which are overlapped by the 28-300mm zoom I mentioned earlier. Even so, you might be willing to carry an extra prime lens or two in order to gain the speed or image quality that lens offers.

- **Image quality.** Prime lenses usually produce better image quality at their focal length than even the most sophisticated zoom lenses at the same magnification. Zoom lenses, with their shifting elements and f/stops that can vary from zoom position to zoom position, are in general more complex to design than fixed focal length lenses. That's not to say that the very best prime lenses can't be complicated as well. However, the exotic designs, aspheric elements, low-dispersion glass, and Canon's new diffraction optics (DO) technology can be applied to improving the quality of the lens, rather than wasting a lot of it on compensating for problems caused by the zoom process itself.

- **Maximum aperture.** Because of the same design constraints, zoom lenses usually have smaller maximum apertures than prime lenses, and the most affordable zooms have a lens opening that grows effectively smaller as you zoom in. The difference in lens speed verges on the ridiculous at some focal lengths. For example, the 18mm-55mm basic zoom gives you a 55mm f/5.6 lens when zoomed all the way out, while prime lenses in that focal length commonly have f/1.8 or faster maximum apertures. Indeed, the fastest f/2, f/1.8, f1/4, and f/1.2 lenses are all primes, and if you require speed, a fixed focal length lens is what you should rely on. Figure 6.7 shows an image taken with a Canon 85mm f/1.8 Series EF USM Telephoto Lens.

- **Speed.** Using prime lenses takes time and slows you down. It takes a few seconds to remove your current lens and mount a new one, and the more often you need to do that, the more time is wasted. If you choose not to swap lenses, when using a fixed focal length lens you'll still have to move closer or farther away from your subject to get the field of view you want. A zoom lens allows you to change magnifications and focal lengths with the twist of a ring and generally saves a great deal of time.

Figure 6.7 An 85mm f/1.8 lens was perfect for this handheld photo of bluesman Tab Benoit.

Categories of Lenses

Lenses can be categorized by their intended purpose—general photography, macro photography, and so forth—or by their focal length. The range of available focal lengths is usually divided into three main groups: wide-angle, normal, and telephoto. Prime lenses fall neatly into one of these classifications. Zooms can overlap designations, with a significant number falling into the catch-all wide-to-telephoto zoom range. This section provides more information about focal length ranges, and how they are used.

Any lens with an equivalent focal length of 10mm to 20mm is said to be an *ultra-wide-angle lens*; from about 20mm to 40mm (equivalent) is said to be a *wide-angle lens*. *Normal lenses* have a focal length roughly equivalent to the diagonal of the film or sensor, in millimeters, and so fall into the range of about 45mm to 60mm (on a full-frame camera). *Telephoto lenses* usually fall into the 75mm and longer focal lengths, while those from about 300mm-400mm and longer often are referred to as *super-telephotos*.

Using Wide-Angle and Wide-Zoom Lenses

To use wide-angle prime lenses and wide zooms, you need to understand how they affect your photography. Here's a quick summary of the things you need to know.

- **More depth-of-field.** Practically speaking, wide-angle lenses offer more depth-of-field at a particular subject distance and aperture. (But see the sidebar below for an important note.) You'll find that helpful when you want to maximize sharpness of a large zone, but not very useful when you'd rather isolate your subject using selective focus (telephoto lenses are better for that).

- **Stepping back.** Wide-angle lenses have the effect of making it seem that you are standing farther from your subject than you really are. They're helpful when you don't want to back up, or can't because there are impediments in your way.

- **Wider field of view.** While making your subject seem farther away, as implied above, a wide-angle lens also provides a larger field of view, including more of the subject in your photos. Table 6.1 shows the diagonal field of view offered by an assortment of lenses, taking into account the crop factor introduced by the EOS 40D's smaller-than-full-frame sensor.

- **More foreground.** As background objects retreat, more of the foreground is brought into view by a wide-angle lens. That gives you extra emphasis on the area that's closest to the camera. Photograph your home with a normal

Table 6.1 Field of View at Various Focal Lengths

Diagonal Field of View	Length at Focal	Focal Length Needed to Produce Same 1X Crop Field of View at 1.6X Crop
107 degrees	16mm	10mm
94 degrees	20mm	12mm
84 degrees	24mm	15mm
75 degrees	28mm	18mm
63 degrees	35mm	22mm
47 degrees	50mm	31mm
28 degrees	85mm	53mm
18 degrees	135mm	85mm
12 degrees	200mm	125mm
8.2 degrees	300mm	188mm

lens/normal zoom setting, and the front yard probably looks fairly conventional in your photo (that's why they're called "normal" lenses). Switch to a wider lens and you'll discover that your lawn now makes up much more of the photo. So, wide-angle lenses are great when you want to emphasize that lake in the foreground, but problematic when your intended subject is located farther in the distance.

- **Super-sized subjects.** The tendency of a wide-angle lens to emphasize objects in the foreground, while de-emphasizing objects in the background can lead to a kind of size distortion that may be more objectionable for some types of subjects than others. Shoot a bed of flowers up close with a wide angle, and you might like the distorted effect of the larger blossoms nearer the lens. Take a photo of a family member with the same lens from the same distance, and you're likely to get some complaints about that gigantic nose in the foreground.

- **Perspective distortion.** When you tilt the camera so the plane of the sensor is no longer perpendicular to the vertical plane of your subject, some parts of the subject are now closer to the sensor than they were before, while other parts are farther away. So, buildings, flagpoles, or NBA players appear to be falling backwards, as you can see in Figure 6.8. While this kind of apparent distortion (it's not caused by a defect in the lens) can happen with any lens, it's most apparent when a wide angle is used.

Figure 6.8
Tilting the camera
back produces this
"falling back" look in
architectural photos.

Figure 6.8
Tilting the camera back produces this "falling back" look in architectural photos.

- **Steady cam.** You'll find that you can handhold a wide-angle lens at slower shutter speeds, without need for image stabilization, than you can with a tele-photo lens. The reduced magnification of the wide-lens or wide-zoom setting doesn't emphasize camera shake like a telephoto lens does.

- **Interesting angles.** Many of the factors already listed combine to produce more interesting angles when shooting with wide-angle lenses. Raising or low-ering a telephoto lens a few feet probably will have little effect on the appear-ance of the distant subjects you're shooting. The same change in elevation can produce a dramatic effect for the much-closer subjects typically captured with a wide-angle lens or wide-zoom setting.

The crop factor strikes again! You can see from this table that wide-angle lenses provide a broader field of view, and that, because of the 40D's 1.6 crop factor, lenses must have a shorter focal length to provide the same field of view. If you like working with a 28mm lens with your full-frame camera, you'll need an 18mm lens for your EOS 40D to get the same field of view. (Some focal lengths have been rounded slightly for simplification.)

DOF IN DEPTH

The DOF advantage of wide-angle lenses is diminished when you enlarge your pic-ture; believe it or not, a wide-angle image enlarged and cropped to provide the same subject size as a telephoto shot would have the *same* depth-of-field. Try it: take a wide-angle photo of a friend from a fair distance, and then zoom in to dupli-cate the picture in a telephoto image. Then, enlarge the wide shot so your friend is the same size in both. The wide photo will have the same depth-of-field (and will have much less detail, too).

Avoiding Potential Wide-Angle Problems

Wide-angle lenses have a few quirks that you'll want to keep in mind when shoot-ing so you can avoid falling into some common traps. Here's a checklist of tips for avoiding common problems:

- **Symptom: converging lines.** Unless you want to use wildly diverging lines as a creative effect, it's a good idea to keep horizontal and vertical lines in land-scapes, architecture, and other subjects carefully aligned with the sides, top, and bottom of the frame. That will help you avoid undesired perspective dis-tortion. Sometimes it helps to shoot from a slightly elevated position so you don't have to tilt the camera up or down.

- **Symptom: color fringes around objects.** Lenses are often plagued with fringes of color around backlit objects, produced by *chromatic aberration*, which comes in two forms: *longitudinal/axial*, in which all the colors of light don't focus in the same plane; and *lateral/transverse*, in which the colors are shifted to one side. Axial chromatic aberration can be reduced by stopping down the lens, but transverse CA cannot. Both can be reduced by using lenses with low diffraction index glass (or UD elements, in Canon nomenclature) and by incorporating elements that cancel the chromatic aberration of other glass in the lens. For example, a strong positive lens made of low dispersion crown glass (made of a soda-lime-silica composite) may be mated with a weaker negative lens made of high-dispersion flint glass, which contains lead.

- **Symptom: lines that bow outward.** Some wide-angle lenses cause straight lines to bow outwards, with the strongest effect at the edges. In fisheye (or *curvilinear*) lenses, this defect is a feature, as you can see in Figure 6.9. When distortion is not desired, you'll need to use a lens that has corrected barrel distortion. Manufacturers like Canon do their best to minimize or eliminate it

Figure 6.9 Many wide-angle lenses cause lines to bow outwards towards the edges of the image; with a fisheye lens, this tendency is considered an interesting feature.

(producing a *rectilinear* lens), often using *aspherical* lens elements (which are not cross-sections of a sphere). You can also minimize barrel distortion simply by framing your photo with some extra space all around, so the edges where the defect is most obvious can be cropped out of the picture.

- **Symptom: dark corners and shadows in flash photos.** The Canon EOS 40D's built-in electronic flash is designed to provide even coverage for lenses as wide as 17mm. If you use a wider lens, you can expect darkening, or *vignetting*, in the corners of the frame. At wider focal lengths, the lens hood of some lenses (my 17mm-85mm lens is a prime offender) can cast a semi-circular shadow in the lower portion of the frame when using the built-in flash. Sometimes removing the lens hood or zooming in a bit can eliminate the shadow. Mounting an external flash unit, such as the mighty Canon 580EX can solve both problems, as it has zoomable coverage up to 114 degrees with the included adapter, sufficient for a 9mm rectilinear lens (14mm equivalent). Its higher vantage point eliminates the problem of lens-hood shadow, too.

- **Symptom: light and dark areas when using polarizing filter.** If you know that polarizers work best when the camera is pointed 90 degrees away from the sun and have the least effect when the camera is oriented 180 degrees from the sun, you know only half the story. With lenses having a focal length of 10mm to 18mm (the equivalent of 16mm-28mm), the angle of view (107 to 75 degrees diagonally, or 97 to 44 degrees horizontally) is extensive enough to cause problems. Think about it: when a 10mm lens is pointed at the proper 90-degree angle from the sun, objects at the edges of the frame will be oriented at 135 to 41 degrees, with only the center at exactly 90 degrees. Either edge will have much less of a polarized effect. The solution is to avoid using a polarizing filter with lenses having an actual focal length of less than 18mm (or 28mm equivalent).

Using Telephoto and Tele-Zoom Lenses

Telephoto lenses also can have a dramatic effect on your photography, and Canon is especially strong in the long-lens arena, with lots of choices in many focal lengths and zoom ranges. You should be able to find an affordable telephoto or tele-zoom to enhance your photography in several different ways. Here are the most important things you need to know. In the next section, I'll concentrate on telephoto considerations that can be problematic—and how to avoid those problems.

- **Selective focus.** Long lenses have reduced depth-of-field within the frame, allowing you to use selective focus to isolate your subject. You can open the lens up wide to create shallow depth-of-field, or close it down a bit to allow more to be in focus. The flip side of the coin is that when you *want* to make a range of objects sharp, you'll need to use a smaller f/stop to get the depth-of-field you need. Like fire, the depth-of-field of a telephoto lens can be friend or foe. Figure 6.10 shows a photo of a piece of antique glassware that couldn't be removed from its display shelf, so I photographed it using a short telephoto lens and wider f/stop to de-emphasize the other glassware in the background.

■ **Getting closer.** Telephoto lenses bring you closer to wildlife, sports action, and candid subjects. No one wants to get a reputation as a surreptitious or "sneaky" photographer (except for paparazzi), but when applied to candids in an open and honest way, a long lens can help you capture memorable moments while retaining enough distance to stay out of the way of events as they transpire.

■ **Reduced foreground/increased compression.** Telephoto lenses have the opposite effect of wide angles: they reduce the importance of things in the foreground by squeezing everything together. This compression even makes distant objects appear to be closer to subjects in the foreground and middle ranges. You can use this effect as a creative tool.

Figure 6.10 A wide f/stop helped isolate this antique glassware from the other items on the display shelf.

- **Accentuates camera shakiness.** Telephoto focal lengths hit you with a double-whammy in terms of camera/photographer shake. The lenses themselves are bulkier, more difficult to hold steady, and may even produce a barely perceptible see-saw rocking effect when you support them with one hand halfway down the lens barrel. Telephotos also magnify any camera shake. It's no wonder that image stabilization is popular in longer lenses.

- **Interesting angles require creativity.** Telephoto lenses require more imagination in selecting interesting angles, because the "angle" you do get on your subjects is so narrow. Moving from side to side or a bit higher or lower can make a dramatic difference in a wide-angle shot, but raising or lowering a telephoto lens a few feet probably will have little effect on the appearance of the distant subjects you're shooting.

Avoiding Telephoto Lens Problems

Many of the "problems" that telephoto lenses pose are really just challenges and not that difficult to overcome. Here is a list of the seven most common picture maladies and suggested solutions.

- **Symptom: flat faces in portraits.** Head-and-shoulders portraits of humans tend to be more flattering when a focal length of 50mm to 85mm is used. Longer focal lengths compress the distance between features like noses and ears, making the face look wider and flat. A wide-angle might make noses look huge and ears tiny when you fill the frame with a face. So stick with 50mm to 85mm focal lengths, going longer only when you're forced to shoot from a greater distance, and wider only when shooting three-quarters/full-length portraits, or group shots.

- **Symptom: blur due to camera shake.** Use a higher shutter speed (boosting ISO if necessary), consider an image-stabilized lens, or mount your camera on a tripod, monopod, or brace it with some other support. Of those three solutions, only the first will reduce blur caused by *subject* motion; an IS lens or tripod won't help you freeze a racecar in mid-lap.

- **Symptom: color fringes.** Chromatic aberration is the most pernicious optical problem found in telephoto lenses. There are others, including spherical aberration, astigmatism, coma, curvature of field, and similarly scary-sounding phenomena. The best solution for any of these is to use a better lens that offers the proper degree of correction, or stop down the lens to minimize the problem. But that's not always possible. Your second-best choice may be to correct the fringing in your favorite RAW conversion tool or image editor. Photoshop CS3's Lens Correction filter (found in the Distort menu) offers sliders that minimize both red/cyan and blue/yellow fringing.

- **Symptom: lines that curve inwards.** Pincushion distortion is found in many telephoto lenses. You might find after a bit of testing that it is worse at certain focal lengths with your particular zoom lens. Like chromatic aberration, it can be partially corrected using tools like Photoshop's Lens Correction filter.

- **Symptom: low contrast from haze or fog.** When you're photographing distant objects, a long lens shoots through a lot more atmosphere, which generally is muddied up with extra haze and fog. That dirt or moisture in the atmosphere can reduce contrast and mute colors. Some feel that a skylight or UV filter can help, but this practice is mostly a holdover from the film days. Digital sensors are not sensitive enough to UV light for a UV filter to have much effect. So you should be prepared to boost contrast and color saturation in your Picture Styles menu or image editor if necessary.

- **Symptom: low contrast from flare.** Lenses are furnished with lens hoods for a good reason: to reduce flare from bright light sources at the periphery of the picture area, or completely outside it. Because telephoto lenses often create images that are lower in contrast in the first place, you'll want to be especially careful to use a lens hood to prevent further effects on your image (or shade the front of the lens with your hand).

- **Symptom: dark flash photos.** Edge-to-edge flash coverage isn't a problem with telephoto lenses as it is with wide angles. The shooting distance is. A long lens might make a subject that's 50 feet away look as if it's right next to you, but your camera's flash isn't fooled. You'll need extra power for distant flash shots, and probably more power than your 40D's built-in flash provides. The shoe-mount Canon 580EX Speedlite, for example, can automatically zoom its coverage down to that of a medium telephoto lens, providing a theoretical full-power shooting aperture of about f/8 at 50 feet and ISO 400. (Try *that* with the built-in flash!)

Telephotos and Bokeh

Bokeh describes the aesthetic qualities of the out-of-focus parts of an image and whether out-of-focus points of light—circles of confusion—are rendered as distracting fuzzy discs or smoothly fade into the background. *Boke* is a Japanese word for "blur," and the h was added to keep English speakers from rendering it mono-syllabically to rhyme with *broke*. Although bokeh is visible in blurry portions of any image, it's of particular concern with telephoto lenses, which, thanks to the magic of reduced depth-of-field, produce more obviously out-of-focus areas.

Bokeh can vary from lens to lens, or even within a given lens depending on the f/stop in use. Bokeh becomes objectionable when the circles of confusion are evenly illuminated, making them stand out as distinct discs, or, worse, when these circles are darker in the center, producing an ugly "doughnut" effect. A lens defect called spherical aberration may produce out-of-focus discs that are brighter on the edges and darker in the center, because the lens doesn't focus light passing through the edges of the lens exactly as it does light going through the center. (Mirror or *catadioptric* lenses also produce this effect.)

Other kinds of spherical aberration generate circles of confusion that are brightest in the center and fade out at the edges, producing a smooth blending effect, as you can see at right in Figure 6.11. Ironically, when no spherical aberration is present at all, the discs are a uniform shade, which, while better than the doughnut effect, is not as pleasing as the bright center/dark edge rendition. The shape of the disc also comes into play, with round smooth circles considered the best, and nonagonal or some other polygon (determined by the shape of the lens diaphragm) considered less desirable.

If you plan to use selective focus a lot, you should investigate the bokeh characteristics of a particular lens before you buy. Canon user groups and forums will usually be full of comments and questions about bokeh, so the research is fairly easy.

Figure 6.11 Bokeh is less pleasing when the discs are prominent (left), and less obtrusive when they blend into the background (right).

Add-ons and Special Features

Once you've purchased your telephoto lens, you'll want to think about some appropriate accessories for it. There are some handy add-ons available that can be valuable. Here are a couple of them to think about.

Lens Hoods

Lens hoods are an important accessory for all lenses, but they're especially valuable with telephotos. As I mentioned earlier, lens hoods do a good job of preserving image contrast by keeping bright light sources outside the field of view from striking the lens and, potentially, bouncing around inside that long tube to generate flare that, when coupled with atmospheric haze, can rob your image of detail and snap. In addition, lens hoods serve as valuable protection for that large, vulnerable, front lens element. It's easy to forget that you've got that long tube sticking out in front of your camera and accidentally whack the front of your lens into something. It's cheaper to replace a lens hood than it is to have a lens repaired, so you might find that a good hood is valuable protection for your prized optics.

When choosing a lens hood, it's important to have the right hood for the lens, usually the one offered for that lens by Canon or the third-party manufacturer. You want a hood that blocks precisely the right amount of light: neither too much light nor too little. A hood with a front diameter that is too small can show up in your pictures as vignetting. A hood that has a front diameter that's too large isn't stopping all the light it should. Generic lens hoods may not do the job.

When your telephoto is a zoom lens, it's even more important to get the right hood, because you need one that does what it is supposed to at both the wide-angle and telephoto ends of the zoom range. Lens hoods may be cylindrical, rectangular (shaped like the image frame), or petal shaped (that is, cylindrical, but with cut-out areas at the corners which correspond to the actual image area). Lens hoods should be mounted in the correct orientation (a bayonet mount for the hood usually takes care of this).

Telephoto Extenders

Telephoto extenders (often called teleconverters outside the Canon world) multiply the actual focal length of your lens, giving you a longer telephoto for much less than the price of a lens with that actual focal length. These extenders fit between the lens and your camera and contain optical elements that magnify the image produced by the lens. Available in 1.4X and 2.0X configurations from

Canon, an extender transforms, say, a 200mm lens into a 280mm or 400mm optic, respectively. Given the 40D's crop factor, your 200mm lens now has the same field of view as a 448mm or 640mm lens on a full-frame camera. At around $300 each, they're quite a bargain, aren't they?

Actually, there are some downsides. While extenders retain the closest focusing distance of your original lens, autofocus is maintained only if the lens's original maximum aperture is f/4 or larger (for the 1.4X extender) or f/2.8 or larger (for the 2X extender). The components reduce the effective aperture of any lens they are used with, by one f/stop with the 1.4X extender, and 2 f/stops with the 2X extender. So, your EF 200mm f/2.8L II USM becomes a 280mm f/4 or 400mm f/5.6 lens. Although Canon extenders are precision optical devices, they do cost you a little sharpness, but that improves when you reduce the aperture by a stop or two. Each of the extenders is compatible only with a particular set of lenses of 135mm focal length or greater, so you'll want to check Canon's compatibility chart to see if the component can be used with the lens you want to attach to it.

If your lenses are compatible and you're shooting under bright lighting conditions, the Canon Extender EF 1.4x II, and Canon Extender EF 2x II make handy accessories.

Macro Focusing

Some telephotos and telephoto zooms available for the EOS 40D have particularly close focusing capabilities, making them *macro* lenses. Of course, the object is not necessarily to get close (get too close and you'll find it difficult to light your subject). What you're really looking for in a macro lens is to magnify the apparent size of the subject in the final image. Camera-to-subject distance is most important when you want to back up farther from your subject (say, to avoid spooking skittish insects or small animals). In that case, you'll want a macro lens with a longer focal length to allow that distance while retaining the desired magnification.

Canon makes 50mm, 60mm, 65mm, 100mm, and 180mm lenses with official macro designations. You'll also find macro lenses, macro zooms, and other close-focusing lenses available from Sigma, Tamron, and Tokina. If you want to focus closer with a macro lens, or any other lens, you can add an accessory called an *extension tube*, like the one shown in Figure 6.12. These add-ons move the lens farther from the focal plane, allowing it to focus more closely. Canon also sells add-on close-up lenses, which look like filters, and allow lenses to focus more closely.

Figure 6.12
Extension tubes
enable any lens to
focus more closely to
the subject.

Image Stabilization

Canon has a burgeoning line of more than a dozen lenses with built-in image stabilization (IS) capabilities. This feature uses lens elements that are shifted internally in response to the motion of the lens during handheld photography, countering the shakiness the camera and photographer produce and which telephoto lenses magnify. However, IS is not limited to long lenses; the feature works like a champ at the 17mm zoom position of Canon's EF-S 17-85MM f4-5.6 IS USM and EF-S 17-55 f/2.8 IS USM lenses. Other Canon IS lenses provide stabilization with zooms that are as wide as 24-28mm.

Image stabilization provides you with camera steadiness that's the equivalent of at least two or three shutter speed increments. (Canon claims four, which I feel may be optimistic.) This extra margin can be invaluable when you're shooting under dim lighting conditions or handholding a long lens for, say, wildlife photography. Perhaps that shot of a foraging deer calls for a shutter speed of 1/1,000 second at f/5.6 with your EF 100-400mm f/4.5-5.6L IS USM lens. Relax. You can shoot at 1/250 second at f/11 and get virtually the same results, as long as the deer doesn't decide to bound off.

Or, maybe you're shooting a high-school play without a tripod or monopod, and you'd really, really like to use 1/15 second at f/4. Assuming the actors aren't flitting around the stage at high speed, your 17mm-85mm IS lens can grab the shot for you at its wide-angle position.

However, keep these facts in mind:

- **IS doesn't stop action.** Unfortunately, no IS lens is a panacea to replace the action-stopping capabilities of a higher shutter speed. Image stabilization applies only to camera shake. You still need a fast shutter speed to freeze action. IS works great in low light, when you're using long lenses, and for macro photography. It's not always the best choice for action photography, unless there's enough light to allow a sufficiently high shutter speed. If so, IS can make your shot even sharper.

- **IS slows you down.** The process of adjusting the lens elements takes time, just as autofocus does, so you might find that IS adds to the lag between when you press the shutter and when the picture is actually taken. That's another reason why image stabilization might not be a good choice for sports.

- **Use when appropriate.** Some IS lenses produce worse results if you use them while you're panning, although newer Canon IS lenses have a mode that works fine when the camera is deliberately moved from side to side during exposure. Older lenses can confuse the motion with camera shake and overcompensate. You might want to switch off IS when panning or when your camera is mounted on a tripod.

- **Do you need IS at all?** Remember that an inexpensive monopod might be able to provide the same additional steadiness as an IS lens, at a much lower cost. If you're out in the field shooting wild animals or flowers and think a tripod isn't practical, try a monopod first.

IMAGE STABILIZATION: IN THE CAMERA OR IN THE LENS?

Sony's acquisition of Konica Minolta's dSLR assets and the introduction of an improved in-camera image-stabilization system has revised an old debate about whether IS belongs in the camera or in the lens. Perhaps it's my Canon bias showing, but I am quite happy not to have image stabilization available in the body itself. Here are some reasons:

- Should in-camera IS fail, you have to send the whole camera in for repair, and camera repairs are generally more expensive than lens repairs. I like being able to simply switch to another lens if I have an IS problem.

- IS in the camera doesn't steady your view in the viewfinder, whereas an IS lens shows you a steadied image as you shoot.

- You're stuck with the IS system built into your camera. If an improved system is incorporated into a lens and the improvements are important to you, just trade in your old lens for the new one.

7

Working with Light

All artists, including sculptors, painters, and photographers, use light as their medium to create images. Each of these types of creative work has its own challenges. Sculptors, for example, don't have control over the light used to illuminate their work, so they must create shapes using planes and curved surfaces so that the form envisioned by the artist comes to life from a variety of viewing and lighting angles. Painters, in contrast, have absolute control over both shape and light in their work, as well as the viewing angle, so they can use both the contours of their two-dimensional subjects and the qualities of the "light" they use to illuminate those subjects to evoke the image they want to produce. Photography is a third form of art. The picture-taker may have little or no control over the subject (other than posing human subjects) but can often adjust both viewing angle *and* the nature of the light source to create a particular image.

But, in all three cases, light, as it appears in the finished product that we see, is a main contributor to the mood, look, and effectiveness of the artwork. In photography, the direction and intensity of the light sources create the shapes and textures that we see. The distribution and proportions determine the contrast and tonal values: whether the image is stark or high key, or muted and low in contrast. The colors of the light (because even "white" light has a color balance that the sensor can detect), and how much of those colors the subject reflects or absorbs, paint the hues visible in the image.

As a Canon EOS 40D photographer, you must learn to be a painter and sculptor of light if you want to move from *taking* a picture to *making* a photograph. This chapter provides an introduction to using the two main types of illumination: *continuous* lighting (such as daylight, incandescent, or fluorescent sources) and the brief, but brilliant snippets of light we call *electronic flash*.

Continuous Illumination versus Electronic Flash

Continuous lighting is light that is available all the time during a shooting session, such as daylight or the artificial lighting encountered both indoors and outdoors. The latter sources embrace both the lights that are there already (such as lamps or overhead fluorescent lights indoors) and fixtures you supply yourself, including photoflood lamps or reflectors you supply to provide light for photography.

Electronic flash includes the flip-up flash unit built into your EOS 40D (see Figure 7.1) or any external flash you choose to couple with it, including those that mount on the accessory shoe on top of the camera and units that are used off-camera. Studio flash units count, too, and aren't limited to "professional" shooters, as there are economical "monolight" (one-piece flash/power supply) flash available in the $200 price range.

There are advantages and disadvantages to each type of illumination. Here's a quick checklist of pros and cons:

■ **Lighting preview.** With continuous lighting, you always know exactly what kind of lighting effect you're going to get and, if multiple lights are used, how they will interact with each other. With electronic flash, the general effect you're going to see may be a mystery until you've built some experience, and you may need to review a shot on the LCD, make some adjustments, and then reshoot to get the look you want. (In this sense, a digital camera's review capabilities replace the Polaroid test shots pro photographers relied on in decades past.) While the 580EX/580 EXII have a modeling light function

Figure 7.1
One form of light that's always available is the flip-up flash on your EOS 40D.

(consisting of a series of low-powered bursts that flash for a period of time), this feature is no substitute for an always-on modeling lamp or continuous illumination.

- **Exposure calculation.** Your 40D has no problem calculating exposure for continuous lighting, because it remains constant. The amount of light available just before the exposure will, in almost all cases, be the same amount of light present when the shutter is released. You can even use a handheld light meter to measure the light yourself, say, when you want to compare the illumination falling on the highlight areas of a subject with the light reaching the shadows in order to calculate the exact amount of contrast to expect. Electronic flash illumination, on the other hand, doesn't exist until the flash fires, and so must be measured using a preflash an instant before the main flash, or measured *during the actual exposure.* In the case of a digital SLR, that is tricky to do in-camera because the mirror has flipped up and is blocking the metering system built into the camera; it's more common, when such a system is used at all, to measure the light by non-through-the-lens means using a light sensor in an external flash unit. If you have a do-it-yourself bent, there are handheld flash meters, too, including models that measure both flash and continuous light.

- **Evenness of illumination.** Of continuous light sources, daylight, in particular, provides illumination that tends to fill an image completely, lighting up the foreground, background, and your subject almost equally. Shadows do come into play, of course, so you might need to use reflectors or fill-in light sources to even out the illumination further, but barring objects that block large sections of your image from daylight, the light is spread fairly evenly. Electronic flash units (as well as continuous light sources such as lamps that don't have the advantage of being 93 million miles from the subject) suffer from the effects of their proximity: the *inverse square law* dictates that as a light source's distance increases from the subject, the amount of light reaching the subject falls off proportionately to the square of the distance. In plain English, that means that a flash or lamp that's eight feet away from a subject provides only one-quarter as much illumination as a source that's four feet away (rather than half as much). This translates into relatively shallow "depth-of-light."

- **Action stopping.** When it comes to the ability to freeze moving objects in their tracks, the advantage goes to electronic flash. As I explained in Chapter 4, the brief duration of electronic flash serves as a very high "shutter speed" when the flash is the main or only source of illumination for the photo. Your

EOS 40D's shutter speed may be set for 1/250th second during a flash exposure, but if the flash illumination predominates, the *effective* exposure time will be the 1/1,000th to 1/50,000th second or less duration of the flash, as you can see in Figure 7.2, because the flash unit reduces the amount of light released by reducing the duration of the flash. Action stopping with continuous light sources, on the other hand, is completely dependent on the shutter speed you've dialed in on the camera. And the speeds available are dependent on the amount of light available and your ISO sensitivity setting. For example, if you're shooting sports indoors, there probably won't be enough available light to allow you to use a 1/2,000th second shutter speed, but applying that effective speed by using a flash unit is no problem at all.

- **Cost.** Incandescent lamps are generally much less expensive than electronic flash units, which can easily cost several hundred dollars. If you want to use more than one light source, the costs mount more quickly with flash.

- **Flexibility.** Because incandescent lamps are not as bright as electronic flash, the slower shutter speeds required (see Action stopping, above) mean that you may have to use a tripod more often, especially when shooting portraits. Electronic flash's action-freezing power allows you to work without a tripod, adding flexibility and speed when choosing angles and positions.

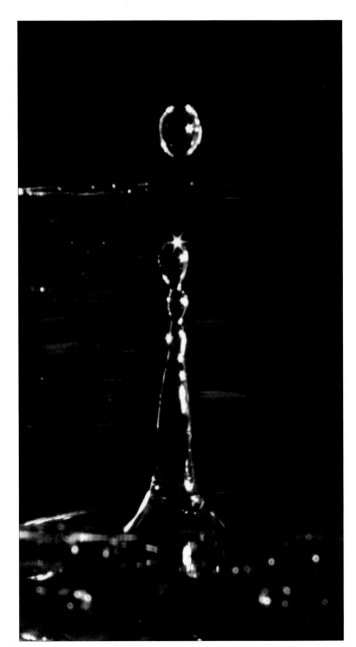

Figure 7.2 Electronic flash can freeze almost any action.

Continuous Lighting Basics

While continuous lighting and its effects are generally much easier to visualize and use than electronic flash, there are some factors you need to take into account, particularly the color temperature of the light. (Color temperature concerns aren't exclusive to continuous light sources, of course, but the variations tend to be more extreme and less predictable than those of electronic flash.)

Color temperature, in practical terms, is how "bluish" or how "reddish" the light appears to be to the digital camera's sensor. Indoor illumination is quite warm, comparatively, and appears reddish to the sensor. Daylight, in contrast, seems much bluer to the sensor. Our eyes (our brains, actually) are quite adaptable to these variations, so white objects don't appear to have an orange tinge when viewed indoors, nor do they seem excessively blue outdoors in full daylight. Yet, these color temperature variations are real and the sensor is not fooled. To capture the most accurate colors, we need to take the color temperature into account in setting the color balance (or *white balance*) of the 40D—either automatically using the camera's smarts, or manually, using our own knowledge and experience.

The only time you need to think in terms of actual color temperature is when you're making adjustments using the Color temp. setting in the Shooting 2 menu (which allows you to dial in exact color temperatures, if known). So, those occasions are the only times you're likely to be confused by a seeming contradiction in how color temperatures are named: warmer (more reddish) color temperatures (measured in degrees Kelvin) are the *lower* numbers, while cooler (bluer) color temperatures are *higher* numbers. It might not make sense to say that 3,400K is warmer than 6,000K, but that's the way it is. If it helps, think of a glowing red ember contrasted with a white-hot welder's torch, rather than fire and ice.

The confusion comes from physics. Scientists calculate color temperature from the light emitted by a mythical object called a black body radiator, which absorbs all the radiant energy that strikes it, and reflects none at all. Such a black body not only *absorbs* light perfectly, but it *emits* it perfectly when heated (and since nothing in the universe is perfect, that makes it mythical).

At a particular physical temperature, this imaginary object always emits light of the same wavelength or color. That makes it possible to define color temperature in terms of actual temperature in degrees on the Kelvin scale that scientists use. Incandescent light, for example, typically has a color temperature of 3,200K to 3,400K. Daylight might range from 5,500K to 6,000K. Each type of illumination we use for photography has its own color temperature range—with some cautions. The next sections will summarize everything you need to know about the qualities of these light sources.

Daylight

Daylight is produced by the sun, and so is moonlight (which is just reflected sunlight). Daylight is present, of course, even when you can't see the sun. When sunlight is direct, it can be bright and harsh. If daylight is diffused by clouds, softened by bouncing off objects such as walls or your photo reflectors, or filtered by shade, it can be much dimmer and less contrasty.

Daylight's color temperature can vary quite widely. It is highest (most blue) at noon when the sun is directly overhead, because the light is traveling through a minimum amount of the filtering layer we call the atmosphere. The color temperature at high noon may be 6,000K. At other times of day, the sun is lower in the sky and the particles in the air provide a filtering effect that warms the illumination to about 5,500K for most of the day. Starting an hour before dusk and for an hour after sunrise, the warm appearance of the sunlight is even visible to our eyes when the color temperature may dip to 5,000-4,500K, as shown in Figure 7.3.

Because you'll be taking so many photos in daylight, you'll want to learn how to use or compensate for the brightness and contrast of sunlight, as well as how to deal with its color temperature. I'll provide some hints later in this chapter.

Figure 7.3 At dawn and dusk, the color temperature of daylight may dip as low as 4,500K.

Incandescent/Tungsten Light

The term incandescent or tungsten illumination is usually applied to the direct descendents of Thomas Edison's original electric lamp. Such lights consist of a glass bulb that contains a vacuum, or is filled with a halogen gas, and contains a tungsten filament that is heated by an electrical current, producing photons and heat. Tungsten-halogen lamps are a variation on the basic light bulb, using a more rugged (and longer-lasting) filament that can be heated to a higher temperature, housed in a thicker glass or quartz envelope, and filled with iodine or bromine ("halogen") gases. The higher temperature allows tungsten-halogen (or quartz-halogen/quartz-iodine, depending on their construction) lamps to burn "hotter" and whiter. Although popular for automobile headlamps today, they've also been popular for photographic illumination.

Although incandescent illumination isn't a perfect black body radiator, it's close enough that the color temperature of such lamps can be precisely calculated and used for photography without concerns about color variation (at least, until the very end of the lamp's life).

The other qualities of this type of lighting, such as contrast, are dependent on the distance of the lamp from the subject, type of reflectors used, and other factors that I'll explain later in this chapter.

Fluorescent Light/Other Light Sources

Fluorescent light has some advantages in terms of illumination, but some disadvantages from a photographic standpoint. This type of lamp generates light through an electro-chemical reaction that emits most of its energy as visible light, rather than heat, which is why the bulbs don't get as hot. The type of light produced varies depending on the phosphor coatings and type of gas in the tube. So, the illumination fluorescent bulbs produce can vary widely in its characteristics.

That's not great news for photographers. Different types of lamps have different "color temperatures" that can't be precisely measured in degrees Kelvin, because the light isn't produced by heating. Worse, fluorescent lamps have a discontinuous spectrum of light that can have some colors missing entirely. A particular type of tube can lack certain shades of red or other colors (see Figure 7.4), which is why fluorescent lamps and other alternative technologies such as sodium-vapor illumination can produce ghastly looking human skin tones. Their spectra can lack the reddish tones we associate with healthy skin and emphasize the blues and greens popular in horror movies.

Figure 7.4
The fluorescent
lighting in the room
where this historical
re-enactor gave his
performance added a
distinct greenish cast
to the image.

Adjusting White Balance

I showed you how to adjust white balance in Chapter 3, using the 40D's built-in presets, white balance shift capabilities, setting exact color temperatures, and white balance bracketing (there's more on bracketing in Chapter 4, too).

In most cases, however, the EOS 40D will do a good job of calculating white balance for you, so Auto can be used as your choice most of the time. Use the preset values or set a custom white balance that matches the current shooting conditions when you need to. The only really problematic light sources are likely to be fluorescents. Vendors, such as GE and Sylvania, may actually provide a figure known as the *color rendering index* (or CRI), which is a measure of how accurately a particular light source represents standard colors, using a scale of 0 (some sodium-vapor lamps) to 100 (daylight and most incandescent lamps). Daylight fluorescents and deluxe cool white fluorescents might have a CRI of about 79 to 95, which is perfectly acceptable for most photographic applications. Warm white fluorescents might have a CRI of 55. White deluxe mercury vapor lights are less suitable with a CRI of 45, while low-pressure sodium lamps can vary from CRI 0-18.

Remember that if you shoot RAW or sRAW, you can specify the white balance of your image when you import it into Photoshop, Photoshop Elements, or another image editor using your preferred RAW converter. While color-balancing filters that fit on the front of the lens exist, they are primarily useful for film cameras, because film's color balance can't be tweaked as extensively as that of a sensor.

Electronic Flash Basics

Until you delve into the situation deeply enough, it might appear that serious photographers have a love/hate relationship with electronic flash. You'll often hear that flash photography is less natural looking, and that the built-in flash in most cameras should never be used as the primary source of illumination because it provides a harsh, garish look. Indeed, most "pro" cameras like the Canon EOS 1D Mark III and 1Ds Mark III don't have a built-in flash at all. Available ("continuous") lighting is praised, and built-in flash photography seems to be roundly denounced.

In truth, however, the bias is against *bad* flash photography. Indeed, flash has become the studio light source of choice for pro photographers, because it's more intense (and its intensity can be varied to order by the photographer), freezes action, frees you from using a tripod (unless you want to use one to lock down a composition), and has a snappy, consistent light quality that matches daylight. (While color balance changes as the flash duration shortens, some Canon flash units can communicate to the camera the exact white balance provided for that shot.) And even pros will cede that the built-in flash of the Canon EOS 40D has some important uses as an adjunct to existing light, particularly to fill in dark shadows.

But electronic flash isn't as inherently easy to use as continuous lighting. As I noted earlier, electronic flash units are more expensive, don't show you exactly what the lighting effect will be (unless you use a second source called a *modeling light* for a preview), and the exposure of electronic flash units is more difficult to calculate accurately.

How Electronic Flash Works

The bursts of light we call electronic flash are produced by a flash of photons generated by an electrical charge that is accumulated in a component called a *capacitor* and then directed through a glass tube containing xenon gas, which absorbs the energy and emits the brief flash. For the pop-up flash built into the EOS 40D, the full burst of light lasts about 1/1,000th of a second and provides enough illumination to shoot a subject 10 feet away at f/4 using the ISO 100 setting. In a more typical situation, you'd use ISO 200, f/5.6 to f/8 and photograph something 8 to 10 feet away. As you can see, the built-in flash is somewhat limited in range; you'll see why external flash units are often a good idea later in this chapter.

An electronic flash (whether built in or connected to the EOS 40D through a cable or the hot shoe) is triggered at the instant of exposure, during a period when the sensor is fully exposed by the shutter. As I mentioned earlier in this book, the 40D has a vertically traveling shutter that consists of two curtains. The first curtain opens and moves to the opposite side of the frame, at which point the shutter is completely open. The flash can be triggered at this point (so-called *first-curtain sync*), making the flash exposure. Then, after a delay that can vary from 30 seconds to 1/250th second (with the EOS 40D; other cameras may sync at a faster or slower speed), a second curtain begins moving across the sensor plane, covering up the sensor again. If the flash is triggered just before the second curtain starts to close, then *second-curtain sync* is used. In both cases, though, a shutter speed of 1/250th second is the maximum that can be used to take a photo.

If you happen to set the 40D's shutter to a faster speed in Tv or M mode, the camera will automatically adjust the shutter speed down to 1/250th second. In Av, P, or any of the Basic Zone modes, the 40D will never select a shutter speed higher than 1/250th second when using flash. Actually, in P mode, shutter speed is automatically set between 1/60th to 1/250th second when using flash.

Ghost Images

The difference might not seem like much, but whether you use first-curtain sync (the default setting) or second-curtain sync (an optional setting) can make a significant difference to your photograph *if the ambient light in your scene also contributes to the image.* At faster shutter speeds, particularly 1/250th second, there isn't much time for the ambient light to register, unless it is very bright. It's likely that the electronic flash will provide almost all the illumination, so first-curtain sync or second-curtain sync isn't very important.

However, at slower shutter speeds, or with very bright ambient light levels, there is a significant difference, particularly if your subject is moving, or the camera isn't steady. In any of those situations, the ambient light will register as a second image accompanying the flash exposure, and if there is movement (camera or subject), that additional image will not be in the same place as the flash exposure. It will show as a ghost image and, if the movement is significant enough, as a blurred ghost image trailing in front of or behind your subject in the direction of the movement.

When you're using first-curtain sync, the flash goes off the instant the shutter opens, producing an image of the subject on the sensor. Then, the shutter remains open for an additional period (30 seconds to 1/250th second, as I noted). If your subject is moving, say, towards the right side of the frame, the ghost image produced by the ambient light will produce a blur on the right side of the original subject image, making it look as if your sharp (flash-produced) image is chasing the ghost. For those of us who grew up with lightning-fast superheroes who always left a ghost trail *behind them*, that looks unnatural (see Figure 7.5).

Figure 7.5 First-curtain sync produces an image that trails in front of the flash exposure (top), while second-curtain sync creates a more "natural looking" trail behind the flash image.

So, Canon provides second-curtain sync to remedy the situation. In that mode, the shutter opens, as before. The shutter remains open for its designated duration, and the ghost image forms. If your subject moves from the left side of the frame to the right side, the ghost will move from left to right, too. *Then*, about 1.5 milliseconds before the second shutter curtain closes, the flash is triggered, producing a nice, sharp flash image *ahead* of the ghost image. Voilà! We have monsieur *le Flash* outrunning his own trailing image.

Exception to the Sync Rule

Triggering the electronic flash only when the shutter is completely open makes a lot of sense if you think about what's going on. To obtain shutter speeds faster than 1/250th second, the 40D exposes only part of the sensor at one time, by starting the second curtain on its journey before the first curtain has completely opened. That effectively provides a briefer exposure as a slit of passes over the surface of the sensor. If the flash were to fire during the time when the first and second curtains partially obscured the sensor, only the slit that was actually open would be exposed.

However, the 40D and certain Canon flashes provide a partial solution, called *high-speed sync* or *FP sync* (focal plane sync). Those flash units can fire a series of flashes consecutively in rapid succession, producing the illusion of a longer continuous flash, although at reduced intensity. These multiple flashes have a duration long enough to allow exposing the area of the sensor revealed by the traveling slit as it makes its full pass. However, the reduced intensity means that your flash's range is greatly reduced.

There is no setting to make on the EOS 40D to use this high-speed sync (other than to dial in a shutter speed higher than 1/250 second). Instead, you need to select this mode on the flash itself. With the 580EX II, the button to press is the High Speed Sync/Shutter Synchronization button, located just below the LCD between the Mode and Zoom buttons. The button is used to select second-curtain sync on the flash unit.

Determining Exposure

Calculating the proper exposure for an electronic flash photograph is a bit more complicated than determining the settings by continuous light. The right exposure isn't simply a function of how far away your subject is (which the 40D can figure out based on the autofocus distance that's locked in just prior to taking the picture). Various objects reflect more or less light at the same distance so, obviously, the camera needs to measure the amount of light reflected back and through the lens. Yet, as the flash itself isn't available for measuring until it's triggered, the 40D has nothing to measure.

The solution is to fire the flash twice. The initial shot is a preflash that can be analyzed, then followed by a main flash that's given exactly the calculated intensity needed to provide a correct exposure. As a result, the primary flash may be longer for distant objects and shorter for closer subjects, depending on the required intensity for exposure. This through-the-lens evaluative flash exposure system is called E-TTL II, and it operates whenever the pop-up internal flash is used, or you have attached a Canon dedicated flash unit to the 40D.

Guide Numbers

Guide numbers, usually abbreviated GN, are a way of specifying the power of an electronic flash in a way that can be used to determine the right f/stop to use at a particular shooting distance and ISO setting. In fact, before automatic flash units became prevalent, the GN was actually used to do just that. A GN is usually given as a pair of numbers for both feet and meters that represent the range at ISO 100. For example, the EOS 40D's built-in flash has a GN of 13/43 (meters/feet) at ISO 100. To calculate the right exposure at that ISO setting, you'd divide the guide number by the distance to arrive at the appropriate f/stop.

Using the 40D's built-in flash as an example, at ISO 100 with its GN of 43, if you wanted to shoot a subject at a distance of 10 feet, you'd use f/4.3 (43 divided by 10; round to f/4 for simplicity's sake). At 8 feet, an f/stop of f/5.4 (round up to f/5.6) would be used. Some quick mental calculations with the GN will give you any particular electronic flash's range. You can easily see that the built-in flash would begin to peter out at about 15 feet, where you'd need an aperture of f/2.8 at ISO 100. Of course, in the real world you'd probably bump the sensitivity up to a setting of ISO 400 so you could use a more practical f/5.6 at that distance.

Today, guide numbers are most useful for comparing the power of various flash units. You don't need to be a math genius to see that an electronic flash with a GN of, say, 165 would be *a lot* more powerful than your built-in flash (at ISO 100, you could use f/11 instead of f/2.8 at 15 feet).

Using the Built-In Flash

The Canon EOS 40D's built-in flash is a handy accessory because it is available as required, without the need to carry an external flash around with you constantly. This section explains how to use the flip-up flash in the various Basic Zone and Creative Zone modes.

Basic Zone Flash

When the 40D is set to one of the Basic Zone modes (except for Landscape, Sports, or Flash Off modes), the built-in flash will pop up when needed to provide extra illumination in low-light situations, or when your subject matter is backlit and could benefit from some fill flash. The flash doesn't pop up in Landscape mode because the flash doesn't have enough reach to have much effect for pictures of distant vistas in any case; nor does the flash pop up automatically in Sports mode, because you'll often want to use shutter speeds faster than 1/250th second and/or be shooting subjects that are out of flash range. Pop-up flash is disabled in Flash Off mode for obvious reasons.

If you happen to be shooting a landscape photo and do want to use flash (say, to add some illumination to a subject that's closer to the camera), or you want flash with your sports photos, or you *don't* want the flash popping up all the time when using one of the other Basic Zone modes, switch to an appropriate Creative Zone mode and use that instead.

Creative Zone Flash

When you're using a Creative Zone mode, you'll have to judge for yourself when flash might be useful, and flip it up yourself by pressing the Flash button on the side of the pentaprism. The behavior of the internal flash varies, depending on which Creative Zone mode you're using.

- **P/A-DEP.** In these modes, the 40D fully automates the exposure process, giving you subtle fill flash effects in daylight, and fully illuminating your subject under dimmer lighting conditions. The camera selects a shutter speed from 1/60th to 1/250th second and sets an appropriate aperture.

- **Av.** In Aperture Priority mode, you set the aperture as always, and the 40D chooses a shutter speed from 30 seconds to 1/250th second. Use this mode with care, because if the camera detects a dark background, it will use the flash to expose the main subject in the foreground, and then leave the shutter open long enough to allow the background to be exposed correctly, too. If you're not using an image-stabilized lens, you can end up with blurry ghost images even of non-moving subjects at exposures longer than 1/30th second, and if your camera is not mounted on a tripod, you'll see these blurs at exposures longer than about 1/8th second even if you are using IS. You can prevent Av mode from using shutter speeds slower than 1/250th second by using Custom Function 03, as described in Chapter 3.

- **Tv.** When using flash in Tv mode, you set the shutter speed from 30 seconds to 1/250th second, and the 40D will choose the correct aperture for the correct flash exposure. If you accidentally set the shutter speed higher than 1/250th second, the camera will reduce it to 1/250th second when you're using the flash.

- **M.** In Manual mode, you select both shutter speed (30 seconds to 1/250th second) and aperture. The camera will adjust the shutter speed to 1/250th second if you try to use a faster speed with flash. The E-TTL II system will provide the correct amount of exposure for your main subject at the aperture you've chosen (if the subject is within the flash's range, of course).

When using Creative Zone modes (or any Basic Zone mode in which flash is used), if Red-Eye Reduction is turned on in the Shooting menu (as described in

Chapter 3), the red-eye reduction lamp will illuminate for about 1.5 seconds when you press down the shutter release halfway, theoretically causing your subjects' irises to contract (if they are looking toward the camera), and thereby reducing the red-eye effect in your photograph.

Using FE Lock and Flash Exposure Compensation

If you want to lock flash exposure for a subject that is not centered in the frame, you can use the FE Lock button (*) to lock in a specific flash exposure. Just depress and hold the shutter button halfway to lock in focus, then center the viewfinder on the subject you want to correctly expose and press the * button. The preflash fires and calculates exposure, displaying the FEL (flash exposure lock) message in the viewfinder. Then, recompose your photo and press the shutter down the rest of the way to take the photo.

You can also manually add or subtract exposure to the flash exposure calculated by the 40D. Just press the Metering Mode/Flash Exposure Compensation button and spin the Main Dial to the left to dial in less exposure, or to the right to add exposure. The exposure index scale on the top panel LCD and in the viewfinder will indicate the change you've made. As with non-flash exposure compensation, the adjustment you make remains in effect for the pictures that follow, and even when you've turned the camera off, remember to cancel the flash exposure compensation adjustment by reversing the steps used to set it when you're done using it.

Using External Electronic Flash

Canon offers a broad range of accessory electronic flash units for the EOS 40D. They can be mounted to the flash accessory shoe, or used off-camera with a dedicated cord that plugs into the flash shoe to maintain full communications with the camera for all special features. They range from the Speedlite 580EX (see Figure 7.6), which can correctly expose subjects up to 24 feet away at f/11 and ISO 200, to the 220EX, which is good out to 9 feet at f/11 and ISO 200. (You'll get greater ranges at even higher ISO settings, of course.) There are also two electronic flash units specifically for specialized close-up flash photography.

Speedlite 580EX II

This flagship of the Canon accessory flash line is the most powerful unit the company offers, with a GN of 190, and a manual/automatic zoom flash head that covers the full frame of lenses from 24mm wide angle to 105mm telephoto. (There's a flip-down wide-angle diffuser that spreads the flash to cover a 14mm lens's field of view, too.) All angle specifications given by Canon refer to full-frame sensors, but this flash unit automatically converts its field of view coverage to accommodate the crop factor of the EOS 40D and the other 1.6X crop Canon dSLRs. Compared to the 580 EX it replaces, the Mark II model recycles (inaudibly—no more hum!) 20 percent faster, and has improved dust- and water-resistance so you can use it in harsher environments.

The unit offers full-swivel, 180 degrees in either direction, and has its own built-in AF assist beam and an exposure system that's compatible with the nine focus points of the 40D. Powered by economical AA-size batteries, the unit recycles in 0.1 to 6 seconds, and can squeeze 100 to 700 flashes from a set of alkaline batteries.

The 580EX automatically communicates white balance information to your camera, allowing it to automatically adjust WB to match the flash output. You can even simulate a modeling light effect: When you press the Depth-of-Field Preview button on the 40D, the 580EX emits a one-second burst of light that allows you to judge the flash effect. If you're using multiple flash units with Canon's wireless E-TTL system, this model can serve as a master flash that controls the slave units you've set up (more about this later) or function as a slave itself.

Figure 7.6 The Canon Speedlite 580EX II is the most powerful shoe-mount flash Canon offers.

It's easy to access all the features of this unit, because it has a large backlit LCD panel on the back that provides information about all flash settings. There are 14 Custom Functions that can be controlled from the flash or using the EOS 40D's menus. The built-in flash must be flipped up and any external flash attached and switched on for the menu options to become available. These functions are (the first setting is the default value):

C.Fn.-01   Automatic cancellation of Flash Exposure Bracketing (Enable/Disable)

C.Fn.-02   Flash Exposure Bracketing Sequence (Metered>Decreased>Increased Exposure or Decreased>Metered>Increased Exposure)

C.Fn.-03   Flash metering exposure (E-TTL II/E-TTL)

C.Fn.-04   Slave unit's auto power off time (60 minutes/10 minutes)

C.Fn.-05   Cancellation of slave unit auto power off by master unit (Within 1 hour/Within 8 Hours)

C.Fn.-06   Modeling Flash (Enable/Disable)

C.Fn.-07   Flash recycling on external power (Use internal and external power/Use only external power)

C.Fn.-08   Quick Flash with continuous shooting (Disable/Enable)

C.Fn.-09   Test firing with autoflash power level (1/32 power/full power)

C.Fn.-10   Modeling flash triggered by test firing button (Disable/Enable)

C.Fn.-11   Auto setting of flash coverage to match image size (Enable/Disable)

C.Fn.-12   AF-assist beam OFF (Disable/Enable)

C.Fn.-13   Flash Exposure Compensation setting button (Flash unit Select/Set with Select Dial/Select Dial only)

C.Fn.-14   Auto Power Off (On/Off)

Speedlite 430EX

This less pricey electronic flash has a GN of 141, with automatic and manual zoom coverage from 24mm to 105mm, and the same wide-angle pullout panel found on the 580EX II that covers the area of a 14mm lens on a full-frame camera, and automatic conversion to the cropped frame area of the 40D and other 1.6X crop Canon dSLRs. The 430EX also communicates white balance information with the camera, and has its own AF assist beam. Compatible with Canon's wireless E-TTL system, it makes a good slave unit, but cannot serve as a master flash. It, too, uses AA batteries, and offers recycle times of 0.1 to 3.7 seconds for 200 to 1,400 flashes, depending on subject distance.

Speedlite 220EX

Unlike the other two units, this one offers automatic operation only, and none of the fancy features of its more expensive siblings. Its 72 guide number is a little beefier than the 40D's built-in flash, making it a good choice as a low-power auxiliary flash unit. It lacks a zoomable flash head and offers fixed coverage equivalent to the field of view of a 28mm full-frame lens. Expect 250 to 1,700 flashes from a set of four AA batteries and recycle times of 0.1 to 4.5 seconds. The built-in AF assist beam is linked to the center focusing point of the 40D only.

More Advanced Lighting Techniques

As you advance in your Canon EOS 40D photography, you'll want to learn more sophisticated lighting techniques, using more than just straight-on flash, or using just a single flash unit. Entire books have been written on lighting techniques, and I've written multiple chapters on them in books of my own. I'm going to provide a quick introduction to some of the techniques you should be considering.

Diffusing and Softening the Light

Direct light can be harsh and glaring, especially if you're using the flash built into your camera, or an auxiliary flash mounted in the hot shoe and pointed directly at your subject. The first thing you should do is stop using direct light (unless you're looking for a stark, contrasty appearance as a creative effect). There are a number of simple things you can do with both continuous and flash illumination.

- **Use window light.** Light coming in a window can be soft and flattering, and a good choice for human subjects. Move your subject close enough to the window that its light provides the primary source of illumination. You might want to turn off other lights in the room, particularly to avoid mixing daylight and incandescent light. (See Figure 7.7.)

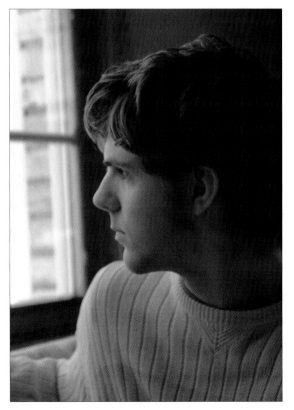

Figure 7.7
Window light makes the perfect diffuse illumination for informal soft-focus portraits like this one.

■ **Use fill light.** Your 40D's built-in flash makes a perfect fill-in light for the shadows, brightening inky depths with a kicker of illumination. (See Figure 7.8.)

Figure 7.8
The flamingo (top) was in shadow. Fill flash (bottom) brightened up the bird, while adding a little catch light to its eye.

■ **Bounce the light.** External electronic flash units mounted on the 40D usually have a swivel that allows them to be pointed up at a ceiling for a bounce light effect. You can also bounce the light off a wall. You'll want the ceiling or wall to be white or have a neutral gray color to avoid a color cast.

■ **Use reflectors.** Another way to bounce the light is to use reflectors or umbrellas that you can position yourself to provide a greater degree of control over the quantity and direction of the bounced light. Good reflectors can be pieces of foamboard, Mylar, or a reflective disk held in place by a clamp and stand. Although some expensive umbrellas and reflectors are available, spending a lot isn't necessary. A simple piece of white foamboard does the job beautifully. Umbrellas have the advantage of being compact and foldable, while providing a soft, even kind of light. They're relatively cheap, too, with a good 40-inch umbrella available for as little as $20.

■ **Use diffusers.** Sto-Fen and some other vendors offer clip-on diffusers like the one shown in Figures 7.9 and 7.10, that fit over your electronic flash head and provide a soft, flattering light. These add-ons are more portable than umbrellas and other reflectors, yet provide a nice diffuse lighting effect.

Figure 7.9 The Sto-Fen OmniBounce is a clip-on diffuser that softens the light of an external flash unit.

Figure 7.10 Softboxes use Velcro strips to attach them to third-party flash units (like the one shown) or any Canon external flash.

Using Multiple Light Sources

Once you gain control over the qualities and effects you get with a single light source, you'll want to graduate to using multiple light sources. Using several lights allows you to shape and mold the illumination of your subjects to provide a variety of effects, from backlighting to side lighting to more formal portrait lighting. You can start simply with several incandescent light sources, bounced off umbrellas or reflectors that you construct. Or you can use more flexible multiple electronic flash setups.

Effective lighting is the one element that differentiates great photography from candid or snapshot shooting. Lighting can make a mundane subject look a little more glamorous. Make subjects appear to be soft when you want a soft look, or bright and sparkly when you want a vivid look, or strong and dramatic if that's what you desire. As you might guess, having control over your lighting means that you probably can't use the lights that are already in the room. You'll need separate, discrete lighting fixtures that can be moved, aimed, brightened, and dimmed on command.

Selecting your lighting gear will depend on the type of photography you do, and the budget you have to support it. It's entirely possible for a beginning 40D photographer to create a basic, inexpensive lighting system capable of delivering high-quality results for a few hundred dollars, just as you can spend megabucks ($1,000 and up) for a sophisticated lighting system.

Basic Flash Setups

If you want to use multiple electronic flash units, the Canon Speedlites described earlier will serve admirably. The two higher-end models can be used with Canon's wireless E-TTL feature, which allows you to set up to three separate groups of flash units (several flashes can be included in each group) and trigger them using a master flash (such as the 580EX II) and the camera. Just set up one master unit (there's a switch on the unit's foot that sets it for master mode) and arrange the compatible slave units around your subject. You can set the relative power of each unit separately, thereby controlling how much of the scene's illumination comes from the main flash, and how much from the auxiliary flash units, which can be used as fill flash, background lights, or, if you're careful, to illuminate the hair of portrait subjects.

Studio Flash

If you're serious about using multiple flash units, a studio flash setup might be more practical. The traditional studio flash is a multi-part unit, consisting of a flash head that mounts on your light stand, and is tethered to an AC (or sometimes battery) power supply. A single power supply can feed two or more flash heads at a time, with separate control over the output of each head.

When they are operating off AC power, studio flash don't have to be frugal with the juice, and are often powerful enough to illuminate very large subjects or to supply lots and lots of light to smaller subjects. The output of such units is measured in watt seconds (ws), so you could purchase a 200ws, 400ws, or 800ws unit, and a power pack to match.

Their advantages include greater power output, much faster recycling, built-in modeling lamps, multiple power levels, and ruggedness that can stand up to transport, because many photographers pack up these kits and tote them around as location lighting rigs. Studio lighting kits can range in price from a few hundred dollars for a set of lights, stands, and reflectors, to thousands for a high-end lighting system complete with all the necessary accessories.

A more practical choice these days are *monolights* (see Figure 7.11), which are "all-in-one" studio lights that sell for about $200-$400. They have the flash tube, modeling light, and power supply built into a single unit that can be mounted on a light stand. Monolights are available in AC-only and battery-pack versions, although an external battery eliminates some of the advantages of having a flash with everything in one unit. They are very portable, because all you need is a case for the monolight itself, plus the stands and other accessories you want to carry along. Because these units are so popular with photographers who are not full-time professionals, the lower-cost monolights are often designed more for lighter

Figure 7.11 All-in-one "monolights" contain flash, power supply, and a modeling light in one compact package (umbrella not included).

duty than professional studio flash. That doesn't mean they aren't rugged; you'll just need to handle them with a little more care, and, perhaps, not expect them to be used eight hours a day for weeks on end. In most other respects, however, monolights are the equal of traditional studio flash units in terms of fast recycling, built-in modeling lamps, adjustable power, and so forth.

Connecting Multiple Units to Your Canon EOS 40D

Non-dedicated electronic flash units can't use the automated E-TTL II features of your EOS 40D; you'll need to calculate exposure manually, through test shots evaluated on your camera's LCD, or by using an electronic flash meter. Moreover, you don't have to connect them to the accessory shoe on top of the camera. Instead, you can use the PC/X connector on the side of the camera under the rubber cover, and a shutter speed of 1/60th second or slower.

You should be aware that older electronic flash units sometimes use a triggering voltage that is too much for your 40D to handle. You can actually damage the camera's electronics if the voltage is too high. You won't need to worry about this if you purchase brand new units from Alien Bees, Adorama, or other vendors. But if you must connect an external flash with an unknown triggering voltage, I recommend using a Wein Safe Sync (see Figure 7.12), which isolates the flash's voltage from the camera triggering circuit.

Figure 7.12

A voltage isolator can prevent frying your 40D's flash circuits if you use an older electronic flash.

Another safe way to connect external cameras is through a radio-control device, such as the transmitter/receiver set shown in Figure 7.13. It clips on the hot shoe and plugs into the 40D's PC/X connector (see Figure 7.14) and transmits a signal to a matching receiver that's connected to your flash unit. The receiver has both a PC connector of its own as well as a "monoplug" connector (it looks like a headphone plug) that links to a matching port on compatible flash units.

Figure 7.13 A radio-control device frees you from a sync cord tether between your flash and camera.

Figure 7.14 The PC/X connector allows attaching studio flash and non-dedicated flash units to the Canon EOS 40D.

Finally, some flash units have an optical slave trigger built in, or can be fitted with one, so that they fire automatically when another flash, including your camera's built-in unit, fires.

Other Lighting Accessories

Once you start working with light, you'll find there are plenty of useful accessories that can help you. Here are some of the most popular that you might want to consider.

Soft Boxes

Soft boxes are large square or rectangular devices that may resemble a square umbrella with a front cover, and produce a similar lighting effect. They can extend from a few feet square to massive boxes that stand five or six feet tall—virtually a wall of light. With a flash unit or two inside a soft box, you have a very large, semi-directional light source that's very diffuse and very flattering for portraiture and other people photography.

Soft boxes are also handy for photographing shiny objects. They not only provide a soft light, but if the box itself happens to reflect in the subject (say you're photographing a chromium toaster), the box will provide an interesting highlight that's indistinct and not distracting.

You can buy soft boxes or make your own. Some lengths of friction-fit plastic pipe and a lot of muslin cut and sewed just so may be all that you need.

Light Stands

Both electronic flash and incandescent lamps can benefit from light stands. These are lightweight, tripod-like devices (but without a swiveling or tilting head) that can be set on the floor, tabletops, or other elevated surfaces and positioned as needed. Light stands should be strong enough to support an external lighting unit, up to and including a relatively heavy flash with soft box or umbrella reflectors. You want the supports to be capable of raising the lights high enough to be effective. Look for light stands capable of extending six to seven feet high. The nine-foot units usually have larger, steadier bases, and extend high enough that you can use them as background supports. You'll be using these stands for a lifetime, so invest in good ones. I bought the light stand shown in Figure 7.15 when I was in college, and I have been using it for decades.

Figure 7.15
Light stands can hold lights, umbrellas, backdrops, and other equipment.

Backgrounds

Backgrounds can be backdrops of cloth, sheets of muslin you've painted yourself using a sponge dipped in paint, rolls of seamless paper, or any other suitable surface your mind can dream up. Backgrounds provide a complementary and non-distracting area behind subjects (especially portraits) and can be lit separately to provide contrast and separation that outlines the subject, or which helps set a mood.

I like to use plain-colored backgrounds for portraits, and white seamless backgrounds for product photography. You can usually construct these yourself from cheap materials and tape them up on the wall behind your subject, or mount them on a pole stretched between a pair of light stands.

Snoots and Barn Doors

These fit over the flash unit and direct the light at your subject. Snoots are excellent for converting a flash unit into a hair light, while barn doors give you enough control over the illumination by opening and closing their flaps that you can use another flash as a background light, with the capability of feathering the light exactly where you want it on the background. Both are shown in Figure 7.16.

Figure 7.16
Snoots and barn doors allow you to modulate the light from a flash or lamp, and they are especially useful for hair lights and background lights.

8

Downloading and Editing Your Images

Taking the picture is only half the work and, in some cases, only half the fun. After you've captured some great images and have them safely stored on your Canon EOS 40D's memory card, you'll need to transfer them from your camera and Compact Flash card to your computer, where they can be organized, fine-tuned in an image editor, and prepared for web display, printing, or some other final destination.

Fortunately, there are lots of software utilities and applications to help you do all these things. This chapter will introduce you to a few of them.

What's in the Box?

Your Canon EOS 40D came with software programs on CD for both Windows PCs and Macs. Pop the CD into your computer and it will self-install a selection of these useful applications and utilities. Manuals for all these programs are included on CD, too, but here's a summary of what you get on the EOS Digital Solutions disk:

Picture Style Editor

The Picture Style Editor, shown in Figure 8.1, allows you to create your own custom Picture Styles, or edit existing styles, including the Standard, Landscape, Faithful, and other predefined settings already present in your EOS 40D. You can change sharpness, contrast, color saturation, and color tone—and a lot more—

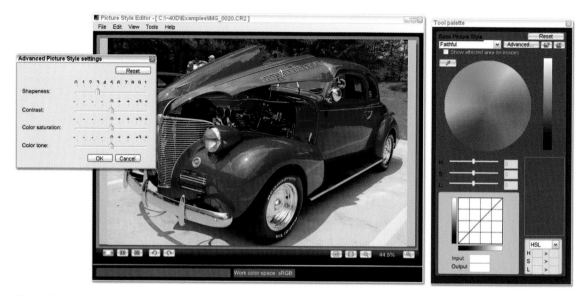

Figure 8.1 The new Picture Style Editor lets you create your own Picture Styles for use by the 40D or Digital Photo Professional when importing image files.

and then save the modifications as a .PF2 file that can be uploaded to the camera, or used by Digital Photo Professional (described later in this chapter) to modify a RAW or sRAW image as it is imported.

You can define your own color response using a color picker in a sample RAW photograph to choose a specific hue, which you can then modify using hue/saturation/luminance adjustments. The range of adjacent colors affected by your new settings can also be specified. Before/after views let you compare the Picture Style settings you've entered with standard settings using a sample image you upload.

Among the most valuable features of the Canon EOS 40D Digital SLR is its compatibility with Canon's Picture Style Editor (PSE, not to be confused with the "other" PSE—Adobe Photoshop Elements) software. With PSE, shooters can actually design the look of their photographs by inputting their own preferred style, color, and tone curves. The EOS 40D Digital SLR also ships with the latest versions of Canon's powerful software applications, including Digital Photo Professional 3.1 and EOS Utility 2.1, which now support the camera's Remote Live View and Dust Delete Data functions, as well as incorporating a broad range of additional improvements designed to improve image quality and speed up workflow. Also included are ZoomBrowser EX 5.8 and ImageBrowser 5.8 for easy browsing, viewing, printing and archiving with compatible computer operating systems, including Microsoft Windows Vista and Windows XP, as well as Mac OS X.

EOS Utility

Both Windows and Mac versions are provided for this useful program. It serves as command center for several useful functions, all available from the main control panel, shown in Figure 8.2. It includes an image downloading module that previews the images in your 40D, and can automatically copy them from the camera to either Digital Photo Professional or ZoomBrowser EX. (See Figure 8.3.)

Figure 8.2

The EOS Utility has a settings/remote shooting function that allows you to control a 40D connected to your computer with the USB cable.

Figure 8.3

The download utility allows transfer of photos from your camera or memory card to Digital Photo Professional or ZoomBrowser EX.

It also includes a camera settings/remote shooting module that allows you to link your computer with the 40D and use a dialog box (see Figure 8.4) to change camera settings and to control the camera for remote shooting. You can have access to many of the 40D's menus right from the software (see Figure 8.5). The settings feature is especially useful for changing Picture Styles quickly, while you'll find the remote shooting capabilities useful when you want to program a delay before the camera takes a picture, or do some interval (time-lapse) shooting. The updated version of the utility (Version 2.1 and later) supports the 40D's Live View and Dust Delete Data functions. It includes many preferences you can use to tailor its operation (see Figure 8.6).

Figure 8.4 The EOS Utility gives you direct control of camera settings for remote shooting.

Figure 8.5 You can access many of the EOS 40D's menu settings from your computer.

Figure 8.6 The EOS Utility five tabs' worth of preferences for modifying how it behaves.

ZoomBrowser/ImageBrowser

This is an image viewing and editing application for Windows PCs (the equivalent program for Macs is called ImageBrowser). You can organize, sort, classify, and rename files, and convert JPEG files in batches. This utility is especially useful for printing index sheets of groups of images (see Figure 8.7). It can also prepare images for e-mailing. It works with RAW Image Task for converting CR2 files to some other format, and it can be used to select images for merging using PhotoStitch.

The simple image editing facilities of ZoomBrowser allow red-eye correction, brightness/contrast and color correction, manipulating sharpness, trimming photos, and a few other functions. For more complex editing, you can transfer images directly from this application to Photoshop or another image editor.

Figure 8.7
ZoomBrowser allows organizing your images and performing simple fixes.

RAW Image Task

This is a simple RAW converter that can be used to create TIFF or JPEG images from RAW files, using the settings you specified in the camera, or tweaked settings that you choose. It can also transfer the converted files to another image editor, such as Photoshop or Photoshop Elements. These functions are available for both Windows PCs and Macs.

PhotoStitch

This Windows/Mac utility allows you to take several JPEG images and combine them to create a panorama in a single new file. You can choose the images to be merged in ZoomBrowser and then transfer them to PhotoStitch, or operate the utility as a standalone module and select the images using the standard File > Open commands (see Figure 8.8).

Digital Photo Professional

While far from a Photoshop replacement, Digital Photo Professional is a useful image editing program that helps you organize, trim, correct, and print images. You can make RAW adjustments, correct tonal curves, color tone, color saturation, sharpness, as well as brightness and contrast. Especially handy are the "recipes" that can be developed and saved so that a given set of corrections can be kept separate from the file itself, and, if desired, applied to other images (see Figure 8.9).

Figure 8.8
Panoramas are easy to create with PhotoStitch.

Figure 8.9
Digital Photo Professional will never replace Photoshop, but it has some basic image editing features.

Transferring Your Photos

While it's rewarding to capture some great images and have them ensconced in your camera, eventually you'll be transferring them to your laptop or PC, whether you're using a Windows or Macintosh machine. You have three options for image transfer: direct transfer over a USB cable, automated transfer using a card reader and transfer software such as the EOS Utility or Adobe Photoshop Elements Photo Downloader, or manual transfer using drag and drop from a memory card inserted in a card reader.

Direct-Direct Transfer/Indirect-Direct Transfer

There are some advantages to transferring photos directly from your EOS 40D to a computer. The destination computer doesn't need to have a card reader; all it requires is a USB port. So, if you have the USB cable that came with your camera, you can transfer photos to any computer that has the Canon utility software (discussed later) installed. However, direct transfer uses your 40D's internal battery power, while removing the card and transferring the photos with a card reader installed on the destination computer does not.

You can select which images are transferred to the computer, or transfer all the images, both RAW and JPEG, that are on the Compact Flash card. Canon gives you two different methods, one using the camera to direct the transfer process (I call this Direct-Direct Transfer), and one using both the camera and software on your computer to manage the transfer (I call this Indirect-Direct Transfer—for no good reason). Both methods require that you install the software furnished with the EOS 40D, including the EOS Utility and Digital Photo Professional. The CD bundled with your camera has versions of each for both Macintosh and Windows.

Direct-Direct Transfer

With this option, you don't have to fiddle with the software on your computer. The camera does all the work (so don't look for options on your computer!). You lose the ability to customize your transfer (say, to rename the files as they are deposited on your computer), but the process is fast and easy. Just follow these steps:

1. Connect the USB cable to the DIGITAL terminal on the left side of the EOS 40D (under the rubber cover), and plug the other end into a USB port on the destination computer (which you have cleverly turned on in anticipation of this transfer).

2. Turn the EOS 40D on. The Direct Transfer screen shown in Figure 8.10 will appear on the camera's LCD screen.

Figure 8.10

You can transfer images directly from your camera to the computer using the EOS 40D as the controller.

3. Choose one of these options:

   ■ **All Images** to transfer all images on the Compact Flash card.

   ■ **New Images** to transfer only images that haven't already been transferred.

   ■ **Transfer Order Images** to transfer images that have already been marked as described in the next section.

   ■ **Select and Transfer** if you'd like to choose specific images to be transferred (This option is not selectable until you've marked at least some images for transfer, as described in the next section).

   ■ **Wallpaper** to create a copy of an image that can be used as wallpaper on the desktop of your computer.

4. Press Set or the Print/Share button (which will be illuminated with a blue LED) to start the transfer.

5. Press the Menu button when finished to exit.

Your photos will be transferred automatically, and Digital Photo Professional will open to display thumbnails of the images.

Indirect-Direct Transfer

You can also use a combination of camera selections and the EOS Utility software included with your camera to transfer photos. This option allows you to choose which images to transfer, and to apply various preferences to the process, such as renaming the files to reflect their content.

Follow these steps to transfer your photos using this method:

1. Press the Menu button and jump/scroll to the Transfer order selection in the Playback menu. Press **Set**. You'll see a screen like the one in Figure 8.11.

Figure 8.11
Choose to copy a transfer order of selected images, or all images.

2. Turn the Quick Control Dial to select either **All image** (if you want to transfer every image) or **Sel. Image** (if you want to transfer the selected images). Press **Set**.

3a. If you've chosen **All image**, choose **Mark All** and press **Set**, then press the Menu button to exit this selection screen and store your choice to the Compact Flash card. Continue with Step 4.

3b. If you've selected **Sel. Image**, the transfer image selection screen appears. Use the Quick Control Dial to scroll through the available images. Press the Thumbnail/Zoom Out button to toggle between a three-image and single-image view. When an image you want to transfer is highlighted, press the Set button to add a checkmark to the box in the upper-left corner of the image. If you change your mind, press **Set** again to unmark the image. Choose all the images you want to transfer, and press **Menu** to exit this selection screen, and **Menu** again to store your choices on the Compact Flash card.

4. Connect the USB cable to the DIGITAL terminal on the left side of the EOS 40D (under the rubber cover) and plug the other end into a USB port on the destination computer.

5. Turn on the EOS 40D. The EOS Utility will appear, ready to download your photos. (If you have another program installed that also has a transfer utility, such as Adobe Photoshop Elements 6.0's Photo Downloader, it may pop up as well. Close that window if you want to use the EOS Utility.)

6. Use the controls within the EOS Utility to activate the transfer process.

Using a Card Reader and Software

You can also use a Compact Flash memory card reader and software to transfer photos and automate the process using the EOS Utility, Photoshop Elements' Photo Downloader, or the downloading program supplied with some other third-party applications. This method is more frugal in its use of your 40D's battery and can be faster if you have a speedy USB 2.0 or FireWire card reader attached to an appropriate port.

The installed software automatically remains in memory as you work, and it recognizes when a Compact Flash card is inserted in your card reader; you don't have to launch it yourself. With Photoshop Elements 6.0's Photo Downloader, you can click **Get Photos** to begin the transfer of all images immediately or choose **Advanced Dialog** to produce a dialog box like the one shown in Figure 8.12, and then select which images to download from the memory card by marking them with a check. You can select the photos you want to transfer, plus options such as Automatically Fix Red Eyes. Start the download, and a confirmation dialog box like the one in Figure 8.13 shows the progress.

Figure 8.12
With Advanced view activated, Photoshop Elements' Photo Downloader allows you to select the photos you want to copy to your computer and apply some options such as new filenames or red-eye fixes automatically.

Figure 8.13
The Photo Downloader's confirmation dialog box shows the progress as images are transferred.

Dragging and Dropping

The final way to move photos from your memory card to your computer is the old-fashioned way: manually dragging and dropping the files from one window on your computer to another. The procedure works pretty much the same whether you're using a Mac or a PC.

1. Remove the Compact Flash card from the EOS 40D and insert it in your memory card reader.

2. Using Windows Explorer, My Computer, or your Mac desktop, open the icon representing the memory card, which appears on your desktop as just another disk drive.

3. Open a second window representing the folder on your computer that you want to use as the destination for the files you are copying or moving.

4. Drag and drop the files from the Compact Flash card window to the folder on your computer. You can select individual files, press Ctrl/Command+A to select all the files, or Ctrl/Command+click to select multiple files.

Editing Your Photos

Image manipulation tasks fall into several categories. You might want to fine-tune your images, retouch them, change color balance, composite several images together, and perform other tasks we know as image editing, with a program like Adobe Photoshop, Photoshop Elements, or Corel Photo Paint.

You might want to play with the settings in RAW files, too, as you import them from their .CR2 state into an image editor. There are specialized tools expressly for tweaking RAW files, ranging from Canon's own Digital Photo Professional to Adobe Camera RAW, and PhaseOne's Capture One Pro (C1 Pro). A third type of manipulation is the specialized task of noise reduction, which can be performed within Photoshop, Adobe Camera RAW, or tools like Bibble Professional. There are also specialized tools just for noise reduction, such as Noise Ninja (also included with Bibble) and Neat Image.

Each of these utilities and applications deserves a chapter of its own, so I'm simply going to enumerate some of the most popular image editing and RAW conversion programs here and tell you a little about what they do.

Image Editors

Image editors are general-purpose photo editing applications that can do color correction, tonal modifications, retouching, combining of several images into one, and usually include tools for working with RAW files and reducing noise. So, you'll find programs like those listed here good for all-around image manipulation. The leading programs are:

Adobe Photoshop CS3/Photoshop Elements 6.0. Photoshop CS3 is the serious photographer's number one choice for image editing, and Elements is an excellent option for those who need most of Photoshop's power, but not all of its professional-level features. Unfortunately, Adobe's releases of Elements for the Macintosh tend to lag behind the Windows version. While Elements 6.0 for

Windows was introduced about a month after the EOS 40D, the Macintosh edition wasn't made available until early 2008. Both editors use the latest version of Adobe's Camera RAW plug-in, which makes it easy to adjust things like color space profiles, color depth (either 8 bits or 16 bits per color channel), image resolution, white balance, exposure, shadows, brightness, sharpness, luminance, and noise reduction. One plus with the Adobe products is that they are available in identical versions for both Windows and Macs (eventually!).

Corel Photo Paint. This is the image-editing program that is included in the popular CorelDRAW Graphics suite. Although a Mac version was available in the past, this is primarily a Windows application today. It's a full-featured photo retouching and image-editing program with selection, retouching, and painting tools for manual image manipulations, and it also includes convenient automated commands for a few common tasks, such as red-eye removal. Photo Paint accepts Photoshop plug-ins to expand its assortment of filters and special effects.

Corel Paint Shop Pro. This is a general-purpose Windows-only image editor that has gained a reputation as the "poor man's Photoshop" for providing a substantial portion of Photoshop's capabilities at a fraction of the cost. It includes a nifty set of wizard-like commands that automate common tasks, such as removing red eye and scratches, as well as filters and effects, which can be expanded with other Photoshop plug-ins.

Macromedia Fireworks. This is the image-editing program for Macs and PCs formerly from Macromedia, and now owned by Adobe, and it is most useful when used with web development and animation software like Dreamweaver and Flash. If you're using your EOS 40D images on web pages, you'll like this program's capabilities in the web graphics arena, such as banners, image maps, and rollover buttons.

Corel Painter. Here's another image-editing program from Corel for both Mac and Windows. This one's strength is in mimicking natural media, such as charcoal, pastels, and various kinds of paint. Painter includes a basic assortment of tools that you can use to edit existing images, but the program is really designed for artists to use in creating original illustrations. As a photographer, you might prefer another image editor, but if you like to paint on top of your photographic images, nothing else really does the job of Painter.

Corel Ulead PhotoImpact. Corel finally brought one of the last remaining non-Adobe image editors into its fold when it acquired PhotoImpact. This is a general-purpose photo editing program for Windows with a huge assortment of brushes for painting, retouching, and cloning in addition to the usual selection, cropping, and fill tools. If you frequently find yourself performing the same image manipulations on a number of files, you'll appreciate PhotoImpact's batch operations. Using this feature, you can select multiple image files and then apply any one of a long list of filters, enhancements, or auto-process commands to all the selected files.

RAW Utilities

Your software choices for manipulating RAW files are broader than you might think. Camera vendors always supply a utility to read their cameras' own RAW files, but sometimes, particularly with those point-and-shoot cameras that can produce RAW files, the options are fairly limited. Most Canon dSLR users have gone beyond the Canon File View Utility to something better from third parties, such as Capture1. Other vendors, such as Nikon (with its Nikon Capture), offer RAW file handling that is much more flexible and powerful.

Because in the past digital camera vendors offered RAW converters that weren't very good (Canon's File View Utility comes to mind), there is a lively market for third-party RAW utilities available at extra cost. However, the EOS Utility and Digital Photo Professional do a good job and may be all that you need.

The third-party solutions are usually available as standalone applications (often for both Windows and Macintosh platforms), as Photoshop-compatible plug-ins, or both. Because the RAW plug-ins displace Photoshop's own RAW converter, I tend to prefer to use most RAW utilities in standalone mode. That way, if I choose to open a file directly in Photoshop, it automatically opens using Photoshop's fast and easy-to-use Adobe Camera RAW (ACR) plug-in. If I have more time or need the capabilities of another converter, I can load that, open the file, and make my corrections there. Most are able to transfer the processed file directly to Photoshop even if you aren't using plug-in mode.

This section provides a quick overview of the range of RAW file handlers, so you can get a better idea of the kinds of information available with particular applications. I'm going to include both high-end and low-end RAW browsers so you can see just what is available.

Digital Photo Professional

Digital Photo Professional, introduced earlier in this chapter (see Figure 8.9), is preferred by many for Canon dSLR cameras like the EOS 40D.

DPP offers much higher-speed processing of RAW images than was available with the late, not lamented, sluggardly File Viewer Utility (as much as six times faster). Canon says this utility rivals third-party standalone and plug-in RAW converters in speed and features. It supports both Canon's original CRW format and the newer CR2 RAW format used by the 40D, along with TIFF, Exif TIFF, and JPEG.

You can save settings that include multiple adjustments and apply them to other images, and use the clever comparison mode to compare your original and edited versions of an image either side by side or within a single split image. The utility allows easy adjustment of color channels, tone curves, exposure compensation, white balance, dynamic range, brightness, contrast, color saturation, ICC Profile embedding, and assignment of monitor profiles. A new feature is the ability to continue editing images while batches of previously adjusted RAW files are rendered and saved in the background.

IrfanView

At the low (free) end of the price scale is IrfanView (see Figure 8.14), a Windows freeware program you can download at www.irfanview.com. It can read many common RAW photo formats. It's a quick way to view RAW files (just drag and drop to the IrfanView window) and make fast changes to the unprocessed file. You can crop, rotate, or correct your image, and do some cool things like swap the colors around (red for blue, blue for green, and so forth) to create false color pictures.

The price is right, and IrfanView has some valuable capabilities.

Figure 8.14

IrfanView is a freeware program that can read many RAW file formats, including the 40D's CR2 format.

Phase One Capture One Pro (C1 Pro)

If there is a Cadillac of RAW converters for Nikon and Canon digital SLR cameras, C1 Pro has to be it. This premium-priced program does everything, does it well, and does it quickly. If you can't justify the price tag of this professional-level software, there are "lite" versions for serious amateurs and cash-challenged professionals called Capture One dSLR and Capture One dSLR SE.

Aimed at photographers with high-volume needs (that would include school and portrait photographers, as well as busy commercial photographers), C1 Pro (shown in Figure 8.15) is available for both Windows and Mac OS X, and supports a broad range of Canon digital cameras. Phase One is a leading supplier of megabucks digital camera backs for medium and larger format cameras, so they really understand the needs of photographers.

The latest features include individual noise reduction controls for each image, automatic levels adjustment, a "quick develop" option that allows speedy conversion from RAW to TIFF or JPEG formats, dual-image side-by-side views for comparison purposes, and helpful grids and guides that can be superimposed over an image. Photographers concerned about copyright protection will appreciate the ability to add watermarks to the output images.

Figure 8.15
Phase One's C1 Pro is fast and sophisticated.

Bibble Pro

One of my personal favorites among third-party RAW converters is Bibble Pro (shown in Figure 8.16), which just came out with a new version as I was writing this book. It supports one of the broadest ranges of RAW file formats available (which can be handy if you find yourself with the need to convert a file from a friend or colleague's non-Canon camera), including NEF files from Nikon D1,D1x/h, D2H, D100; .CRW files from the Canon C30/D60/10D/300D; .CR2 files from the Canon EOS 40D and other newer models; .ORF files from the Olympus E10/E20/E1/C5050/C5060; .DCR files from the Kodak 720x/760/14n; .RAF files from the Fuji S2Pro; .PEF files from Pentax ISTD; .MRW files from the Minolta Maxxum; and .TIF from Canon 1D/1DS.

Figure 8.16

Bibble Pro supports a broad range of RAW file formats.

The utility supports lots of different platforms, too. It's available for Windows, Mac OS X, and, believe it or not, Linux.

Bibble works fast because it offers instantaneous previews and real-time feedback as changes are made. That's important when you have to convert many images in a short time (event photographers will know what I am talking about!). Bibble's batch-processing capabilities also let you convert large numbers of files using settings you specify without further intervention.

Its customizable interface lets you organize and edit images quickly and then output them in a variety of formats, including 16-bit TIFF and PNG. You can even create a web gallery from within Bibble. I often find myself disliking the generic filenames applied to digital images by cameras, so I really like Bibble's ability to rename batches of files using new names that you specify.

Bibble is fully color managed, which means it can support all the popular color spaces (Adobe sRGB and so forth) and use custom profiles generated by third-party color-management software. There are two editions of Bibble, a Pro version and a Lite version. Because the Pro version is reasonably priced at $129, I don't really see the need to save $60 with the Lite edition, which lacks the top-line's options for tethered shooting, embedding IPTC-compatible captions in images, and can also be used as a Photoshop plug-in (if you prefer not to work with the application in its standalone mode). Bibble Pro now incorporates Noise Ninja technology, so you can get double-duty from this valuable application.

BreezeBrowser

BreezeBrowser, shown in Figure 8.17, was long the RAW converter of choice for Canon dSLR owners who run Windows and who were dissatisfied with Canon's lame antique File Viewer Utility. It works quickly and has lots of options for converting CRW and CR2 files to other formats. You can choose to show highlights

Figure 8.17
BreezeBrowser makes converting Canon RAW files a breeze.

that will be blown out in your finished photo as flashing areas (so they can be more easily identified and corrected), use histograms to correct tones, add color profiles, auto rotate images, and adjust all those raw image parameters, such as white balance, color space, saturation, contrast, sharpening, color tone, EV compensation, and other settings.

You can also control noise reduction (choosing from low, normal, or high reduction), evaluate your changes in the live preview, and then save the file as a compressed JPEG or as either an 8-bit or 16-bit TIFF file. BreezeBrowser can also create HTML web galleries directly from your selection of images.

Photoshop CS3

The latest version of Photoshop includes a built-in RAW plug-in that is compatible with the proprietary formats of a growing number of digital cameras, both new and old. This plug-in also works with Photoshop Elements 6.0.

To open a RAW image in Photoshop CS3, just follow these steps (Elements 5.0 and 6.0 users can use much the same workflow, although fewer settings are available):

1. Transfer the RAW images from your camera to your computer's hard drive.

2. In Photoshop, choose Open from the File menu, or use Bridge.

3. Select a RAW image file. The Adobe Camera Raw plug-in will pop up, showing a preview of the image, like the one shown in Figure 8.18.

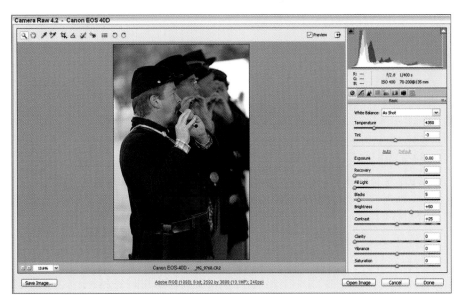

Figure 8.18
The basic ACR dialog box looks like this when processing a single image.

4. If you like, use one of the tools found in the toolbar at the top left of the dialog box. From left to right, they are:

- **Zoom.** Operates just like the Zoom tool in Photoshop.

- **Hand.** Use like the Hand tool in Photoshop.

- **White Balance.** Click an area in the image that should be neutral gray or white to set the white balance quickly.

- **Color Sampler.** Use to determine the RGB values of areas you click with this eyedropper.

- **Crop.** Pre-crops the image so that only the portion you specify is imported into Photoshop. This option saves time when you want to work on a section of a large image, and you don't need the entire file.

- **Straighten.** Drag in the preview image to define what should be a horizontal or vertical line, and ACR will realign the image to straighten it.

- **Retouch.** Used to heal or clone areas you define.

- **Red-Eye Removal.** Quickly zap red pupils in your human subjects.

- **ACR Preferences.** Produces a dialog box of Adobe Camera Raw preferences.

- **Rotate Counter-clockwise.** Rotates counter-clockwise in 90-degree increments with a click.

- **Rotate Clockwise.** Rotates clockwise in 90-degree increments with a click.

5. Using the Basic tab, you can have ACR show you red and blue highlights in the preview that indicate shadow areas that are clipped (too dark to show detail) and light areas that are blown out (too bright). Click the triangles in the upper-left corner of the histogram display (shadow clipping) and upper-right corner (highlight clipping) to toggle these indicators on or off.

6. Also in the Basic tab you can choose white balance, either from the drop-down list or by setting a color temperature and green/magenta color bias (tint) using the sliders.

7. Other sliders are available to control exposure, recovery, fill light, blacks, brightness, contrast, vibrance, and saturation. A checkbox can be marked to convert the image to grayscale.

8. Make other adjustments (described in more detail below).

9. ACR makes automatic adjustments for you. You can click Default and make the changes yourself or click the Auto link (located just above the Exposure slider) to reapply the automatic adjustments after you've made your own modifications.

10. If you've marked more than one image to be opened, the additional images appear in a "filmstrip" at the left side of the screen. You can click on each thumbnail in the filmstrip in turn and apply different settings to each.

11. Click Open Image/Open image(s) into Photoshop using the settings you've made.

The Basic tab is displayed by default when the ACR dialog box opens, and it includes most of the sliders and controls you'll need to fine-tune your image as you import it into Photoshop. These include:

- **White Balance.** Leave it As Shot or change to a value such as Daylight, Cloudy, Shade, Tungsten, Fluorescent, or Flash. If you like, you can set a custom white balance using the Temperature and Tint sliders.

- **Exposure.** This slider adjusts the overall brightness and darkness of the image.

- **Recovery.** Restores detail in the red, green, and blue color channels.

- **Fill Light.** Reconstructs detail in shadows.

- **Blacks.** Increases the number of tones represented as black in the final image, emphasizing tones in the shadow areas of the image.

- **Brightness.** This slider adjusts the brightness and darkness of an image.

- **Contrast.** Manipulates the contrast of the midtones of your image.

- **Convert to Grayscale.** Mark this box to convert the image to black and white.

- **Vibrance.** Prevents over-saturation when enriching the colors of an image.

- **Saturation.** Manipulates the richness of all colors equally, from zero saturation (gray/black, no color) at the −100 setting to double the usual saturation at the +100 setting.

Additional controls are available on the Tone Curve, Detail, HSL/Grayscale, Split Toning, Lens Corrections, Camera Calibration, and Presets tabs, shown in Figure 8.19. The Tone Curve tab can change the tonal values of your image. The Detail tab lets you adjust sharpness, luminance smoothing, and apply color noise reduction. The HSL/Grayscale tab offers controls for adjusting hue, saturation, and lightness and converting an image to black and white. Split Toning helps you colorize an image with sepia or cyanotype (blue) shades. The Lens Corrections tab has sliders to adjust for chromatic aberrations and vignetting. The Camera Calibration tab provides a way for calibrating the color corrections made in the Camera Raw plug-in. The Presets tab (not shown) is used to load settings you've stored for reuse.

Figure 8.19 More controls are available within the additional tabbed dialog boxes in Adobe Camera Raw.

9

Canon EOS 40D: Troubleshooting and Prevention

One of the nice things about modern electronic cameras like the Canon EOS 40D is that they have fewer mechanical moving parts to fail, so they are less likely to "wear out." No film transport mechanism, no wind lever or motor drive, no complicated mechanical linkages from camera to lens to physically stop down the lens aperture. Instead, tiny, reliable motors are built into each lens (and you lose the use of only that lens should something fail), and one of the few major moving parts in the camera itself is a lightweight mirror (its small size one of the advantages of the 40D's 1.6X crop factor) that flips up and down with each shot.

Of course, the camera also has a moving shutter that can fail, but the shutter is built rugged enough that you can expect it to last 100,000 shutter cycles or more. Unless you're shooting sports in continuous mode day in and day out, the shutter on your 40D is likely to last as long as you expect to use the camera.

The only other things on the camera that move are switches, dials, buttons, the flip-up electronic flash, and the door that slides open to allow you to remove and insert the Compact Flash card. Unless you're extraordinarily clumsy or unlucky and manage to bend the internal pins in the CF card slot, or give your built-in flash a good whack while it is in use, there's not a lot that can go wrong mechanically with your EOS 40D.

On the other hand, one of the chief drawbacks of modern electronic cameras is that they are modern *electronic* cameras. Your 40D is fully dependent on two different batteries. Without them, the camera can't be used. There are numerous other electrical and electronic connections in the camera (many connected to those mechanical switches and dials), and components like the color LCD and top panel status LCD that can potentially fail or suffer damage. The camera also relies on its "operating system," or *firmware*, which can be plagued by bugs that cause unexpected behavior. Luckily, electronic components are generally more reliable and trouble-free, especially when compared to their mechanical counterparts from the pre-electronic film camera days. (Film cameras of the last 10 to 20 years have had almost as many electronic features as digital cameras, but, believe it or not, there were whole generations of film cameras that had *no* electronics or batteries.)

Digital cameras have problems unique to their breed, too; the most troublesome being the need to clean the sensor of dust and grime periodically. This chapter will show you how to diagnose problems, fix some common ills, and, importantly, learn how to avoid them in the future.

Update Your Firmware

As I said, the firmware in your EOS 40D is the camera's operating system, which handles everything from menu display (including fonts, colors, and the actual entries themselves), what languages are available, and even support for specific devices and features. Upgrading the firmware to a new version makes it possible to add new features while fixing some of the bugs that sneak in. For example, a firmware update for the 20D added the ability to use the WFT-E1 wireless file transmitter.

Sometimes firmware updates happen during product development; I received my EOS 40D a few weeks after it was introduced, and it already had firmware Version 1.0.3 installed. Even more interesting are some of the "bootleg" firmware upgrades that become available from time to time. The most notorious examples apply to the original Digital Rebel, which was basically equipped with the same firmware (and much of the electronics) found in the contemporary Canon EOS 10D. Clever souls produced hacked firmware (which was unsupported by Canon) that restored to the Digital Rebel/300D features that had been disabled, such as ISO 3200 capabilities, flash exposure control, mirror lockup, and single-shot autofocus. (Quite an impressive list!)

While there are no hacked firmware upgrades for the 40D I am aware of, this model is so similar to the previous EOS 30D model that there was a tremendous amount of speculation that someone would alter the 40D's firmware so it can be loaded into the 30D. But don't hold your breath. There are some fundamental differences, particularly in hardware, between the 30D and 40D. In any case, hacked firmware can be dangerous—potentially killing your camera if the unauthorized "operating system" has bugs in it that might prevent reloading the factory firmware in case of failure.

Official Firmware

Official firmware for your 40D is given a version number that you can view by turning the power on, pressing the Menu button, and scrolling to **Firmware Ver. x.x.x** in the Set-up menu. As I write this, the current version is 1.0.3, shown in Figure 9.1. The first number in the string represents the major release number, while the second and third represent less significant upgrades and minor tweaks, respectively. Theoretically, a camera should have a firmware version number of 1.0.0 when it is introduced, but vendors have been known to do some minor fixes during testing and unveil a camera with a 1.0.1 firmware designation (or even 1.0.3 in the case of the 40D). If a given model is available long enough, as the EOS 20D was, it can evolve into significant upgrades, such as 2.0.3.

Oddly enough, sometimes an update is so minor that it doesn't earn an upgraded number. When Canon introduced firmware version 1.0.4 for the previous model 30D, it discovered that some of the characters for Simplified Chinese and

Figure 9.1
You can view the current firmware version in the Set-up menu.

Traditional Chinese languages caused problems when displayed on the LCD monitor, and issued a *new* Version 1.0.4. It recommended installing this fixed firmware for anyone experiencing the problem, even if the user had already upgraded to Version 1.0.4.

Firmware upgrades are used most frequently to fix bugs in the software, and much less frequently to add or enhance features. For example, previous firmware upgrades for Canon cameras have mended things like incorrect color temperature reporting when using specific Canon Speedlites, or problems communicating with Compact Flash cards under certain conditions. The exact changes made to the firmware are generally spelled out in the firmware release announcement. You can examine the remedies provided and decide if a given firmware patch is important to you. If not, you can usually safely wait a while before going through the bother of upgrading your firmware—at least long enough for the early adopters to report whether the bug fixes have introduced new bugs of their own. Each new firmware release incorporates the changes from previous releases, so if you skip a minor upgrade you should have no problems.

Upgrading Your Firmware

If you're computer savvy, you might wonder how your EOS 40D is able to overwrite its own operating system—that is, how can the existing firmware be used to load the new version on top of itself? It's a little like lifting yourself by reaching down and pulling up on your bootstraps. Not ironically, that's almost exactly what happens: At your command (when you start the upgrade process), the 40D shifts into a special mode in which it is no longer operating from its firmware but, rather, from a small piece of software called a *bootstrap loader*, a separate, protected software program that functions only at startup or when upgrading firmware. The loader's function is to look for firmware to launch or, when directed, to copy new firmware from a Compact Flash card to the internal memory space where the old firmware is located. Once the new firmware has replaced the old, you can turn your camera off and then on again, and the updated operating system will be loaded.

Because the loader software is small in size and limited in function, there are some restrictions on what it can do. For one thing, it recognizes only Compact Flash cards that have been formatted using an organizational system called FAT16 (which again, you might be familiar with if you're comfortable with hard disk technology). To ensure that the Compact Flash card is formatted using FAT16, you must upgrade using a CF card at least 8MB in size and no larger than 2GB, and then format the card in your camera. Memory cards that are smaller or larger might be formatted using a different FAT system (FAT12 or FAT32, respectively).

In addition, the loader software isn't set up to go hunting through your Compact Flash card for the firmware file. It looks only in the top or root directory of your card, so that's where you must copy the firmware you download. Once you've determined that a new firmware update is available for your camera and that you want to install it, just follow these steps. (If you chicken out, any Canon Service Center can install the firmware upgrade for you.)

1. Download the firmware from Canon (you'll find it in the Downloads section of the Support portion of Canon's website) and place it on your computer's hard drive. The firmware is contained in a self-extracting file for either Windows or Mac OS. It will have a name such as 40D00104.fir.

2. In your camera, format a Compact Flash card that's larger than 8MB and smaller than 2GB to ensure that the proper file system has been formatted onto the card. Choose **Format** from the Set-up menu, and initialize the card (make sure you don't have images you want to keep before you do this!).

3. You can copy the upgrade software to the card either using a CF card reader or by connecting the camera to your computer with a USB cable and using the EOS Utility application furnished with your camera (as described next).

4. Insert the CF card in the camera and then turn the camera on. Press **Menu** and scroll to **Firmware Ver. x.x.x** in the Set-up menu and press the **Set** button. Choose **OK** and press the **Set** button to begin loading the update program.

5. A final confirmation screen will appear. Press **Set** to confirm. The firmware will be updated.

6. When you see the completion screen press the **Set** button to complete the process.

7. Turn off the EOS 40D, remove the AC adapter, if used, and replace the battery. Then turn the camera on to boot up your camera with the new firmware update.

8. Be sure and reformat the card before returning it to regular use to remove the firmware software.

WARNING

Use a fully charged battery or Canon's optional ACK-E2 AC adapter kit to ensure that you'll have enough power to operate the camera for the entire upgrade. Moreover, you should not turn off the camera while your old firmware is being overwritten. Don't open the Compact Flash card door or do anything else that might disrupt operation of the 40D while the firmware is being installed.

Using Direct Camera USB Link to Copy the Software

The procedure is slightly different (and a little more automated) if you choose to transfer the firmware software to the camera through a USB linkup. Follow these instructions to get started:

1. Connect the camera (with a freshly charged battery or attached to AC Adapter ACK-E2) to the computer using the USB cable and turn it on.

2. Load the EOS Utility.

3. Click the Camera/Settings/Remote Shooting button.

4. Select the firmware update option. When the Update Firmware window appears at the bottom of the EOS Utility, choose OK.

5. Click Yes in the confirmation screen (see Figure 9.2).

6. Follow the instructions in the dialog boxes that pop up next by pressing the Set button on the camera.

Protect Your LCD

The color LCD on the back of your EOS 40D almost seems like a target for banging, scratching, and other abuse. Fortunately, it's quite rugged, and a few errant knocks are unlikely to shatter the protective cover over the LCD, and scratches won't easily mar its surface. However, if you want to be on the safe side, there are a number of protective products you can purchase to keep your LCD safe—and, in some cases, make it a little easier to view. Here's a quick overview of your options.

Figure 9.2 In the EOS Utility, choose the Camera Settings tool to update firmware.

- **Plastic overlays.** The simplest solution (although not always the cheapest), is to apply a plastic overlay sheet or "skin" cut to fit your LCD. These adhere either by static electricity or through a light adhesive coating that's even less clingy than stick-it notes. You can cut down overlays made for PDAs (although these can be pricey at up to $19.95 for a set of several sheets), or purchase overlays sold specifically for digital cameras. Vendors such as Hoodman (www.hoodmanusa.com) and Delkin (www.delkin.com) and Belkin (www.belkin.com) offer overlays of this type. These products will do a good job of shielding your 40D's LCD screen from scratches and minor impacts, but will not offer much protection from a good whack.

- **Acrylic shields.** These scratch-resistant acrylic panels, laser cut to fit your camera perfectly, are my choice as the best protection solution, and what I use on my own 40D. At about $6 each, they also happen to be the least expensive option as well. I get mine, shown in Figure 9.3, from a company called 'da Products (www.daproducts.com). They attach using strips of sticky adhesive that hold the panel flush and tight, but which allow the acrylic to be pried off and the adhesive removed easily if you want to remove or replace the shield. They don't attenuate your view of the LCD and are non-reflective enough for use under a variety of lighting conditions.

■ **Flip-up hoods.** These protectors slip on using the flanges around your 40D's eyepiece, and provide a cover that completely shields the LCD, but unfolds to provide a three-sided hood that allows viewing the LCD while minimizing the extraneous light falling on it and reducing contrast. They're sold for about $40 by Belkin and Hoodman. If you want to completely protect your LCD from hard knocks and need to view the screen outdoors in bright sunlight, there is nothing better. However, I have a couple problems with these devices. First, with the cover closed, you can't peek down after taking a shot to see what your image looks like during picture review. You must open the cap each time you want to look at the LCD. Moreover, with the hood unfolded, it's difficult to look through the viewfinder: Don't count on being able to use the viewfinder *and* the LCD at the same time with one of these hoods in place.

■ **Magnifiers.** If you look hard enough, you should be able to find an LCD magnifier that fits over the monitor panel and provides a 2X magnification. These often strap on clumsily, and serve better as a way to get an enlarged view of the LCD than as protection. Hoodman, Photodon (www.photodon.com), and other suppliers offer these specialized devices.

Figure 9.3
A tough acrylic shield, here shown with a piece of plastic containing a set of peel-off sticky strips to help it adhere to the camera, can protect your LCD from scratches.

Troubleshooting Memory Cards

Sometimes good memory cards go bad. Sometimes good photographers can treat their memory cards badly. It's possible that a memory card that works fine in one camera won't be recognized when inserted into another. In the worst case, you can have a card full of important photos and find that the card seems to be corrupted and you can't access any of them. Don't panic! If these scenarios sound horrific to you, there are lots of things you can do to prevent them from happening, and a variety of remedies available if they do occur. You'll want to take some time—before disaster strikes—to consider your options.

All Your Eggs in One Basket?

The debate about whether it's better to use one large memory card or several smaller ones has been going on since even before there were memory cards. I can remember when computer users wondered whether it was smarter to install a pair of 200MB (not *gigabyte*) hard drives in their computer, or if they should go for one of those new-fangled 500MB models. By the same token, a few years ago the user groups were full of proponents who insisted that you ought to use 128MB Compact Flash cards rather than the huge 512MB versions. Today, most of the arguments involve 4GB cards versus 2GB cards, and I expect that as prices for 8GB CF cards continue to drop, they'll find their way into the debate as well.

Why all the fuss? Are 4GB memory cards more likely to fail than 2GB cards? Are you risking all your photos if you trust your images to a larger card? Isn't it better to use several smaller cards, so that if one fails you lose only half as many photos? Or, isn't it wiser to put all your photos onto one larger card, because the more cards you use, the better your odds of misplacing or damaging one and losing at least some pictures?

In the end, the "eggs in one basket" argument boils down to statistics, and how you happen to use your 40D. The rationales can go both ways. If you have multiple smaller cards, you do increase your chances of something happening to one of them, so, arguably, you might be boosting the odds of losing some pictures. If all your images are important, the fact that you've lost 100 rather than 200 pictures isn't very comforting.

Also consider that the eggs/basket scenario assumes that the cards that are lost or damaged are always full. It's actually likely that your 4GB card might suffer a mishap when it's less than half full (indeed, it's more likely that a large card won't be completely filled before it's offloaded to a computer), so you really might not lose any more shots with a single 4GB card than with multiple 2GB cards.

If you shoot photojournalist-type pictures, you probably change memory cards when they're less than completely full in order to avoid the need to do so at a crucial moment. (When I shoot sports, my cards rarely reach 80 to 90 percent of capacity before I change them.) Using multiple smaller cards means you have to change them that more often, which can be a real pain when you're taking a lot of photos. As an example, if you use 1GB memory cards with an EOS 40D and shoot RAW+JPEG FINE, you may get only 68 pictures on the card. That's not even twice the capacity of a 36-exposure roll of film (remember those?). In my book, I prefer keeping all my eggs in one basket, and then making very sure that nothing happens to that basket.

There are only two really good reasons to justify limiting yourself to smaller memory cards when larger ones can be purchased at the same cost per-gigabyte. One of them is when every single picture is precious to you and the loss of any of them would be a disaster. If you're a wedding photographer, for example, and unlikely to be able to restage the nuptials if a memory card goes bad, you'll probably want to shoot no more pictures than you can afford to lose on a single card, and have an assistant ready to copy each card removed from the camera onto a backup hard drive or DVD onsite.

To be even more safe, you'd want to alternate cameras or have a second photographer at least partially duplicating your coverage so your shots are distributed over several memory cards simultaneously. (Strictly speaking, the safest route of all is to spend some significant bucks on Canon's Wireless File Transmitter WFT-E3/WFT-E3A, and beam the images over to a computer as you shoot them. Although pricey, this kind of accessory previously required purchasing a Canon EOS 1-Ds Mark II or Mark III camera for about $7,000 more, as it didn't work with "lesser" cameras!)

If none of these options are available to you, consider *interleaving* your shots. Say you don't shoot weddings, but you do go on vacation from time to time. Take 50 or so pictures on one card, or whatever number of images might fill about 25 percent of its capacity. Then, replace it with a different card and shoot about 25 percent of that card's available space. Repeat these steps with diligence (you'd have to be determined to go through this inconvenience), and, if you use four or more memory cards you'll find your pictures from each location scattered among the different Compact Flash cards. If you lose or damage one, you'll still have *some* pictures from all the various stops on your trip on the other cards. That's more work than I like to do (I usually tote around a portable hard disk and copy the files to the drive as I go), but it's an option.

The second good reason to use smaller memory cards is owning a camera that is incompatible with Compact Flash cards larger than 2GB. The Canon EOS 40D isn't one of these, so you're stuck with reason #1.

What Can Go Wrong?

There are lots of things that can go wrong with your memory card, but the ones that aren't caused by human stupidity are statistically very rare. Yes, a Compact Flash card's internal bit bin or controller can suddenly fail due to a manufacturing error or some inexplicable event caused by old age. However, if your CF card works for the first week or two that you own it, it should work forever. There's really not a lot that can wear out.

The typical Compact Flash card is rated for a Mean Time Between Failures of 1,000,000 hours of use. That's constant use 24/7 for more than 100 years! According to the manufacturers, they are good for 10,000 insertions in your camera, and should be able to retain their data (and that's without an external power source) for something on the order of 11 years. Of course, with the millions of CF cards in use, there are bound to be a few lemons here or there.

Those mini-hard drives with a Compact Flash form factor are a special case. They really are hard disk drives with moving parts and are subject to the same kinds of failure that their bigger siblings inside your computer can suffer. You'll find many, many happy users of mini-disks who have never had a problem, but anecdotal evidence suggests that they do fail significantly more often than solid-state memory cards. Mini-drives are slower and their price and capacity advantages are fading, so I find little reason to use them for serious work.

Given the reliability of solid-state memory, compared to magnetic memory, though, it's more likely that your Compact Flash problems will stem from something that you do. Although they're not as tiny as the SD and xD cards a few other digital SLRs use, CF cards are still small and easy to misplace if you're not careful. For that reason, it's a good idea to keep them in their original cases or a "card safe" offered by Gepe (www.gepecardsafe.com), Pelican (www.pelican.com), and others. Always placing your memory card in a case can provide protection from the second-most common mishap that befalls Compact Flash cards: the common household laundry. If you slip a memory card in a pocket, rather than a case or your camera bag often enough, sooner or later it's going to end up in the washing machine and probably the clothes dryer, too. There are plenty of reports of relieved digital camera owners who've laundered their memory cards and found they still worked fine, but it's not uncommon for such mistreatment to do some damage.

Memory cards can also be stomped on, accidentally bent, dropped into the ocean, chewed by pets, and otherwise rendered unusable in myriad ways. It's also possible to force a card into your 40D's CF card slot incorrectly if you're diligent enough, doing little damage to the card itself, but bending the connector pins in the camera, eliminating its ability to read or write to any memory card. Or, if the card is formatted in your computer with a memory card reader, your 40D may fail to recognize it. Occasionally, I've found that a memory card used in one camera would fail if used in a different camera (until I reformatted it in Windows, and then again in the camera). Every once in awhile, a card goes completely bad and—seemingly—can't be salvaged.

Another way to lose images is to do commonplace things with your CF card at an inopportune time. If you remove the card from the 40D while the camera is writing images to the card, you'll lose any photos in the buffer and may damage the file structure of the card, making it difficult or impossible to retrieve the other pictures you've taken. The same thing can happen if you remove the CF card from your computer's card reader while the computer is writing to the card (say, to erase files you've already moved to your computer). You can avoid this by *not* using your computer to erase files on a Compact Flash card but, instead, always reformatting the card in your 40D before you use it again.

What Can You Do?

Pay attention: If you're having problems, the *first* thing you should do is *stop* using that memory card. Don't take any more pictures. Don't do anything with the card until you've figured out what's wrong. Your second line of defense (your first line is to be sufficiently careful with your cards that you avoid problems in the first place) is to *do no harm* that hasn't already been done. Read the rest of this section and then, if necessary, decide on a course of action (such as using a data recovery service or software described later) before you risk damaging the data on your card further.

Now that you've calmed down, the first thing to check is whether you've actually inserted a card in the camera. If you've set the camera in the Shooting menu so that Shoot w/o card has been turned on, it's entirely possible (although not particularly plausible) that you've been snapping away with no memory card to store the pictures to, which can lead to massive disappointment later on. Of course, the No CF card message appears on the LCD when the camera is powered up, and it is superimposed on the review image after every shot, but maybe you're inattentive, aren't using picture review, or have purchased one of those LCD fold-up hoods mentioned earlier in this chapter. You can avoid all this by turning the Shoot w/o card feature off and leaving it off.

Things get more exciting when the card itself is put in jeopardy. If you lose a card, there's not a lot you can do other than take a picture of a similar card and print up some Have You Seen This Lost Flash Memory? flyers to post on utility poles all around town.

If all you care about is reusing the card, and have resigned yourself to losing the pictures, try reformatting the card in your camera. You may find that reformatting removes the corrupted data and restores your card to health. Sometimes I've had success reformatting a card in my computer using a memory card reader (this is normally a no-no because your operating system doesn't understand the needs of your 40D), and *then* reformatting again in the camera.

If your Compact Flash card is not behaving properly, and you *do* want to recover your images, things get a little more complicated. If your pictures are very valuable, either to you or to others (for example, a wedding), you can always turn to professional data recovery firms. Be prepared to pay hundreds of dollars to get your pictures back, but these pros often do an amazing job. You wouldn't want them working on your memory card on behalf of the police if you'd tried to erase some incriminating pictures. There are many firms of this type, and I've never used them myself, so I can't offer a recommendation. Use a Google search to turn up a ton of them.

THE ULTIMATE IRONY

I recently purchased an 8GB Kingston memory card that was furnished with some nifty OnTrack data recovery software. The first thing I did was format the card to make sure it was OK. Then I hunted around for the free software, only to discover it was preloaded onto the memory card. I was supposed to copy the software to my computer before using the memory card for the first time.

Fortunately, I had the OnTrack software that would reverse my dumb move, so I could retrieve the software. No, wait. I *didn't* have the software I needed to recover the software I erased. I'd reformatted it to oblivion. Chalk this one up as either the ultimate irony or Stupid Author Trick #523.

A more reasonable approach is to try special data recovery software you can install on your computer and use to attempt to resurrect your "lost" images yourself. They may not actually be gone completely. Perhaps your CF card's "table of contents" is jumbled, or only a few pictures are damaged in such a way that your camera and computer can't read some or any of the pictures on the card. Some of the available software was written specifically to reconstruct lost pictures, while other utilities are more general-purpose applications that can be used with any media, including floppy disks and hard disk drives. They have names like OnTrack, Photo Rescue 2, Digital Image Recovery, MediaRecover, Image Recall, and the aptly named Recover My Photos. You'll find a comprehensive list and links, as well as some picture-recovery tips at www.ultimateslr.com/memory-card-recovery.php.

DIMINISHING RETURNS

Usually, once you've recovered any images on a Compact Flash card, reformatted it, and returned it to service, it will function reliably for the rest of its useful life. However, if you find a particular card going bad more than once, you'll almost certainly want to stop using it forever. See if you can get it replaced by the manufacturer, if you can, but, in the case of CF card failures, the third time is never the charm.

Replacing Your Clock Battery

In addition to the large rechargeable lithium ion battery that provides most of the power for your Canon EOS 40D, a second battery nestles in the same compartment to provide enough power to retain your current settings and preferences, as well as the local date and time. This coin-sized *clock* battery is a long-lived C2016 3-volt lithium manganese dioxide cell, located in a slide-out carrier near the hinge of the battery door, shown in Figure 9.4.

Figure 9.4
Your clock battery is located in the main battery compartment.

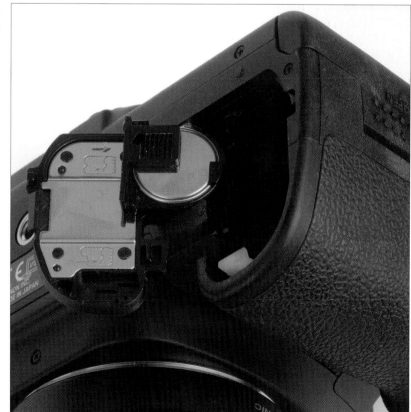

You may never notice this battery at all, as it may last several years without needing replacement. Your first clue will be when you switch on your 40D and a message on your LCD asks you to input the date and time. That's your cue to trot down to the electronics store and buy a new one.

To install it, just slide out the plastic carrier and remove the old battery. There is a pair of plastic tabs holding it in tight, and you may have to pry one up to free the dead cell. Then slide the new one in and return the carrier to your camera. When you turn the power on, you'll need to enter the current date and time. Don't forget to choose OK when finished; if you simply exit the settings screen by pressing the Menu button, your time setting will not be entered. You'll also have to re-enter other camera and user settings that the EOS 40D normally "remembers."

Clean Your Sensor

There's no avoiding dust. No matter how careful you are, some of it is going to settle on your camera and on the mounts of your lenses, eventually making its way inside your camera to settle in the mirror chamber. As you take photos, the mirror flipping up and down causes the dust to become airborne and eventually make its way past the shutter curtain to come to rest on the anti-aliasing filter atop your sensor. There, dust and particles can show up in every single picture you take at a small enough aperture to bring the foreign matter into sharp focus. No matter how careful you are and how cleanly you work, eventually you will get some of this dust on your camera's sensor. Some say that CMOS sensors, like the one found in the EOS 40D, "attract" less dust than CCD sensors found in cameras from other vendors. But even the cleanest-working photographers using Canon cameras are far from immune.

Fortunately, one of the EOS 40D's most useful new features is the automatic sensor cleaning system that reduces or eliminates the need to clean your camera's sensor manually. As I mentioned in Chapter 3, Canon has applied anti-static coatings to the sensor and other portions of the camera body interior to counter charge build-ups that attract dust. A separate filter over the sensor vibrates ultrasonically each time the 40D is powered on or off, shaking loose any dust.

Although the automatic sensor cleaning feature operates when you power the camera up or turn it off, you can activate it at any time. Choose **Sensor Cleaning** from the Set-up 2 menu, and select **Clean now**. If you'd rather turn the feature on or off, choose **Auto cleaning** instead, and then choose either **Enable** or **Disable** with the Quick Control Dial. Press **Set**, then press the Menu button to return to the Set-up 2 menu. (See Figure 9.5.)

Figure 9.5

You can activate automatic sensor cleaning immediately or enable/disable the feature.

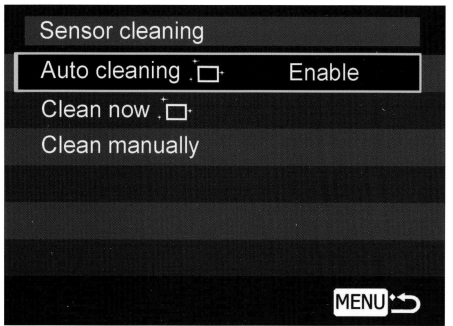

If some dust does collect on your sensor, you can often map it out of your images (making it invisible) using software techniques with the Dust Delete Data feature in the Shooting Menu 2. Operation of this feature is described in Chapter 3. Of course, even with the EOS 40D's automatic sensor cleaning/dust resistance features, you may still be required to manually clean your sensor from time to time. This section explains the phenomenon and provides some tips on minimizing dust and eliminating it when it begins to affect your shots. I also cover this subject in my book, *Digital SLR Pro Secrets*, with complete instructions for constructing your own sensor cleaning tools. However, I'll provide a condensed version here of some of the information in that book, because sensor dust and sensor cleaning are two of the most contentious subjects Canon EOS 40D owners have to deal with.

Dust the FAQs, Ma'am.

Here are some of the most frequently asked questions about sensor dust issues.

Q. I see tiny specks in my viewfinder. Do I have dust on my sensor?

A. If you see sharp, well-defined specks, they are clinging to the underside of your focus screen and not on your sensor. They have absolutely no effect on your photographs, and are merely annoying or distracting.

Q. **I can see dust on my mirror. How can I remove it?**

A. Like focus-screen dust, any artifacts that have settled on your mirror won't affect your photos. You can often remove dust on the mirror or focus screen with a bulb air blower, which will loosen it and whisk it away. Stubborn dust on the focus screen can sometimes be gently flicked away with a soft brush designed for cleaning lenses. I don't recommend brushing the mirror or touching it in any way. The mirror is a special front-surface-silvered optical device (unlike conventional mirrors, which are silvered on the back side of a piece of glass or plastic) and can be easily scratched. If you can't blow mirror dust off, it's best to just forget about it. You can't see it in the viewfinder, anyway.

Q. **I see a bright spot in the same place in all of my photos. Is that sensor dust?**

A. You've probably got either a "hot" pixel or one that is permanently "stuck" due to a defect in the sensor. A hot pixel is one that shows up as a bright spot only during long exposures as the sensor warms. A pixel stuck in the "on" position always appears in the image. Both show up as bright red, green, or blue pixels, usually surrounded by a small cluster of other improperly illuminated pixels, caused by the camera's interpolating the hot or stuck pixel into its surroundings, as shown in Figure 9.6. A stuck pixel can also be permanently dark. Either kind is likely to show up when they contrast with plain, evenly colored areas of your image.

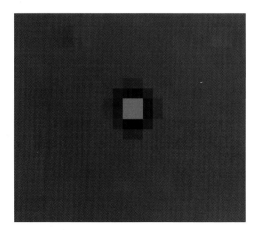

Figure 9.6 A stuck pixel is surrounded by improperly interpolated pixels created by the 40D's demosaicing algorithm.

Finding one or two hot or stuck pixels in your sensor is unfortunately fairly common. They can be "removed" by telling the 40D to ignore them through a simple process called *pixel mapping*. If the bad pixels become bothersome, Canon can remap your sensor's pixels with a quick trip to a service center.

Bad pixels can also show up on your camera's color LCD panel, but, unless they are abundant, the wisest course is to just ignore them.

Q. **I see an irregular out-of-focus blob in the same place in my photos. Is that sensor dust?**

A. Yes. Sensor contaminants can take the form of tiny spots, larger blobs, or even curvy lines if they are caused by minuscule fibers that have settled on the sensor. They'll appear out of focus because they aren't actually on the sensor surface but, rather, a fraction of a millimeter above it on the filter that covers the sensor. The smaller the f/stop used, the more in-focus the dust becomes. At large apertures, it may not be visible at all.

Q. I never see any dust on my sensor. What's all the fuss about?

A. Those who never have dust problems with their EOS 40D fall into one of four categories: those for whom the camera's automatic dust removal features are working well; those who seldom change their lenses and have clean working habits that minimize the amount of dust that invades their cameras in the first place; those who simply don't notice the dust (often because they don't shoot many macro photos or other pictures using the small f/stops that makes dust evident in their images); and those who are very, very lucky.

Identifying and Dealing with Dust

Sensor dust is less of a problem than it might be because it shows up only under certain circumstances. Indeed, you might have dust on your sensor right now and not be aware if it. The dust doesn't actually settle on the sensor itself, but, rather, on a protective filter a very tiny distance above the sensor, subjecting it to the phenomenon of *depth-of-focus*. Depth-of-focus is the distance the focal plane can be moved and still render an object in sharp focus. At f/2.8 to f/5.6 or even smaller, sensor dust, particularly if small, is likely to be outside the range of depth-of-focus and blur into an unnoticeable dot.

However, if you're shooting at f/16 to f/22 or smaller, those dust motes suddenly pop into focus. Forget about trying to spot them by peering directly at your sensor with the shutter open and the lens removed. The period at the end of this sentence, about .33mm in diameter, could block a group of pixels measuring 40 × 40 pixels (160 pixels in all!). Dust spots that are even smaller than that can easily show up in your images if you're shooting large, empty areas that are light colored. Dust motes are most likely to show up in the sky, as in Figure 9.7, or in white backgrounds of your seamless product shots and are less likely to be a problem in images that contain lots of dark areas and detail.

To see if you have dust on your sensor, take a few test shots of a plain, blank surface (such as a piece of paper or a cloudless sky) at small f/stops, such as f/22, and a few wide open. Open Photoshop, copy several shots into a single document in separate layers, then flip back and forth between layers to see if any spots you see are present in all layers. You may have to boost contrast and sharpness to make the dust easier to spot.

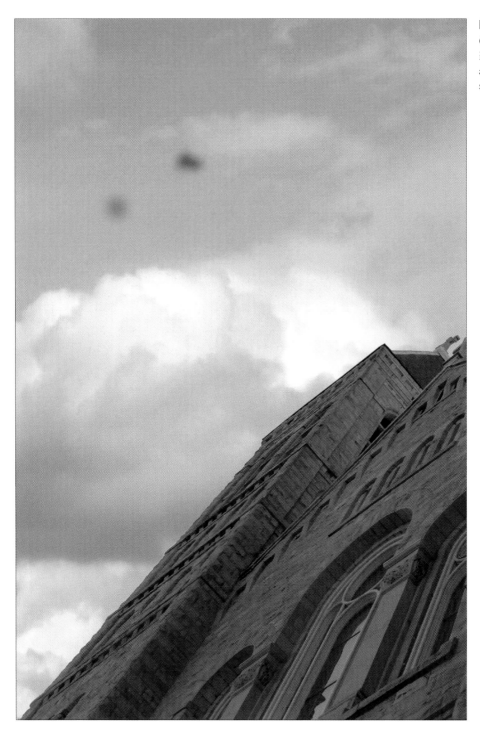

Figure 9.7
Only the dust spots in the sky are apparent in this shot.

Avoiding Dust

Of course, the easiest way to protect your sensor from dust is to prevent it from settling on the sensor in the first place. Some Canon lenses come with rubberized seals around the lens mounts that help keep dust from infiltrating, but you'll find that dust will still find a way to get inside. Here are my stock tips for eliminating the problem before it begins.

- **Clean environment.** Avoid working in dusty areas if you can do so. Hah! Serious photographers will take this one with a grain of salt, because it usually makes sense to go where the pictures are. Only a few of us are so paranoid about sensor dust (considering that it is so easily removed) that we'll avoid moderately grimy locations just to protect something that is, when you get down to it, just a tool. If you find a great picture opportunity at a raging fire, during a sandstorm, or while surrounded by dust clouds, you might hesitate to take the picture, but, with a little caution (don't remove your lens in these situations, and clean the camera afterwards!) you can still shoot. However, it still makes sense to store your camera in a clean environment. One place cameras and lenses pick up a lot of dust is inside a camera bag. Clean your bag from time to time, and you can avoid problems.

- **Clean lenses.** There are a few paranoid types that avoid swapping lenses in order to minimize the chance of dust getting inside their cameras. It makes more sense just to use a blower or brush to dust off the rear lens mount of the replacement lens first, so you won't be introducing dust into your camera simply by attaching a new, dusty lens. Do this before you remove the lens from your camera, and then avoid stirring up dust before making the exchange.

- **Work fast.** Minimize the time your camera is lens-less and exposed to dust. That means having your replacement lens ready and dusted off, and a place to set down the old lens as soon as it is removed, so you can quickly attach the new lens.

- **Let gravity help you.** Face the camera downward when the lens is detached so any dust in the mirror box will tend to fall away from the sensor. Turn your back to any breezes, indoor forced air vents, fans, or other sources of dust to minimize infiltration.

- **Protect the lens you just removed.** Once you've attached the new lens, quickly put the end cap on the one you just removed to reduce the dust that might fall on it.

- **Clean out the vestibule.** From time to time, remove the lens while in a relatively dust-free environment and use a blower bulb like the one shown in Figure 9.8 (*not* compressed air or a vacuum hose) to clean out the mirror box area. A blower bulb is generally safer than a can of compressed air, or a strong positive/negative airflow, which can tend to drive dust further into nooks and crannies.

- **Be prepared.** If you're embarking on an important shooting session, it's a good idea to clean your sensor *now*, rather than come home with hundreds or thousands of images with dust spots caused by flecks that were sitting on your sensor before you even started. Before I left on my recent trip to Spain, I put both cameras I was taking through a rigid cleaning regimen, figuring they could remain dust-free for a measly 10 days. I even left my bulky blower bulb at home. It was a big mistake, but my intentions were good.

Figure 9.8 Use a robust air bulb like the Giottos Rocket for cleaning your sensor.

- **Clone out existing spots in your image editor.** Photoshop and other editors have a clone tool or healing brush you can use to copy pixels from surrounding areas over the dust spot or dead pixel. This process can be tedious, especially if you have lots of dust spots and/or lots of images to be corrected. The advantage is that this sort of manual fix-it probably will do the least damage to the rest of your photo. Only the cloned pixels will be affected.

- **Use filtration in your image editor.** A semi-smart filter like Photoshop's Dust & Scratches filter can remove dust and other artifacts by selectively blurring areas that the plug-in decides represent dust spots. This method can work well if you have many dust spots, because you won't need to patch them manually. However, any automated method like this has the possibility of blurring areas of your image that you didn't intend to soften.

Sensor Cleaning

Those new to the concept of sensor dust actually hesitate before deciding to clean their camera themselves. Isn't it a better idea to pack up your 40D and send it to a Canon service center so their crack technical staff can do the job for you? Or, at the very least, shouldn't you let the friendly folks at your local camera store do it?

Of course, if you choose to let someone else clean your sensor, they will be using methods that are more or less identical to the techniques you would use yourself. None of these techniques are difficult, and the only difference between their cleaning and your cleaning is that they might have done it dozens or hundreds of times. If you're careful, you can do just as good a job.

Of course vendors like Canon won't tell you this, but it's not because they don't trust you. It's not that difficult for a real goofball to mess up their camera by hurrying or taking a shortcut. Perhaps the person uses the "Bulb" method of holding the shutter open and a finger slips, allowing the shutter curtain to close on top of a sensor cleaning brush. Or, someone tries to clean the sensor using masking tape, and ends up with goo all over its surface. If Canon recommended *any* method that's mildly risky, someone would do it wrong, and then the company would face lawsuits from those who'd contend they did it exactly in the way the vendor suggested, so the ruined camera is not their fault. If you visit Canon's website, you'll find this recommendation: "If the image sensor needs cleaning, we recommend having it cleaned at a Canon service center, as it is a very delicate component."

You can see that vendors like Canon tend to be conservative in their recommendations, and, in doing so, make it seem as if sensor cleaning is more daunting and dangerous than it really is. Some vendors recommend only dust-off cleaning, through the use of reasonably gentle blasts of air, while condemning more serious scrubbing with swabs and cleaning fluids. However, these cleaning kits for the exact types of cleaning they recommended against are for sale in Japan only, where, apparently, your average photographer is more dexterous than those of us in the rest of the world. These kits are similar to those used by official repair staff to clean your sensor if you decide to send your camera in for a dust-up.

As I noted, sensors can be affected by dust particles that are much smaller than you might be able to spot visually on the surface of your lens. The filters that cover sensors tend to be fairly hard compared to optical glass. Cleaning the 22.5mm × 15mm sensor in your Canon 40D within the tight confines of the mirror box can call for a steady hand and careful touch. If your sensor's filter becomes scratched through inept cleaning, you can't simply remove it yourself and replace it with a new one.

There are four basic kinds of cleaning processes that can be used to remove dusty and sticky stuff that settles on your dSLR's sensor. All of these must be performed with the shutter locked open. I'll describe these methods and provide instructions for locking the shutter later in this section.

- **Air cleaning.** This process involves squirting blasts of air inside your camera with the shutter locked open. This works well for dust that's not clinging stubbornly to your sensor.

- **Brushing.** A soft, very fine brush is passed across the surface of the sensor's filter, dislodging mildly persistent dust particles and sweeping them off the imager.

- **Liquid cleaning.** A soft swab dipped in a cleaning solution such as ethanol is used to wipe the sensor filter, removing more obstinate particles.

■ **Tape cleaning.** There are some who get good results by applying a special form of tape to the surface of their sensor. When the tape is peeled off, all the dust goes with it. Supposedly. I'd be remiss if I didn't point out right now that this form of cleaning is somewhat controversial; the other three methods are much more widely accepted. Now that Canon has equipped the front-sensor filter with a special anti-dust coating, I wouldn't chance damaging that coating by using any kind of adhesive tape.

Placing the Shutter in the Locked and Fully Upright Position for Landing

Make sure you're using a fully charged battery or the optional AC Adapter Kit ACK-E2.

1. Remove the lens from the camera and then turn the camera on.

2. Set the EOS 40D to any one of the Creative Zone exposure modes. The shutter cannot be locked open in any of the Basic Zone modes.

3. You'll find the **Clean Manually** menu choice in the Set-up 2 menu under **Sensor Cleaning** (see Figure 9.5). Press the **Set** button.

4. Select **OK** and press **Set** again. The mirror will flip up and the shutter will open.

5. Use one of the methods described below to remove dust and grime from your sensor. Be careful not to accidentally switch the power off or open the Compact Flash card or battery compartment doors as you work. If that happens, the shutter may be damaged if it closes onto your cleaning tool.

6. When you're finished, turn the power off, replace your lens, and switch your camera back on.

Air Cleaning

Your first attempts at cleaning your sensor should always involve gentle blasts of air. Many times, you'll be able to dislodge dust spots, which will fall off the sensor and, with luck, out of the mirror box. Attempt one of the other methods only when you've already tried air cleaning and it didn't remove all the dust.

Here are some tips for doing air cleaning:

■ **Use a clean, powerful air bulb.** Your best bet is bulb cleaners designed for the job, like the Giottos Rocket shown in Figure 9.8. Smaller bulbs, like those air bulbs with a brush attached sometimes sold for lens cleaning or weak nasal aspirators may not provide sufficient air or a strong enough blast to do much good.

- **Hold the EOS 40D upside down.** Then look up into the mirror box as you squirt your air blasts, increasing the odds that gravity will help pull the expelled dust downward, away from the sensor. You may have to use some imagination in positioning yourself.

- **Never use air canisters.** The propellant inside these cans can permanently coat your sensor if you tilt the can while spraying. It's not worth taking a chance.

- **Avoid air compressors.** Super-strong blasts of air are likely to force dust under the sensor filter.

Figure 9.9 A proper brush is required for dusting off your sensor.

Brush Cleaning

If your dust is a little more stubborn and can't be dislodged by air alone, you may want to try a brush, charged with static electricity, which can pick off dust spots by electrical attraction. One good, but expensive, option is the Sensor Brush sold at www.visibledust.com. A cheaper version can be purchased at www.copperhillimages.com. You need a 16mm version, like the one shown in Figure 9.9, which can be stroked across the short dimension of your 40D's sensor.

Ordinary artist's brushes are much too coarse and stiff and have fibers that are tangled or can come loose and settle on your sensor. A good sensor brush's fibers are resilient and described as "thinner than a human hair." Moreover, the brush has a wooden handle that reduces the risk of static sparks. Check out my *Digital SLR Pro Secrets* book if you want to make a sensor brush (or sensor swabs) yourself.

Brush cleaning is done with a dry brush by gently swiping the surface of the sensor filter with the tip. The dust particles are attracted to the brush particles and cling to them. You should clean the brush with compressed air before and after each use, and store it in an appropriate air-tight container between applications to keep it clean and dust-free. Although these special brushes are expensive, one should last you a long time.

Liquid Cleaning

Unfortunately, you'll often encounter really stubborn dust spots that can't be removed with a blast of air or flick of a brush. These spots may be combined with some grease or a liquid that causes them to stick to the sensor filter's surface. In such cases, liquid cleaning with a swab may be necessary. During my first clumsy attempts to clean my own sensor, I accidentally got my blower bulb tip too close to the sensor, and some sort of deposit from the tip of the bulb ended up on the sensor. I panicked until I discovered that liquid cleaning did a good job of removing whatever it was that took up residence on my sensor.

You can make your own swabs out of pieces of plastic (some use fast food restaurant knives, with the tip cut at an angle to the proper size) covered with a soft cloth or Pec-Pad, as shown in Figures 9.10 and 9.11. However, if you've got the bucks to spend, you can't go wrong with good-quality commercial sensor cleaning swabs, such as those sold by Photographic Solutions, Inc. (www.photosol.com/swabproduct.htm).

Figure 9.10
You can make your own sensor swab from a plastic knife that's been truncated.

Figure 9.11
Carefully wrap a Pec-Pad around the swab.

You want a sturdy swab that won't bend or break so you can apply gentle pressure to the swab as you wipe the sensor surface. Use the swab with methanol (as pure as you can get it, particularly medical grade; other ingredients can leave a residue), or the Eclipse solution also sold by Photographic Solutions. Eclipse (see Figure 9.12) is actually quite a bit purer than even medical-grade methanol. A couple drops of solution should be enough, unless you have a spot that's extremely difficult to remove. In that case, you may need to use extra solution on the swab to help "soak" the dirt off.

Once you overcome your nervousness at touching your 40D's sensor, the process is easy. You'll wipe continuously with the swab in one direction, then flip it over and wipe in the other direction. Figure 9.13 shows a swab being lowered past the lens mount down to the sensor. You need to completely wipe the entire surface; otherwise, you may end up depositing the dust you collect at the far end of your stroke. Wipe; don't rub.

Figure 9.12 Pure Eclipse solution makes the best sensor cleaning liquid.

Figure 9.13 Carefully swab off the dust.

Tape Cleaning

There are people who absolutely swear by the tape method of sensor cleaning. The concept seems totally wacky, and I have never tried it personally, so I can't say with certainty that it either does or does not work. In the interest of completeness, I'm including it here. I can't give you a recommendation, so if you have problems, please don't blame me. The EOS 40D is still too new to have generated any reports of users accidentally damaging the anti-dust coating on the sensor filter using this method.

Tape cleaning works by applying a layer of Scotch Brand Magic Tape to the sensor. This is a minimally sticky tape that some of the tape cleaning proponents claim contains no adhesive. I did check this out with 3M, and can say that Magic Tape certainly *does* contain an adhesive. The question is whether the adhesive comes off when you peel back the tape, taking any dust spots on your sensor with it. The folks who love this method claim there is no residue. There have been reports from those who don't like the method that residue is left behind. This is all anecdotal evidence, so you're pretty much on your own in making the decision whether to try out the tape cleaning method.

Upgrading to the Canon EOS 40D

Are you ready to upgrade to the Canon EOS 40D from an EOS 30D, or, even, an earlier model like the 20D or 10D? Perhaps you own a Digital Rebel in one of its incarnations, and lust for some of the muscular new features found in the 40D. You might even be a die-hard film camera owner with an earlier EOS model, and lots of EF lenses that will work great on the new Canon 40D. If you fall into any one of these categories, you probably want to know "what's new?" before you make the jump.

This appendix provides the information you need. I've placed it here at the end of the book, rather than as the first chapter because not every reader will need this upgrading advice. In addition, most of the descriptions of features and differences between the 40D and its immediate predecessor the 30D also appear in the main body of the text. I've collected all the relevant comparisons and considerations here in one place, where they are readily accessible for those considering an upgrade.

Is This Trip Really Necessary?

If you're a photographic old-timer (say, with more than 10 years' experience under your belt), you may feel that upgrades have become more frequent (and urgent) than they were in the relatively recent past. One of the most dramatic differences between film and digital single lens reflexes (other than the sensor) is that the rapid advances in digital technology have made upgrading a way of life for many. Even though it's been half a decade since the first Digital Rebel made the dSLR practical and affordable for the masses, the digital SLR is still in its infancy, and subject to rapid change and improvements. Resolution has leaped from the 3.1MP of the EOS D30 (*not* 30D!), introduced in April, 2000, to the 10.1MP of the 40D and astounding 21.1MP boasted by the Canon EOS-1Ds Mark III. Features like faster frame rates, Live View, improved high-ISO performance, and enhanced custom features have made upgrading on a 24- to 36-month schedule positively alluring.

In contrast, the improvements in *35mm film* SLRs over the past 70-plus years (the first successful 35mm SLR, the Kine-Exakta, was introduced in 1936) have been much slower in coming. Film cameras represented a relatively stable technology prior to the electronic/digital age. Gaps of five to ten years between introduction of major new features (like through-the-lens metering, automatic exposure, and autofocus) were common. Indeed, film cameras I purchased at the beginning of my career were, other than a few mechanical refinements, virtually state-of-the-art 15 years later, and I used them professionally for an even longer period. In the film era, upgrading to improve your results often meant buying a better lens, using a newer film, or replacing a camera that had simply worn out from use. *Obsolescence* was a term that was rarely applied to cameras using film.

That started to change when manufacturers like Canon began replacing mechanical components with improved and more versatile electronic counterparts. Recent film cameras share a lot of technology with their digital counterparts. A modern high-end film camera, like the Canon EOS-1v shoots at 10 frames per second, has a 45-point autofocus system (which evaluates the image on a CMOS sensor!), offers AI One Shot or AI Servo modes, and *six* metering modes (Evaluative, Partial, Center Spot, Spot, Multi-Spot, and Center-Weighted). You'll find Programmed, Shutter Priority, Aperture Priority, and Depth-of-Field exposure modes, just like the EOS 40D, along with automatic exposure bracketing, and many other features that new photographers have come to associate with "digital" cameras. If a wholesale transition to digital SLRs hadn't taken place, more frequent upgrading might have become part of the film SLR regimen, as well.

So, take heart. Upgrading to the Canon EOS 40D from whatever you were using before isn't an annoying necessity of the digital world. It's an *opportunity* that you can choose to embrace or to ignore. Your Canon EOS 30D or Digital Rebel XTi (see Figure A.1) still is capable of taking the exact same photos as it did the day you bought it. Neither is obsolete. But if you want or need a particular feature that the 40D has, the upgrade path is open to you. Your current camera can serve as an excellent backup, or it can be passed along to a friend or family member who will treasure it as much as you have.

Figure A.1 The Canon EOS 40D (left) is a logical upgrade from either the 30D (center), Digital Rebel XTi (right), or perhaps some other camera.

Canon EOS 40D vs. EOS 30D...et al.

The EOS 40D is a significant upgrade from its predecessor, the 30D. The differences between the two models are much greater than was evident between the 20D and 30D, as the 30D was considered a minor upgrade, at best. So, I'm going to start with a quick review of the improvements that were available when the EOS 30D was introduced in February, 2006:

- **Resolution:** The Canon 30D offered 8.2MP of resolution, compared to the 20D's 6.3MP.

- **Metering:** The 30D added a 3.5 percent image area "Spot" metering mode to the 20D's complement of 35-Zone Evaluative, Partial, and Center-Weighted average metering. The 30D offered both luminance (brightness) and RGB histograms for evaluating exposure; the 20D had only a luminance histogram.

- **ISO:** The 30D's ISO settings could be adjusted in 1/3 stop increments, rather than full stops.

- **Image Parameters:** Where the 20D had two default parameter settings, plus three "user" parameter custom settings, and black-and-white, the 30D switched to a new Picture Style system with Standard, Portrait, Landscape, Neutral, Faithful, Monochrome, and three user-definable styles. In addition, the parameters themselves were given a new, wider range of adjustability.

- **LCD:** The 30D's back-panel LCD was significantly improved at 2.5-inches and 230,000 pixels, compared to the 20D's tiny 1.8-inch LCD with just 118,000 pixels.

- **Shooting speed:** While the 20D had a single continuous shooting speed of 5 frames per second (for up to 23 JPEG or 6 RAW images), the 30D had both 5 fps and 3 fps, and could suck 30 JPEG or 11 RAW images into its buffer in one burst.

- **Playback:** The 30D's Jump button would leap ahead 10 images, just like the 20D, but also could jump 100 images, or advance by date. Images could be magnified during picture review, if desired.

- **Minor differences:** The 30D had 19 Custom Functions and a choice of 53 settings (instead of 18 custom functions and 50 settings), was 2mm thicker, and 37 grams heavier.

Other than the upgrade from 6.3MP to 8.2MP, the easier-to-view LCD, and the more flexible image parameters settings, the EOS 30D offered little that made it a compelling upgrade from the earlier 20D model. Even so, the 30D was especially successful among first-time digital SLR buyers, and those upgrading from earlier Digital Rebel models. The desire for a "real" upgrade hit a fever pitch when the Digital Rebel XTi was introduced, which, at 10.2 MP, had better resolution than the 30D, and leap-frogged its older sibling with features like automatic sensor cleaning and the simpler tabbed menu settings (rather than the continuous scrolling menu of the 30D) found in other Canon EOS digital cameras.

The EOS 40D satisfied most of those who awaited its arrival. It blended a satisfying array of brand-new capabilities with a list of enhancements to existing features. Overall, the 40D is a worthy successor to the 20D and 30D. The next three sections will summarize the changes found in the new camera.

All-New Features

The Canon EOS 40D, like its predecessors, is a mid-level digital SLR, intended as a step up from entry-level cameras like the Digital Rebels. It's suitable for more advanced photographers, especially those who can live without the most advanced features found in Canon's "pro" line, such as the Canon EOS-1D Mark III or Canon EOS-1Ds Mark III. Even so, the 40D is upscale enough to excite any avid photographer. For example, its magnesium alloy body and weatherproofing of the battery compartment and Compact Flash doors make it eminently suitable for professional use, too, either as a main camera or back up. In fact, because the 40D accepts both EF-style lenses and newer "digital only" EF-S lenses (the "pro" cameras can use only the EF-class optics), it offers a tad more flexibility in lens choice. (Chapter 6 has more detail about lenses.)

Here's a quick rundown of the cool new capabilities found in the EOS 40D that the older 30D lacks.

- **Live View:** Those who want or need to be able to see what the sensor is seeing in real-time while composing an image will be pleased with the Live View feature. With Live View, the mirror is elevated (blanking the optical viewfinder), and the shutter opens, allowing the LCD to display a preview image, with optional grid lines if you want them. Although the 40D defaults to manual focusing when Live View is active, you can access autofocus by pressing the AF-ON button, which lowers the mirror to focus the image, then lifts it again to restore Live View. You can magnify the live image 5X or 10X, and access a quieter mirror cycle for "silent shooting" mode. I think Live View is most practical when the 40D is mounted on a tripod, but it works much better than I expected.

- **Dust Reduction:** As with all the other current models in the Canon product line, the 40D features an anti-static coating on the low-pass (anti-aliasing) filter that covers the sensor, and a piezoelectric element that vibrates this filter to remove any stubborn dust and particles when the camera is turned on or off. You can also perform this anti-dust operation manually, or turn it off entirely.

- **DIGIC III processor:** The Live View feature is actually part of the new DIGIC III digital image processor included in the 40D. The processor uses a 14-bit (rather than 12-bit) analog-to-digital converter that is faster and provides an improved dynamic range.

- **sRAW format:** The sRAW format is a reduced-size RAW file containing about 25% of the pixels found in a full-size .CR2 file. This option is useful when you need an image with less resolution, but still want the ability to tweak the camera settings when importing the photo into your image editor. You can shoot sRAW only, or sRAW+Large, Medium, or Small JPEGs using Fine or Normal JPEG compression. Don't be confused by the fact that regular RAW can also be captured at the same time as Large, Medium, and Small resolution JPEGs; in all cases the conventional RAW file is a full resolution image, regardless of the resolution of the accompanying JPEG. If you want your RAW file to match your JPEG file in resolution, use sRAW instead.

- **Interchangeable focus screens:** The EOS 40D now can be fitted with three different focus screens. These include the EF-A Standard Precision Matte screen furnished with the camera, and two optional screens: the EF-S Super Precision Matte, which has a coarser texture that makes manual focus easier; and the EF-D Precision Matte with Grid, which has embedded grid lines that make it easier to align vertical and horizontal subjects. (See Figure A.2.)

Figure A.2
The Canon EOS 40D can be fitted with three different focus screens, including this one with an alignment grid.

- **Main LCD shooting information display:** While the 40D retains the top panel information status display, it now features an optional info display on the color LCD, with much of the same data and settings in a format that may be easier to see and interpret, especially when the camera is mounted high on a tripod, so that the top panel LCD is not visible.

- **Mode dial camera user settings:** The mode dial includes C1, C2, and C3 positions that can be programmed to contain three different groups of settings. If you want to file away your 40D's current shooting parameters, you can pop into a menu and define those settings in one of the three user slots.

- **AF-ON button:** While the 40D can be set so that pressing the shutter release halfway locks in autofocus and exposure, the new AF-ON button simplifies separating the two functions. A Custom Function option can set the AF-ON button to either *start* or *stop* autofocus, as well as work in conjunction with the shutter release in several different combinations of metering/autofocus activation. This feature adds extra flexibility when shooting fast-moving action, as you can choose when to lock in focus and/or exposure. If you don't like the position of the AF-ON button, the 40D lets you move the function to another button.

■ **New Picture Style button:** If you want to switch among Picture Styles quickly (or often), press this button to produce the Picture Style menu on the color LCD. You can choose or define a Picture Style with the exact sharpness, color, and tonal settings you want.

■ **Picture Style Editor Software:** Creating custom Picture Styles has become even easier with this software utility that allows you to define the settings you want and upload them to the EOS 40D.

Physical Improvements

If the array of new features isn't enough to excite you, the Canon EOS 40D bristles with a tempting group of physical enhancements that make this camera much better than its predecessor. This next section explains what the most important improvements are, and why they are significant.

■ **10.1 MP vs. 8.2 MP:** Unless you make huge prints or crop images severely, you're not likely to notice the difference in megapixels. But the jump to10.1 MP does bring the 40D in line with all its competition, as well as its junior sibling, the Digital Rebel XTi.

■ **Faster continuous shooting:** If you don't believe that 6.5 frames per second is a significant improvement over the maximum 5 fps available with the EOS 30D, try firing the two cameras side by side at their maximum burst rates. Shazam! The speedier frame rate helps reduce the chances that the critical moment will occur *between* frames, which is common with fast-moving sports like baseball or track. The 40D also has *slower* continuous shooting, with an optional 3 fps mode to capture more leisurely activities. The slower rate is especially handy when you don't want to sort through a gazillion shots to find the best one.

■ **Larger buffer:** A larger internal memory buffer works hand-in-hand with the 40D's continuous shooting modes to allow you to capture more frames in a row before shooting halts to allow the camera to store the pictures you've already taken on the Compact Flash card. The camera can grab as many as 75 JPEG Large/Fine shots in one burst, compared to just 30 shots with the EOS 30D.

■ **Improved Focus Points:** While the EOS 40D has a nine-point focus system that's similar to the 30D's, all nine function as more sensitive cross-type focus sensors with lenses having a maximum aperture of f/5.6 or larger. Cross sensors detect focus in both horizontal and vertical directions, rather than in just a single orientation. The 40D's center focus point has additional sensitivity when used with lenses having an f/2.8 or larger aperture.

- **Expanded metering sensitivity:** The EOS 40D's exposure metering range extends from 0.0 to 20 EV, rather than EV 1.0 to 20 (with the 30D). In very dim light, the 40D can calculate an exposure of eight seconds at f/2.8 at ISO 100 (EV 0.0), while the 30D won't register an exposure of less than four seconds at f/2.8 at ISO 100 (EV 1.0). Both cameras can meter at brightness levels up to 1/4,000 second at f/16 at ISO 100 (EV 20), which is roughly 32 times as much illumination as you can expect under bright daylight.

- **Improved view:** The viewfinder magnification of the EOS 40D has been boosted to 95 percent of life-size (when using a focal length of 50mm focused at infinity). The eyepoint (the distance you can move your eye from the viewfinder and still see the entire image) has increased from 20mm to 22mm. All in all, the 40D's view is bigger and easier to see.

- **Larger LCD screen:** The improved 3-inch LCD screen can be viewed from a wider viewing angle. The resolution remains the same as in the 30D at 230,000 pixels. Half an inch diagonally may not sound like much, but the new screen is a huge enhancement (see Figure A.3).

- **Improved mirror action:** The EOS 40D uses a motor to raise and lower its mirror (instead of springs), producing a much quieter mechanism, and a significantly shorter blackout time between shots. The motor's action is damped, too, which creates less vibration from potential mirror bounce. In addition, the mirror can be locked up for single or multiple exposures.

Figure A.3　The Canon EOS 40D (left) has a 3-inch LCD, compared to the 2.5-inch LCD on the EOS 30D (right).

- **Wireless and USB Device Support:** Would you like to store your photos to an external USB storage device, such as a hard drive or flash drive? All you need is the Canon WFT-E3/E3A wireless transmitter/vertical grip and suitable media. The transmitter/grip's internal PB-511 battery can power a solid-state flash drive, but if you connect a hard drive it will need its own power supply. If you're shooting in a studio, the accessory grip can connect to your 11b or 11g wireless network, or wired Ethernet connection. Expect to pay a considerable fraction of what you laid out for your EOS 40D camera body for this useful add-on.

- **More road-hugging weight:** Okay, this isn't exactly an advantage, but the EOS 40D is a full 2mm wider and taller (about a tenth of an inch in either direction), and 37 grams (about 1.3 ounces) heavier.

Operational Enhancements

The Canon EOS 40D has lots of operational improvements, too. These enhancements make the camera easier to use and add capabilities. Here are the key changes you'll want to know about.

- **Added viewfinder information:** The current ISO setting is visible in the viewfinder when the display is active, and an icon has been added that shows when the 40D has been set to black-and-white mode.

- **Flexible Auto ISO function:** The EOS 30D can adjust ISO for you automatically within the range of ISO 100 to 400, but only in Auto and other Basic Zone modes. The 40D has additional options: It can choose between ISO 100-800 in certain Basic Zone modes (Auto, Landscape, Close-up, Night Portrait, and Flash Off); adjust between ISO 400-800 in Sports mode; lock sensitivity at ISO 100 in Portrait or ISO 400 in Tv (Shutter Priority) and Manual modes; and roam among ISO 400-800 in Program, Av (Aperture Priority), and A-DEP modes. (A-DEP is the mode both cameras use to choose an f/stop that will provide the best depth-of-field for shots with several subjects at varying distances.)

- **Tabbed menus:** Instead of the long scrolling menu system found in the EOS 30D and earlier models in this line, the 40D now uses tabbed menus like those found in the EOS 1D and (even) the Digital Rebels. Moreover, each tab displays only a single screen of options, so you won't need to scroll down past the bottom entry to see all the menu items on a tab.

- **Five more Custom Functions:** The EOS 40D has 24 Custom Functions (instead of 19), with some new functions replacing three of the C. Fn. settings of the 30D that were moved into the Flash Control entry in the Set-up 2 menu. The C. Fn settings are divided into four separate screens (numbered I, II, III, and IV) instead of crowding them into a single page. Most of the new Custom Functions deal with new and improved features, such as the behavior of Live View and the AF-ON button, and which interchangeable focus screen is installed.

- **Extra noise reduction:** Custom Function II 02 includes an option for specifying additional high ISO noise reduction.

- **Tilt!:** The EOS 40D's in-camera trimming function allows you to rotate the cropping rectangle up to plus or minus ten degrees in 0.5 degree increments, allowing you to correct tilted images. The capability is especially useful if you plan to print photos directly from the camera, rather than fixing them in an image editor first.

- **No more lost photos!:** The 40D will warn you if you open the Compact Flash card door to change cards while photos are still being written to the buffer, and count down the remaining images on the LCD screen until it's safe to proceed. The EOS 30D had this nasty habit of shutting down instantly when the card door was opened, losing all remaining images in the buffer.

With a little planning, your upgrade to the Canon EOS 40D from whatever camera you're using now (or, even, no camera at all) can proceed smoothly.

Glossary

Here are some terms you might encounter while reading this book or working with your Canon EOS 40D.

additive primary colors The red, green, and blue hues, which are used alone or in combinations to create all other colors that you capture with a digital camera, view on a computer monitor, or work with in an image-editing program, such as Photoshop. *See also* CMYK color model.

A-DEP A Creative Zone mode that analyzes your scene and attempts to choose an f/stop and focus distance that will allow all the important subjects to be in sharp focus.

Adobe RGB One of two color space choices offered by the Canon EOS 40D. Adobe RGB is an expanded color space useful for commercial and professional printing, and it can reproduce a larger number of colors. Canon recommends against using this color space if your images will be displayed primarily on your computer screen or output by your personal printer. *See also* sRGB.

AE/FE A control on the Canon EOS 40D that lets you lock the current autoexposure or flash exposure settings prior to taking a picture, freeing you from having to hold the shutter release partially depressed.

AEB Automatic exposure bracketing, which takes a series of pictures at different exposure increments to improve the chances of producing one picture that is perfectly exposed.

ambient lighting Diffuse, non-directional lighting that doesn't appear to come from a specific source but, rather, bounces off walls, ceilings, and other objects in the scene when a picture is taken.

analog/digital converter The electronics built into a camera that convert the analog information captured by the 40D's sensor into digital bits that can be stored as an image bitmap.

angle of view The area of a scene that a lens can capture, determined by the focal length of the lens. Lenses with a shorter focal length have a wider angle of view than lenses with a longer focal length.

anti-alias A process that smoothes the look of rough edges in images (called *jaggies* or *staircasing*) by adding partially transparent pixels along the boundaries of diagonal lines that are merged into a smoother line by our eyes. *See also* jaggies.

Aperture Preferred A camera setting that allows you to specify the lens opening or f/stop that you want to use, with the camera selecting the required shutter speed automatically based on its light-meter reading. This setting is represented by the abbreviation Av on the 40D's Mode Dial. *See also* Shutter Preferred.

artifact A type of noise in an image, or an unintentional image component produced in error by a digital camera during processing, usually caused by the JPEG compression process in digital cameras.

aspect ratio The proportions of an image as printed, displayed on a monitor, or captured by a digital camera.

autofocus A camera setting that allows the Canon EOS 40D to choose the correct focus distance for you, based on the contrast of an image (the image will be at maximum contrast when in sharp focus). The camera can be set for One Shot (generically known as *Single Autofocus*, in which the lens is not focused until the shutter release is partially depressed), AI Servo (known as *Continuous Autofocus*, in which the lens refocuses constantly as you frame and reframe the image), or AI/AF, which allows the camera to switch back and forth between One Shot and AI Servo based on subject movement.

backlighting A lighting effect produced when the main light source is located behind the subject. Backlighting can be used to create a silhouette effect, or to illuminate translucent objects. *See also* front lighting *and* sidelighting.

barrel distortion A lens defect that causes straight lines at the top or side edges of an image to bow outward into a barrel shape. *See also* pincushion distortion.

Basic Zone modes The EOS 40D's automated shooting modes, such as Landscape and Sports, which select lens opening, shutter, speed, exposure, and other parameters for you.

blooming An image distortion caused when a photosite in an image sensor has absorbed all the photons it can handle so that additional photons reaching that pixel overflow to affect surrounding pixels, producing unwanted brightness and overexposure around the edges of objects.

blur To soften an image or part of an image by throwing it out of focus, or by allowing it to become soft due to subject or camera motion. Blur can also be applied in an image-editing program.

bokeh A term derived from the Japanese word for blur, which describes the aesthetic qualities of the out-of-focus parts of an image. Some lenses produce "good" bokeh and others offer "bad" bokeh. Some lenses produce uniformly illuminated out-of-focus discs. Others produce a disc that has a bright edge and a dark center, producing a "doughnut" effect, which is the worst from a bokeh standpoint. Lenses that generate a bright center that fades to a darker edge are favored, because their bokeh allows the circle of confusion to blend more smoothly with the surroundings. The bokeh characteristics of a lens are most important when you're using selective focus (say, when shooting a portrait) to deemphasize the background, or when shallow depth-of-field is a given because you're working with a macro lens, with a long telephoto, or with a wide-open aperture. *See also* circle of confusion.

bounce lighting Light bounced off a reflector, including ceiling and walls, to provide a soft, natural-looking light.

bracketing Taking a series of photographs of the same subject at different settings, including exposure and white balance, to help ensure that one setting will be the correct one. The Canon EOS 40D allows you to choose the order in which bracketed settings are applied, or bracket sequence.

buffer The digital camera's internal memory where an image is stored immediately after it is taken until it can be written to the camera's non-volatile (semi-permanent) memory or a memory card.

burst mode The digital camera's equivalent of the film camera's motor drive, used to take multiple shots within a short period of time, each stored in a memory buffer temporarily before writing it to the media.

calibration A process used to correct for the differences in the output of a printer or monitor when compared to the original image. Once you've calibrated your scanner, monitor, and/or your image editor, the images you see on the screen more closely represent what you'll get from your printer, even though calibration is never perfect.

Camera Raw A plug-in included with Photoshop and Photoshop Elements that can manipulate the unprocessed images captured by digital cameras, such as the Canon EOS 40D's .CR2 files. The latest versions of this module can also work with JPEG and TIFF images.

camera shake Movement of the camera, aggravated by slower shutter speeds, which produces a blurred image.

CCD *See* charge-coupled device (CCD).

center-weighted meter A light-measuring device that emphasizes the area in the middle of the frame when calculating the correct exposure for an image. *See also* spot meter.

charge-coupled device (CCD) A type of solid-state sensor that captures the image used in scanners and digital cameras.

chromatic aberration   An image defect, often seen as green or purple fringing around the edges of an object, caused by a lens failing to focus all colors of a light source at the same point. *See also* fringing.

circle of confusion   A term applied to the fuzzy discs produced when a point of light is out of focus. The circle of confusion is not a fixed size. The viewing distance and amount of enlargement of the image determine whether we see a particular spot on the image as a point or as a disc. *See also* bokeh.

close-up lens   A lens add-on that allows you to take pictures at a distance that is less than the closest-focusing distance of the lens alone.

CMOS   *See* complementary metal-oxide semiconductor (CMOS).

CMYK color model   A way of defining all possible colors in percentages of cyan, magenta, yellow, and frequently, black. (K represents black, to differentiate it from blue in the RGB color model.) Black is added to improve rendition of shadow detail. CMYK is commonly used for printing (both on press and with your inkjet or laser color printer).

color correction   Changing the relative amounts of color in an image to produce a desired effect, typically a more accurate representation of those colors. Color correction can fix faulty color balance in the original image, or compensate for the deficiencies of the inks used to reproduce the image.

complementary metal-oxide semiconductor (CMOS)   A method for manufacturing a type of solid-state sensor that captures the image, used in scanners and digital cameras such as those from Canon.

compression   Reducing the size of a file by encoding using fewer bits of information to represent the original. Some compression schemes, such as JPEG, operate by discarding some image information, while others, such as RAW, preserve all the detail in the original, discarding only redundant data.

Continuous Autofocus   An automatic focusing setting (AI Servo) in which the camera constantly refocuses the image as you frame the picture. This setting is often the best choice for moving subjects. *See also* Single Autofocus.

contrast   The range between the lightest and darkest tones in an image. A high-contrast image is one in which the shades fall at the extremes of the range between white and black. In a low-contrast image, the tones are closer together.

Custom Functions   A group of 24 different settings you can make to specify how the EOS 40D behaves, such as the function of certain controls, electronic flash features, and other customizable attributes.

dedicated flash   An electronic flash unit, such as the Canon 580EX Speedlight, designed to work with the automatic exposure features of a specific camera.

depth-of-field A distance range in a photograph in which all included portions of an image are at least acceptably sharp. With the Canon EOS 40D, you can see the available depth-of-field at the taking aperture by pressing the Depth-of-Field Preview button, or estimate the range by viewing the depth-of-field scale found on many lenses.

diaphragm An adjustable component, similar to the iris in the human eye, which can open and close to provide specific-sized lens openings, or f/stops and thus control the amount of light reaching the sensor or film.

diffuse lighting Soft, low-contrast lighting.

digital processing chip A solid-state device found in digital cameras (such as the EOS 40D's DIGIC III module) that's in charge of applying the image algorithms to the raw picture data prior to storage on the memory card.

diopter A value used to represent the magnification power of a lens, calculated as the reciprocal of a lens's focal length (in meters). Diopters are most often used to represent the optical correction used in a viewfinder to adjust for limitations of the photographer's eyesight, and to describe the magnification of a close-up lens attachment.

equivalent focal length A digital camera's focal length translated into the corresponding values for a 35mm film camera. This value can be calculated for lenses used with the Canon EOS 40D by multiplying by 1.6.

evaluative metering A system of exposure calculation that looks at many different segments of an image to determine the brightest and darkest portions. The EOS 40D uses this system with an Evaluative Metering mode.

exchangeable image file format (Exif) Developed to standardize the exchange of image data between hardware devices and software. A variation on JPEG, Exif is used by most digital cameras, and includes information such as the date and time a photo was taken, the camera settings, resolution, amount of compression, and other data.

Exif *See* exchangeable image file format (Exif).

exposure The amount of light allowed to reach the film or sensor, determined by the intensity of the light, the amount admitted by the iris of the lens, and the length of time determined by the shutter speed.

exposure values (EV) EV settings are a way of adding or decreasing exposure without the need to reference f/stops or shutter speeds. For example, if you tell your camera to add +1EV, it will provide twice as much exposure, either by using a larger f/stop, slower shutter speed, or both.

fill lighting In photography, lighting used to illuminate shadows. Reflectors or additional incandescent lighting or electronic flash can be used to brighten shadows. One common technique outdoors is to use the camera's flash as a fill.

filter In photography, a device that fits over the lens, changing the light in some way. In image editing, a feature that changes the pixels in an image to produce blurring, sharpening, and other special effects. Photoshop includes several interesting filter effects, including Lens Blur and Photo Filters.

flash sync The timing mechanism that insures that an internal or external electronic flash fires at the correct time during the exposure cycle. A digital SLR's flash sync speed is the highest shutter speed that can be used with flash, ordinarily 1/250th of a second with the Canon EOS 40D. *See also* front-curtain sync *and* rear-curtain sync.

focal plane An imaginary line, perpendicular to the optical access, which passes through the focal point forming a plane of sharp focus when the lens is set at infinity. A focal plane indicator is etched into the Canon EOS 40D at the left side of the pentaprism, next to the Mode Dial.

focal length The distance between the film and the optical center of the lens when the lens is focused on infinity, usually measured in millimeters.

focus tracking The ability of the automatic focus feature of a camera to change focus as the distance between the subject and the camera changes. One type of focus tracking is *predictive,* in which the mechanism anticipates the motion of the object being focused on, and adjusts the focus to suit.

format To erase a memory card and prepare it to accept files.

fringing A chromatic aberration that produces fringes of color around the edges of subjects, caused by a lens's inability to focus the various wavelengths of light onto the same spot. Purple fringing is especially troublesome with backlit images.

front-curtain sync (first-curtain sync) The default kind of electronic flash synchronization technique, originally associated with focal plane shutters, which consists of a traveling set of curtains, including a *front curtain* (1st Curtain in the 40D's menus), which opens to reveal the film or sensor, and a *rear curtain* (2nd Curtain in the 40D's menus), which follows at a distance determined by shutter speed to conceal the film or sensor at the conclusion of the exposure. For a flash picture to be taken, the entire sensor must be exposed at one time to the brief flash exposure, so the image is exposed after the front curtain has reached the other side of the focal plane, but before the rear curtain begins to move. Front-curtain sync causes the flash to fire at the beginning of this period when the shutter is completely open, in the instant that the first curtain of the focal plane shutter finishes its movement across the film or sensor plane. With slow shutter speeds, this feature can create a blur effect from the ambient light, showing as patterns that follow a moving subject with the subject shown sharply frozen at the beginning of the blur trail. *See also* rear-curtain sync.

front lighting Illumination that comes from the direction of the camera. *See also* backlighting *and* sidelighting.

f/stop The relative size of the lens aperture, which helps determine both exposure and depth-of-field. The larger the f/stop number, the smaller the f/stop itself.

graduated filter A lens attachment with variable density or color from one edge to another. A graduated neutral density filter, for example, can be oriented so the neutral density portion is concentrated at the top of the lens's view with the less dense or clear portion at the bottom, thus reducing the amount of light from a very bright sky while not interfering with the exposure of the landscape in the foreground. Graduated filters can also be split into several color sections to provide a color gradient between portions of the image.

gray card A piece of cardboard or other material with a standardized 18-percent reflectance. Gray cards can be used as a reference for determining correct exposure or for setting white balance.

high contrast A wide range of density in a print, negative, or other image.

highlights The brightest parts of an image containing detail.

high-speed sync A method for synching Canon EX-series flashes at shutter speeds higher than 1/250th second by increasing the flash duration to match the speed of the focal plane shutter.

histogram A kind of chart showing the relationship of tones in an image using a series of 256 vertical bars, one for each brightness level. A histogram chart, such as the one the Canon EOS 40D can display during picture review, typically looks like a curve with one or more slopes and peaks, depending on how many highlight, midtone, and shadow tones are present in the image. The 40D can also display separate histograms for the red, green, and blue channels of an image.

hot shoe A mount on top of a camera used to hold an electronic flash, while providing an electrical connection between the flash and the camera.

hyperfocal distance A point of focus where everything from half that distance to infinity appears to be acceptably sharp. For example, if your lens has a hyperfocal distance of four feet, everything from two feet to infinity would be sharp. The hyperfocal distance varies by the lens and the aperture in use. If you know you'll be making a grab shot without warning, sometimes it is useful to turn off your camera's automatic focus, and set the lens to infinity, or, better yet, the hyperfocal distance. Then, you can snap off a quick picture without having to wait for the lag that occurs with most digital cameras as their autofocus locks in.

image rotation A feature that senses whether a picture was taken in horizontal or vertical orientation. That information is embedded in the picture file so that the camera and compatible software applications can automatically display the image in the correct orientation.

image stabilization A technology that compensates for camera shake, usually by adjusting the position of the camera sensor or lens elements in response to movements of the camera.

incident light Light falling on a surface.

International Organization for Standardization (ISO) A governing body that provides standards used to represent film speed, or the equivalent sensitivity of a digital camera's sensor. Digital camera sensitivity is expressed in ISO settings.

interpolation A technique digital cameras, scanners, and image editors use to create new pixels required whenever you resize or change the resolution of an image based on the values of surrounding pixels. Devices such as scanners and digital cameras can also use interpolation to create pixels in addition to those actually captured, thereby increasing the apparent resolution or color information in an image.

ISO *See* International Organization for Standardization (ISO).

ISO Expansion A Custom Function that extends the EOS 40D's available ISO settings to ISO 3200 (H).

jaggies Staircasing effect of lines that are not perfectly horizontal or vertical, caused by pixels that are too large to represent the line accurately. *See also* anti-alias.

JPEG A file "lossy" format (short for Joint Photographic Experts Group) that supports 24-bit color and reduces file sizes by selectively discarding image data. Digital cameras generally use JPEG compression to pack more images onto memory cards. You can select how much compression is used (and, therefore, how much information is thrown away) by selecting from among the Standard, Fine, Super Fine, or other quality settings offered by your camera. *See also* RAW.

Kelvin (K) A unit of measure based on the absolute temperature scale in which absolute zero is zero; it's used to describe the color of continuous-spectrum light sources and applied when setting white balance. For example, daylight has a color temperature of about 5,500K, and a tungsten lamp has a temperature of about 3,400K.

lag time The interval between when the shutter is pressed and when the picture is actually taken. During that span, the camera may be automatically focusing and calculating exposure. With digital SLRs like the Canon EOS 40D, lag time is generally very short; with non-dSLRs, the elapsed time easily can be one second or more.

latitude The range of camera exposures that produces acceptable images with a particular digital sensor or film.

lens flare A feature of conventional photography that is both a bane and a creative outlet. It is an effect produced by the reflection of light internally among elements of an optical lens. Bright light sources within or just outside the field of view cause lens flare. Flare can be reduced by the use of coatings on the lens elements or with the use of lens hoods. Photographers sometimes use the effect as a creative technique, and Photoshop includes a filter that lets you add lens flare at your whim.

lighting ratio The proportional relationship between the amount of light falling on the subject from the main light and other lights, expressed in a ratio, such as 3:1.

Live View The ability of some Canon cameras to provide a real-time preview image, as seen by the sensor, on the rear panel color LCD, achieved by flipping up the mirror and opening the shutter.

lossless compression An image-compression scheme, such as TIFF, that preserves all image detail. When the image is decompressed, it is identical to the original version.

lossy compression An image-compression scheme, such as JPEG, that creates smaller files by discarding image information, which can affect image quality.

macro lens A lens that provides continuous focusing from infinity to extreme close-ups, often to a reproduction ratio of 1:2 (half life-size) or 1:1 (life-size).

maximum burst The number of frames that can be exposed at the current settings until the buffer fills.

midtones Parts of an image with tones of an intermediate value, usually in the 25 to 75 percent brightness range. Many image-editing features allow you to manipulate midtones independently from the highlights and shadows.

mirror lock-up The ability of the 40D to retract its mirror to reduce vibration prior to taking the photo and to allow access to the sensor for cleaning.

neutral color A color in which red, green, and blue are present in equal amounts, producing a gray.

neutral density filter A gray camera filter reduces the amount of light entering the camera without affecting the colors.

noise In an image, pixels with randomly distributed color values. Noise in digital photographs tends to be the product of low-light conditions and long exposures, particularly when you've set your camera to a higher ISO rating than normal.

noise reduction A technology used to cut down on the amount of random information in a digital picture, usually caused by long exposures at increased sensitivity ratings. In the Canon EOS 40D, noise reduction is automatically applied for long exposures, and it involves the camera automatically taking a second blank/dark exposure at the same settings that contain only noise, and then using the blank photo's information to cancel out the noise in the original picture. Although the process is very quick, it does double the amount of time required to take the photo.

normal lens   A lens that makes the image in a photograph appear in a perspective that is like that of the original scene, typically with a field of view of roughly 45 degrees.

overexposure   A condition in which too much light reaches the film or sensor, producing a dense negative or a very bright/light print, slide, or digital image.

pincushion distortion   A type of lens distortion in which lines at the top and side edges of an image are bent inward, producing an effect that looks like a pincushion. *See also* barrel distortion.

polarizing filter   A filter that forces light, which normally vibrates in all directions, to vibrate only in a single plane, reducing or removing the specular reflections from the surface of objects.

RAW   An image file format, such as the CR2 format in the Canon EOS 40D, which includes all the unprocessed information captured by the camera after conversion to digital form. RAW files are very large compared to JPEG files and must be processed by a special program such as Canon Digital Photo Pro or Adobe's Camera RAW filter after being downloaded from the camera.

rear-curtain sync (second-curtain sync)   An optional kind of electronic flash synchronization technique, originally associated with focal plane shutters, which consists of a traveling set of curtains, including a *front (first) curtain* (which opens to reveal the film or sensor) and a *rear (second) curtain* (which follows at a distance determined by shutter speed to conceal the film or sensor at the conclusion of the exposure). For a flash picture to be taken, the entire sensor must be exposed at one time to the brief flash exposure, so the image is exposed after the front curtain has reached the other side of the focal plane, but before the rear curtain begins to move. Rear-curtain sync causes the flash to fire at the end of the exposure, an instant before the second or rear curtain of the focal plane shutter begins to move. With slow shutter speeds, this feature can create a blur effect from the ambient light, showing as patterns that follow a moving subject with the subject shown sharply frozen at the end of the blur trail. If you were shooting a photo of The Flash, the superhero would appear sharp, with a ghostly trail behind him. *See also* front-curtain sync (first-curtain sync).

red-eye   An effect from flash photography that appears to make a person's eyes glow red, or an animal's yellow or green. It's caused by light bouncing from the retina of the eye and is most pronounced in dim illumination (when the irises are wide open) and when the electronic flash is close to the lens and, therefore, prone to reflect directly back. Image editors can fix red-eye through cloning other pixels over the offending red or orange ones.

RGB color A color model that represents the three colors—red, green, and blue—used by devices such as scanners or monitors to reproduce color. Photoshop works in RGB mode by default, and even displays CMYK images by converting them to RGB.

saturation The purity of color; the amount by which a pure color is diluted with white or gray.

selective focus Choosing a lens opening that produces a shallow depth-of-field. Usually this is used to isolate a subject in portraits, close-ups, and other types of images, by causing most other elements in the scene to be blurred.

self-timer A mechanism that delays the opening of the shutter for some seconds after the release has been operated.

sensitivity A measure of the degree of response of a film or sensor to light, measured using the ISO setting.

shadow The darkest part of an image, represented on a digital image by pixels with low numeric values.

sharpening Increasing the apparent sharpness of an image by boosting the contrast between adjacent pixels that form an edge.

shutter In a conventional film camera, the shutter is a mechanism consisting of blades, a curtain, a plate, or some other movable cover that controls the time during which light reaches the film. Digital cameras, including the Canon EOS 40D, use actual mechanical shutters for the slower shutter speeds (less than 1/250th second) and an electronic shutter for higher speeds.

Shutter Preferred An exposure mode, represented by the letters Tv (Time Value) on the 40D's Mode Dial, in which you set the shutter speed and the camera determines the appropriate f/stop. *See also* Aperture Preferred.

sidelighting Applying illumination from the left or right sides of the camera. *See also* backlighting *and* front lighting.

slave unit An accessory flash unit that supplements the main flash, usually triggered electronically when the slave senses the light output by the main unit, or through radio waves.

slow sync An electronic flash synchronizing method that uses a slow shutter speed so that ambient light is recorded by the camera in addition to the electronic flash illumination. This allows the background to receive more exposure for a more realistic effect.

specular highlight Bright spots in an image caused by reflection of light sources.

spot meter An exposure system that concentrates on a small area in the image, represented by the circle in the center of the EOS 40D's viewfinder. *See also* center-weighted meter.

sRAW A reduced-size RAW format file option that contains one-quarter as many pixels as a standard RAW file, while retaining all the settings information captured by the camera. *See also* RAW.

sRGB One of two color space choices available with the Canon EOS 40D. The sRGB setting is recommended for images that will be output locally on the user's own printer, as this color space matches that of the typical inkjet printer and a properly calibrated monitor fairly closely. *See also* Adobe RGB.

subtractive primary colors Cyan, magenta, and yellow, which are the printing inks that theoretically absorb all color and produce black. In practice, however, they generate a muddy brown, so black is added to preserve detail (especially in shadows). The combination of the three colors and black is referred to as CMYK. (K represents black, to differentiate it from blue in the RGB model.)

time exposure A picture taken by leaving the shutter open for a long period, usually more than one second. The camera is generally locked down with a tripod to prevent blur during the long exposure.

through the lens (TTL) A system of providing viewing and exposure calculation through the actual lens taking the picture.

tungsten light Light from ordinary room lamps and ceiling fixtures, as opposed to fluorescent illumination.

underexposure A condition in which too little light reaches the film or sensor, producing a thin negative, a dark slide, a muddy-looking print, or a dark digital image.

unsharp masking The process for increasing the contrast between adjacent pixels in an image, increasing sharpness, especially around edges.

vignetting Dark corners of an image, often produced by using a lens hood that is too small for the field of view, a lens that does not completely fill the image frame, or generated artificially using image-editing techniques.

white balance The adjustment of a digital camera to the color temperature of the light source. Interior illumination is relatively red; outdoor light is relatively blue. Digital cameras like the EOS 40D set correct white balance automatically or let you do it through menus. Image editors can often do some color correction of images that were exposed using the wrong white balance setting, especially when working with RAW files that contain the information originally captured by the camera before white balance was applied.

Index